FINDING GENIUS

Kunal Mehta

ISBN 978-1-099-63824-4

www.kunalrmehta.com

For my nephews and my nieces, and to the entrepreneurs working hard to make this world a better place for this generation to live in.

VENTURE CAPITALISTS

RICK HEITZMANN
FirstMark Capital

KEITH RABOIS
Founders Fund

BETH FERREIRA
FirstMark Capital

REBECCA KADEN
Union Square
Ventures

TRAE STEPHENS
Founders Fund

ANDY WEISSMAN
Union Square
Ventures

ANDREW PARKER
Spark Capital

NIHAL MEHTA
Eniac Ventures

JENNY ABRAMSON
ReThink Impact

NICHOLAS CHIRLS
Notation

ROY BAHAT
Bloomberg Beta

SPENCER LAZAR
General Catalyst

BRIAN LAUNG AOAEH
KEC Ventures

ELLIE WHEELER
Greycroft

JEREMY LIEW
Lightspeed Venture Partners

FRAN HAUSER

ILYA FUSHMAN
Kleiner Perkins

VISHAL VASHISHT
Obvious Ventures

ZAVAIN DAR
LUX Capital

TAYLOR GREENE
Collaborative Fund

LINDSEY GRAY
Two Sigma Ventures

BRETT MARTIN
Charge VC

WILLIAM MCQUILLAN
Frontline Ventures

DAVID ROSE
New York Angels

AJAY AGARWAL

Bain Capital Ventures

JACOB YORMAK

Story Ventures

MATT HARTMAN

Betaworks

DANIEL PIANKO

University Ventures

PETER ROJAS

Betaworks

JOSH NUSSBAUM

Compound Ventures

CO-CONTRIBUTORS

WENDY XIAO SCHADECK

Northzone VC

NITYA RAJENDARAN

Tribeca Venture Partners

MICHAEL RAAB

Sinai Ventures

RAYE GASPAR-ASAOKA

Canaan Partners

ANDREW KANGPAN

Two Sigma Ventures

SHEFALI BHARDWAJ

ZS Associates

LAURA CHAU

Canaan Partners

GRACE CHOU

Felicis Ventures

ADRIEL BERCOW

Flybridge VC

BRIAN YORMAK

Story Ventures

FOREWORD

FOREWORD
Sutian Dong, Female Founders Fund

Kunal and I met when he was writing his first book, *Disruptors*, and interviewing startup founders to unpack how passion and meaning have, against many odds, driven success on their entrepreneurial journeys. When Kunal told me he was writing *Finding Genius*, I knew there was no better person with the innate curiosity to tell other people's stories than Kunal.

The funny truth about venture capital is that it is both an art and a science, and for decades has been an industry where expertise is built from apprenticeship. As a consequence, the industry behind almost all successful technology companies has, for too long, been insular and tribal, and the answers to the questions that strike many entrepreneurs — What is venture capital? Why should I raise venture capital? How do I do it? — have been hard to access in a single, easy way.

It's been a long time since I've read a book that was this useful and actionable, and I suspect that is because there are only a few people in the world who excel at both research and practice. In *Finding Genius*, Kunal manages to walk us so much deeper and further into the practice of venture capital than books normally do. He uses his own experience as a VC to guide readers through the case studies and examples that explain how a fund operates, what types of businesses they invest in, and why the right alignment between a fund and a founder can create extraordinary returns for the company and the investors.

Reading *Finding Genius* is less like reading a how-to manual, but rather like participating in an exploration of the big questions that venture capitalists themselves are grappling with: What is genius, and how is it being redefined over time? How is venture capital as an industry evolving? And where do VCs push themselves, as their roles — as financial stewards to their limited partners, and as thought partners to the founders they invest in — continue to shift with the ever-changing needs of rapidly scaling startups?

Think about how much you retain when you hear stories instead of scripts of right versus wrong, or what to do versus what not to do. This book offers so much more than single-point answers by capturing a series of experiences from senior-level investors that shed light on the subtleties of identifying, investing in, and supporting the next generation of entrepreneurial talent.

While *Finding Genius* is built on scenarios and first-hand accounts, at the core it is a book concerned with sharing principles. Grasp these principles, and you will have an understanding of the frameworks with which the best venture capitalists operate, which will guide you whether you are an aspiring VC, a founder seeking capital, or a curious onlooker to the rapidly changing startup ecosystem.

Besides being a gifted and intuitive venture investor, Kunal is a natural storyteller. There is something compelling in the way Kunal shares these principles — especially in his ability to break down the ephemeral nature of "finding genius" to actionable steps that, combined, can create the conditions for venture capitalists to invest in the next Pinterest, Rent the Runway, and Airbnb of the world.

In the end, Kunal believes that venture is a balance between an art and a science, the knowable and unknowable, which combined with hard work, good timing, and luck can create the circumstances that enable the next generation of genius to flourish. He has managed to bring both his intelligence and curiosity about venture capital to the page, and the result is a book that educates the reader while exploring the evolution of venture and the ways that the industry itself might be disrupted in the future.

I predict that this book will make its way onto the must-read lists of VCs new and old, aspiring investors, and entrepreneurs of all stripes who seek to understand the other side of the table. I hope you enjoy reading as much as I have.

PREFACE
Kunal Mehta

In the back of an empty classroom at Indiana University's Kelley School of Business, four students sit together with an ambitious dream to join the entrepreneurial ranks of individuals like Sara Blakely or Mark Zuckerberg. With napkin sketches and books written by former entrepreneurs spread across the table, this group has their heads together crafting a story. What story can they tell about themselves or their business idea that will resonate with an investor?

Brainstorm sessions like these have become a common after-school activity. These four students are like hundreds of thousands of upstarts across the country, weighing an entrepreneurial dream against a morbid corporate recruiting cycle. Every large university offers classes on entrepreneurship and in recent years, many have added seminars on venture capital to syllabi to meet growing demand. This motivated group of individuals remains hopeful that they can build things that solve real problems. To them, anything less radical would be old fashioned, narrow minded, and not a valuable use of their talent. They want to join the ranks of entrepreneurial geniuses who have forever changed the fabric of society.

It is the true hopefulness of these entrepreneurs that inspired me to write my first book, *Disruptors*, which tells the stories of 50 entrepreneurs and the failures they faced when they first pursued entrepreneurial stardom. What did the first six to 12 months of uncertainty look like? In the book, these founders, some of whom went on to start billion-dollar companies, offer candid accounts of bankruptcies, divorces, insurmountable credit card debt, investor and founder feuding, all while maintaining that entrepreneurship was a path worth pursuing, despite the risks. These men and women found satisfaction in their work and were excited to pursue meaningful causes. The stories within those pages revealed that entrepreneurship is an exciting and viable career path, but a founder should be aware of all that is entailed in the unstructured path for non-conformists with bold dreams. There is no such thing as an overnight success story. *Disruptors* was one of many proof points. As a venture capitalist who now invests in founders for a living, I have witnessed the trials and tribulations of founders firsthand.

Disruptors brought me into classrooms like the one at Indiana University, into well-funded programs at Harvard, Stanford, Duke, Columbia, Princeton, and New York University, and into entrepreneurial hubs across the country in Kentucky, Chicago, Virginia, and North Dakota. Across these diverse populations, the common denominator remains the same — entrepreneurs sought to make a lasting imprint through their own ideas and visions, but they lacked the capital to do so. It became clear that entrepreneurship was no longer only a possibility on the coasts or in elite universities; Startups were emerging in every corner of the country, but capital had yet to follow.

The entrepreneurial dreams of the students I met hinged on one question — can you tell us more about venture capitalists? Some of the students I talked to had signed agreements that were destructive to their companies, flown to San Francisco in hopes of meeting an investor on a coffee line, and hired virtual assistants to cold-email anyone with 'investor' in their professional title. The allure of power-yielding venture capitalists was high, but students' understanding of venture capital was slim.

Finding Genius was conceived from my desire to demystify venture capital and provide a roadmap for future entrepreneurs to follow. Through discussions with a growing number of students, disenchanted consultants, lawyers, bankers, doctors, and other corporate escapees, it was clear people saw opportunity through entrepreneurship but were stymied by a venture industry that was opaque, elite, and discriminating. These conversations evolved into interviews with top investors in a format similar to *Disruptors* — a series of conversations with a diverse group of professionals that offer a more candid look into financing entrepreneurial dreams. The venture capitalists featured in this book have invested in the founders behind companies like Facebook, Tesla, Space-X, Twitter, Snapchat, Pinterest, LinkedIn, Airbnb, Uber, Lyft, and other game-changing enterprises that have forever changed humanity. Given that the job of these men and women is to meet with founders every single day, I wanted to know: What patterns do they see from one founder to the next? What qualities or traits stand out that catalyzes them to make an investment?

Through the pages of *Finding Genius*, an esteemed group of venture capitalists will provide insights that begin to answer these questions. When I wrote *Disruptors*, I wrote it with the candor and humility of an aspiring entrepreneur searching for answers. Similarly, I wrote *Finding Genius* with the same undertones of transparency and curiosity — to break through the façade of venture capital to identify and share genuine morsels of wisdom.

FINDING GENIUS

Kunal Mehta

SECTION 1
THE TRAIL-WISE SIDEKICKS

CHAPTER 1
VENTURE CAPITALISTS: THE TRAILWISE SIDEKICKS

In 1998, the *Harvard Business Review* dramatically described venture capital and its place in history amongst American entrepreneurs:

"The popular press is filled with against-all-odds stories of Silicon Valley entrepreneurs. In these sagas, the entrepreneur is the modern-day cowboy, roaming new industrial frontiers much the same way the earlier Americans explored the West. At his side stands the venture capitalist, a trail-wise sidekick ready to help the hero through all the tight spots — in exchange, of course, for a piece of the action."

The venture capitalist and entrepreneur relationship has been romanticized and widely covered in the entrepreneurial boom that has gripped our imaginations. Mark Zuckerberg's relationship to his early investors was documented in the biopic, *The Social Network*. Silicon Valley, a popular HBO series, captures the interactions between eccentric investors and founders who dream of changing the world. Startup mania has led some venture capitalists to crave and get stardom with their own television shows, podcasts, and web series featuring cringe-worthy power dynamics with the founders they meet. While often satirized, the obligations between an investor and a founder are understatedly complex. The history of this asset class remains largely untold and the incentives that drive a venture capitalist are often opaque, leading to a Hollywood-esque representation about the role a venture capitalist plays.

For the stories that do malign the founder and investor relationship, there are the recognizable 'against-all-odds' partnerships over the past few decades that ring true to the *Harvard Business Review* description. Venture investors have helped establish companies such as Google, Facebook, Twitter, Tesla, and Apple as central to our society by making the initial capital investment in a founder's company and supporting them through the 'tight spots' of starting that venture. As Keith Rabois, an investor in Twitter, Airbnb, Square, Yelp, and LinkedIn, describes it, his sole purpose as an investor is to do his best to remove any foreseeable headaches and roadblocks in front of the founders he invests in. His job is to complement a founder's skill set and help guard against their blind spots. Like other seasoned investors, Rabois is qualified to do this because he has witnessed multiple times the cycle of launching and scaling a company from a rough idea to the first 10,000 customers.

Finding Genius is a glimpse into this knowledge that venture veterans have accumulated over these repeat cycles of working with radical, genius entrepreneurs to answer strategic questions: What traits of entrepreneurial genius appeal to a venture capitalist? How do venture capitalists distinguish between idealistic dreams of grandeur from the cold, hard reality of entrepreneurship (the path that often succeeds)? How do entrepreneurs who possess true genius avoid being exploited by investors posing as 'trail-wise sidekicks'?

While these learnings are valuable, a challenge emerged as I began to delve deeper into the venture industry through a series of candid conversations: How do I establish a definition of genius that is robust enough given that venture capital is not fairly spread across race, geography or gender?

From its humble beginnings in the 1940s, as a means to democratize startup capital beyond the American elite, who already fared well with banks and family wealth, venture capital was concepted as a Post-World War II catalyst for innovation. It was a response to support creativity, competition, diversity in thought and process; to challenge the status quo cherished by families such as the Rockefellers and Carnegies; and to provide opportunity to the next generation of American entrepreneurs through mentorship and access. As some still idealistically define it, the venture capital opportunity would be equally available to any gender, geography, or race, but it would be a selective process to back a handful of 'geniuses'.

Yet nearly 80 years later, in speaking with a growing population of entrepreneurs, aspiring venture capitalists, and students across the country for *Disruptors*, I learned that the majority views venture capital as unattainable startup capital that operates in the shadows and continues to preclude large swaths of people from pursuing their entrepreneurial dreams. While 'genius' is defined as the few outliers who will stand apart from the masses to gain access, there exists an underlying knowledge and opportunity gap that has acted as a fortified barrier for some entrepreneurs to recognize their true genius. Over the past few decades, the definition of entrepreneurial genius has been narrowly limited to certain geographies, races, genders, and the flow of venture capital has tipped the scales in their favor. Sadly, there are still some, including investors featured in this project, who scoff at this remark because they believe hard work, execution, and genius ideas will always get funded. The data suggests otherwise: in 2018, funding for female founders capped out at 2.2% of total venture capital dollars. Data suggests similar funding disparities for people of color, people over the age of 40, and founders outside of New York City or San Francisco. If venture capital was truly efficient and the dollars only went to 'geniuses', then genius would be defined as young males who lived on a coast of the United States. Today, more than ever before, people are working to bring efficiency and transparency to venture capital and my hope is that this book serves that purpose.

One goal that drove this project forward was to reveal the inner workings of the venture industry exclusively through diverse perspectives, shared by men and women who believe shining a light on venture capital will enable it to function as it was originally intended. As a result, entrepreneurial genius, as you will see throughout this book, continues to evolve and expand as a new generation of venture investors weighs in and broadens its sample size to surface the true outliers.

While the *Harvard Business Review* aptly described the personas of the two individuals in the entrepreneurial saga, the reality is far more complicated than stereotypical, surface-level descriptions would suggest. This distinction will be covered throughout this book. Entrepreneurs are generally the bold risk takers who shy away from a traditional path, require little structure, and balk at conformity. Venture investors, at least the successful ones, are willing to embark on these new paths with founders to break down their barriers to market success. The stories of entrepreneurs and investors have been told on multiple occasions, but as this relationship has grown more intertwined, venture capital's history, incentives and intended purpose have been overlooked. Prior to signing up to work with venture capitalists, entrepreneurs should be more informed on how this asset class emerged and how it has changed over time.

The History of Venture Capital

Now the dominant source of financing for companies within the global economy, venture capital was initially designed to accelerate the process of building and scaling a high-risk venture and stress test a business model over five to seven years. The simple truth is that most businesses that receive venture funding will fail and entrepreneurs who deploy this form of capital are okay with that fact. While most investors strive for balanced portfolios, these investments are speculative: venture capitalists use a minimal amount of available data to make a series of investments in companies with the conviction that one or two of those, across a portfolio of several companies, will be a runaway success.

Traditionally, and for several reasons why financiers preferred this method, entrepreneurial endeavors were often financed through credit instead of equity. Banks provided loans to American entrepreneurs but were less vested in the growth of the company. They were conservative and myopically concerned with cash balances. This often led to a conflict for entrepreneurs who sought to invest in company growth but were instead now servicing interest payments and managing debt. Phil Knight, the founder of Nike, captured the essence of what it was like to grow a business on credit with banks in his memoir, Shoe Dog. Most banks turned down the opportunity to finance the vision for Nike, and the one that hesitatingly took the risk urged Knight to take a more conservative approach to growth. Knight recounts how the bank was focused on cash balances, not on extraordinary growth; the push-and-pull with bankers often cost him the business in the earliest days of Nike's history. This conflict became the bane of Knight's existence as he scaled Nike at a time when the venture capital industry was non-existent.

While classic American companies such as Ford or General Electric found their startup capital through traditional means as Nike did, the U.S. venture capital industry sprung into existence through a regulatory change called the Prudent Man Rule, which allowed pension funds to invest in venture capital. Simultaneously, the 1978 Revenue Act decreased capital gains tax from 49.5% to 28%, making these sorts of investments more attractive. As this unfolded from the 1950s through the 1980s, venture capital funds in the U.S. exploded with capital ready to be deployed to entrepreneurs. Pension funds were also a factor, as they controlled over $3 trillion by the end of the 1980s and were searching for higher returns during the poor performance of stocks and bonds in the decade prior. Venture capitalists were willing to oblige. While the Prudent Man Rule, favorable tax structures, and an increased appetite for this risky asset class were the catalysts behind the rise of venture capital, the industry began with a sense of humility that it now so often lacks.

The venture capital industry begins with the story of Georges Doriot. In his book *Creative Capital: Georges Doriot and the Birth of Venture Capital*, author Spencer E. Ante captures the founding principles of venture capital as the catalyst to jump start American innovation after World War II. Antes profiles Georges Doriot, a World War II veteran and innovator, who "came to believe in a future of financing entrepreneurs in an organized way." Doriot, born in Paris to the son of an entrepreneur in the automobile industry, went on to turn down a job as the head of the post-World War II U.S. Department of Research and Development, returning instead to his post as a celebrated professor at Harvard Business School. Boston — a hub of intellectual and scientific talent drawn to MIT and Harvard University — became the ideal backdrop for entrepreneurship and venture capital to begin its launch.

As Ante puts it, Doriot recognized the importance of creativity, innovation, and technology in the business world, and at the behest of the New England elite, ran one of Boston's first venture funds: the American Research and

Development Corporation (ARD) in the early 1940s. ARD was the first professional venture capital fund that raised capital outside of non-family resources, but instead through insurance companies, educational institutions, and investment trusts. Concepted by the president of MIT, ARD was designed to 'solve a major imperfection of modern U.S. capitalism' and address the plight of a growing class of American entrepreneurs. Ante describes how the U.S. had dreamers, brilliant minds, innovators, and hard-working men and women who had been re-invigorated to take risks but lacked access to capital and mentorship:

"New companies were starved for money and professional management... ARD promised to break down the walls of an elitist, insular world, reviewing ideas from thousands of companies across the country... In his personal life, Doriot was cautious to a fault at times. But in his professional life, Doriot realized venture capital was all about taking huge but calculated risks."

One of the founding members of ARD spoke publicly in 1945, cautioning that the country should not rest on its laurels and expect existing U.S. industries to continue to remain competitive. He wanted to disrupt traditional American industry, saying:

"We cannot depend safely for an indefinite time on the expansion of our old big industries alone. We need new strength, energy and ability from below. We need to marry some small part of our enormous fiduciary resources to new ideas which are seeking support."

Venture capital would become the bridge between these groups of people. It would "marry money with people and their crazy, new ideas and the result would be a stronger country with a growing supply of well-paying jobs." Venture capital was born to increase competition, disrupt the status quo, and support American innovation.

ARD began humbly with a $3.4 million fund and went on to seed the inception of over a hundred American companies. Doriot referred to his companies as 'children,' worked with them for over a decade, and maintained a patient investment philosophy to build companies for the long haul. He viewed 'returns as the by-product of hard labor, not a goal.' One such company within Doriot's portfolio, Digital Equipment Corporation, established itself on a $70,000 investment from ARD in exchange for 70% of the company. When ARD liquidated its stake in Digital, the company was worth more than $400 million, yielding a return of more than 70,000%! While regulation, public perception, and investor appetite for venture capital would continue to evolve over the next decade, Ante places the inception of venture capital and its role in American entrepreneurship squarely on the shoulders of Georges Doriot. He writes:

"Doriot's influence persisted through the work of his disciples, as various ARD alumni founded and ran the second generation of successful VC firms, including Greylock and Fidelity Ventures... Doriot was the prophet of this new "Start-up Nation," the leader of a social and economic crusade that democratized the clubby world of finance. More than any other person, Doriot — through his teaching, writing and leadership in the military, academic, and financial worlds — pioneered the transition to an economy built on entrepreneurship and innovation."

Booms & Busts

What began as a 'cottage industry,' with a $3.4 million fund in 1946, has since exploded with an abundance of capital chasing those 70,000% returns. In a similar problem that still plagues investors in 2018, the sudden surplus of capital perversely affected investment decisions and portfolio theory through the late 1900s. As more cash was available to be deployed, certain industries came into favor and investors flocked towards them with herd mentality, driving up valuations for which venture investors paid far too much.

This cyclical nature of the industry is something which has had 'experts' claiming, every few decades, that the venture capital model is dead. And yet, over time, it's clear that high-growth business models have become more attractive for financing for two reasons: the decreasing cost of starting and operating companies and the ebb and flow in phases of technology. The MIT Technology Review reflected that in the 1990s, 'venture capitalists seemed like genuine alchemists, able to turn even startup dross into purest gold.' Just prior to this boom, Paul Gompers, a professor of business administration at the University of Chicago, published a study of the industry titled "The Rise and Fall of Venture Capital." His pessimism was followed by a decade that saw public offerings of venture-backed companies such as 'Juniper Networks, foundational to the Internet organizations such as Netscape, and others that would generate solid returns for their investors, but did not perform well in the public markets such as Pets.Com.' Years followed by extreme exuberance in entrepreneurs is often followed by a bust, in which technology companies that were well-funded were not worth their lofty valuations.

Josh Lerner, an economist with Harvard Business School, wrote that "time and again groups raised huge amounts of capital that they invested foolishly, either funding entrepreneurs who never should have raised capital in the first place, or else giving far too much money to promising entrepreneurs." As this phase of the startup bubble burst and public offerings slowed down, many would proclaim that the end had once again come for venture capital as an asset class. In the 2000s, the industry progressed slowly. *MIT Technology Review* captured that sentiment:

"The word crisis has become ubiquitous. Matrix Capital founder Paul Ferri told the Wall Street Journal in 2006 that the industry does not now have 'an economically viable business model.' In the June 2005 issue of this magazine, Yankee Group founder Howard Anderson bid 'goodbye to venture capital.' And when the executive search firm Polachi and Co. asked a thousand VCs last summer 'Is the venture capital business broken?' more than half said it was. When you consider the key role that venture capital has played in funding American innovation over the last 50 years, that conclusion seems ominous."

Describing a slowdown in venture capital in the early 90s, many at the time believed that the role of a venture capitalist was to invest in risky projects, which led to issues within the industry. Yet again, with the entrepreneurial fabric that ran through American society in the early 2000s, venture capital too made a resurgence.

Some of these booms and busts have happened with each phase of the Internet, and the introduction of new applications built on top of the Internet — including mobile, virtual reality (VR), artificial intelligence, blockchain — or even across new business models. The herd mentality of venture capital often begins with a unique 'thesis' about an industry that drives up valuations with an expectation of large exits in the future. More recently a venture investment boom existed in the VR and augmented reality (AR) sector as investors expected strong consumer adoption in the short term. Over $3 billion in venture funding was poured into AR/VR in 2017, but by 2018 that euphoria had waned as valuation write-downs and product disappointments weighed on the market. Investors remained hopeful but held off from further investments, dampening the expectations of entrepreneurs in the space.

This valuation shift happens to promising entrepreneurs behind game-changing movements more frequently than one would hope. Given that the venture capital model is based on seeking higher valuations, founders and venture capitalists alike can fall victim to chasing the hype of a vision over true progress of a company. The valuation of a company is often not based on a mathematical or logical exercise but instead based on the prospect of how attractive a business might be in the future. Sustaining these over-inflated valuations becomes more difficult as investors and public investors begin to seek real results.

Christopher Altchek, the co-founder and CEO of Mic, a fast-growing media company for Millennials, raised over $100 million as investors poured money into 'future of media' companies such as BuzzFeed, Circa, Flipboard, Vice

Media, and others that sought to capitalize on media and content consumption behaviors. In late 2018, Mic was sold for close to $5 million, Circa shut its operations, and BuzzFeed and Vice Media both reported growth and valuation concerns. As these shifts occur, former darlings of the venture capital industry go out of favor, which reduces the likelihood of similar business models from being funded in the future.

Still, the venture model is built to withstand these booms and busts because there are often experiments and risks in which winners in each of these nascent categories emerge. In the end, the goal of venture financing is to sort through the 'losers' to find the diamond in the rough and have the foresight to identify those winners while the industry is still seemingly crowded with dozens of competitors. In the years that followed the early 2000 crash, the world would again see companies such as Facebook, Twitter, Tesla, and Google IPO. Google, which offered shares publicly for the first time in the summer of 2004, received $12.5 million in venture capital from Kleiner Perkins and Sequoia in 1999. At the time of the public offering, this $12.5 million stake was worth well over $2 billion. The Facebook IPO returning capital to its investors, a booming technology scene out of China, and exuberance around valuations of private companies such as Uber, Airbnb, Paytm, Lyft, Stripe, WeWork, and more had venture investors once again pouring capital into startup ventures hoping for similar returns. In 2017, over $72 billion in venture capital was invested into startups in the U.S. and $165 billion was invested globally, and there were no signs of slowing down. In 2018, some funds raised in excess of $3 billion for the first time in the history of venture capital. From 2011-2018, over 250 new micro-venture funds, or funds that would deploy $100,000 to $250,000 in a few companies, sprouted up. In 2019, the exuberance for venture capital is high and in line with Lerner's thoughts on capital deployed, where some founders are raising excess capital, just because they can.

In 2019, venture capitalists are backing geniuses to the tune of billions of dollars and as history has shown time and again, this cycle too will come to an end. But until then, venture capitalists continue to search for entrepreneurial geniuses to accompany on this journey. As in the examples of media, VR/

AR, artificial intelligence, and other sectors that have produced more losers than winners, this is a fundamental truth of venture capital. Venture capitalists, spread across hundreds of funds, will invest heavily in spaces or industries where they see potential and often times, only few winners will emerge. These winners, however, can return 500-700 times an initial investment. Venture capital is built on a winner take all mentality and these investors are racing to find those winners. As was the case at the time of Georges Doriot, this asset class is meant to be the startup capital to allow individuals to take outsized risks in the name of innovation.

In the short history of venture capital, there have been many fits and starts with even more 'pundits' claiming that the market for venture capital is dead. While there have been disruptive forces from within the industry that have forced it to evolve, venture capital is now synonymous with global innovation. Through the history of venture capital, one thing has remained true: profit incentives drive all investor decisions.

Commitment to Outsized Returns

"I've seen Venture Capitalists make wild decisions under the guise of being founder friendly. If some of the Limited Partners were around that table, they would have been shocked. A venture capitalist's most important responsibility is to the Limited Partners — to drive investor capital wisely, to get the best, but fair deal and to do this with a long-term view of the relationship with that company, not just a loyalty to the CEO."

Rick Heitzmann, FirstMark Capital

Venture capitalists choose the entrepreneurs they back through differentiated channels, but they are all driven by a single performance metric: generating outsized returns for their investors, with an emphasis on the word 'outsized.' Given that the return on investment is the common qualifying denominator amongst all investors, it automatically excludes a meaningful group of promising entrepreneurs: those men and women who aspire to create brilliant businesses but will plateau at sub-$100 million valuations because of execution, market opportunity, state of technology, or competitive landscape. Matthew Hartman of Betaworks, a startup incubator and venture fund based in New York City, discusses incentives:

"What entrepreneurs need to understand is that by going with venture capital, everyone is agreeing to take a bet that they're going to try to build something very fast and there may or may not be a company there. If demand is scaling quickly, we'll pour more money to see it through. Everyone has to be on the same page on what the goals are. With venture capital, investors have said they'll return five times the investment to their Limited Partners within five years. They need to now find investments that will return 100 times the money invested and have to find crazy bets to do so. Everything is possible as long as the objectives are explicit and the same. The reality is that when someone is waving a check in front of you for financing, it becomes hard to see past that."

Venture capitalists pursue risky investments that have the potential to reach the unicorn stage of a $1 billion valuation or more. They search for the highest return on their capital within the shortest period of time. It is often said that investors treat each investment as if it can return the value of an entire fund. For example, if a venture capitalist raises a $250 million fund, a venture capitalist's goal should be to find one single investment out of that fund to create returns that would match the entire fund size. In an era where fund sizes have ballooned, so too has the demand for higher returns from start-ups. This requires a certain breed of founders who can withstand the pressure cooker of a venture-backed startup while remaining ethical and focused while commandeering a ship through a storm.

The primary investors in a venture fund and the ones who the entrepreneurs most commonly interface with are known as General Partners (GPs). These individuals raise capital from Limited Partners (LP) and agree to share a percentage of the profits of the investments they make. While GPs are most often former entrepreneurs or operators or have risen up through the ranks in a career in venture capital, LPs can be high net worth individuals, pension funds, sovereign wealth funds, corporate balance sheets, university endowments, and/or other sources of capital. While the LPs operate in the shadows to most of these venture funds, the GPs are the ones entrepreneurs liaise with. At a structural level, the LP and GP relationship is opaque to most entrepreneurs. How do the investors, or limited partners, that a venture fund chooses determine the investments they will make? What time horizons do the LPs want to see a return on the capital they invested? Can these LPs be strategically aligned, or misaligned, with the startup company within a portfolio and how will that impact the founder, for better or worse? Brett Martin, a serial entrepreneur turned venture investor, reveals a common and exaggerated misnomer some founders still have about venture investors:

> "There is a false perception that investors and venture capitalists are like ATM Machines — walk up to them, input data or a slide deck, and cash comes flying out. That's not how it works but I'm shocked that so many founders think it's still that easy."

As far as incentives are concerned, in every case as it relates to traditional venture capital, the LPs and GPs are financially motivated and are looking to generate returns on their capital. The GPs are the contractual decision makers for the fund and receive carried interest paid by the fund, typically 20% of the profits earned through liquidation events. The management company, or the business unit of this partnership between the LPs and GPs, absorbs about 2% of the total assets under management to finance the overhead costs of the fund, including staff salaries, office space, marketing, etc. This incentive structure is often where venture capitalists can be misaligned with founders at any stage of the company's growth.

Venture funds receive equity from a company in exchange for capital, but the venture fund cannot recognize any gains on their investment until there is a liquidation event. Liquidation events generally occur through a strategic acquisition by another market player, an initial public offering of equity, or through a share purchase where an investor's position, or ownership within a company, is bought out by a new investor. As valuations creep higher, investors are faced with the growing dilemma of what valuation an exit/liquidation event will occur at, in what time horizon, and if it will be enough of a return to justify the investment in the first place. Just as founders know that starting a company can be a risky proposition, investors have an appetite for risk as they try to maximize returns. Venture capitalists filter thousands of deals each year, searching for those specific geniuses amongst the masses of entrepreneurs that approach them. Venture funds run an extensive diligence process prior to making an investment and attempt to minimize the risks that come with their investments. Pocket Sun of SoGal Ventures boils this level of risk down:

"Over 70% of startups fail or die. 3% of companies exit above $100 million, 0.7 % exit above $500 million, 0.2% exit above $1 billion, 0.06% exit above $2 billion. In the 1,000 companies hand-selected and funded by venture capital, only two of them can get to an exit over $1 billion. Five companies exit between $500 million and $1 billion. A total of 30 lucky ones exit for over $100 million. Another 70 have some sort of an exit. That leaves us 900 companies with no exit."

Given that 90% of venture funded companies fail, investors are thereby further inclined to find the outsized returns one or two companies can deliver to them.

While understanding the structural returns and portfolio theory of investing is important, the timeline of a fund is also critical to an entrepreneur. Most funds last for seven to 10 years but are generally active in the first three to four years. At the end of year four, the majority of the fund will already be invested. The rest of the fund enters a harvest period for follow-on investments in a few good performers. Many VC funds reserve about 50% to support existing portfolio companies. A smaller fund may not even do follow-on investments because they require a larger capital for a small incremental ownership. In other words, ownership gets more expensive and the economics do not always make sense. As an entrepreneur, you need to do your research and know a fund's vintage, which refers to the year the fund was raised.

Entrepreneurs should be aware that at the end of this lifecycle, depending on the history of the fund and their LPs, the GPs will need to go out and raise more capital from LPs in order to stay in business. While this has minimal impact on the founders from a day-to-day perspective, it is important as some venture investors may attempt to force a liquidation event in order to generate an actual return to LPs. Also, should the fund not be able to successfully raise additional capital, the founder may lose the interest of that investor as they move on to their next endeavor. The LP makeup, GP backgrounds, past investments, liquidation events, and fund timeline are all important points for an entrepreneur to consider prior to partnering with a venture capitalist. Most entrepreneurs see any capital infusion as cash flow to their business and are unbiased when accepting it, regardless of where this capital is coming from. However, some of the fund differentiators listed above may lead to a strategic misalignment and cost a founder their company.

Measuring and Reacting to Risk

As for the statements around venture capitalists taking outsized risks to find these returns, Brad Feld, an investor with the Foundry Group who has invested in Zynga, Fitbit, and MakerBot, disputes this claim. He believes that the successful venture investors are smartly placing their predictions for the future as opposed to a spray-and-pray mentality:

> " 'A venture capitalist's job is to invest in risky projects.' This statement is scary to me. We should be risk evaluators, not risk takers. We should invest where our background and instincts and due diligence convince us the anticipated return will far exceed our evaluation of the risk. There are five key risks in any deal: market, product, management, business model, and capital. Taking all five at once is crazy. Most

losses happen when you combine market and product risk — take one, not both, and take it with a proven entrepreneur."

As we will see throughout this book with the 'calculated risks' that entrepreneurs take, venture capitalists also need to learn to manage this risk as they swing for the fences with their investments. In discussing his career over a 20 year period, Fred Wilson, the founder of Union Square Ventures (USV) offers insight into how venture capitalists approach an entire portfolio of companies:

"I remember back in the mid 90s, I used to say with some pride that I had not lost money on any of my VC investments. Then one day, someone told me 'then you are not taking enough risk.' I ended that streak of not losing money on VC investments in the late 90s in a series of epic flameouts. I lost somewhere between $25 million and $30 million on one single investment. I am not proud of those mistakes. They were stupid. I am ashamed of them to be honest. But I learned a lot from them. Not only was my "winning streak" a case of not taking enough risk, it was also a case of not enough learning. The go-go Internet era of the late 90s fixed both of those things for me. I took more risk and learned a ton."

Wilson's first fund with USV, launched in 2004, turned out to be the best fund that the firm has ever invested out of. Wilson recounts in his blog that of the 21 investments made from that fund, 12 of those made money for the fund and the fund lost their entire investments in the other nine companies. The fund's performance, however, was based on five investments in which they made returns of 115x, 82x, 68x, 30x, and 21x. Similarly, in the 2008 fund launched out of USV, a fund that is projected to be another high-performer based on companies within that portfolio, USV has 'completely written off' six companies as losses. In sharing these performance metrics, Wilson reveals that portfolio theory of venture capital is to explain that 'losing money is part of being an investor'. In his decades of experience as a venture capitalist, Fred

Wilson shares a unique perspective on managing risk and swinging for the fences:

> "There are some things you can do with your winners and losers to drive up your performance. The first and most important thing you can do is minimize the amount of money you invest in your losers. In our 2004 fund, we invested a total of $50 million out of $120 million of total investment in our nine losers. That wasn't so good. We could have, and should have, recognized our bad investments earlier and cut them off. In our 2008 fund, I think we will invest roughly $35 million out of roughly $140 million of total investments in failed investments. So even though our loss ratio on "names" is around 40%, our loss ratio on dollars will be around 20%. We did a good job of not allocating too much of the fund's capital to losers in our 2008 fund."

In speaking with other venture capitalists, I came to understand how investors approach companies that are perceived to be 'failures' within a portfolio. The investors generally agreed that a venture capitalist should minimize their exposure and gain clarity quickly on whether or not a company is hitting its metrics and still has the same potential as when the investment was made. Wilson says he is a big believer in 'loving your losers' in that companies should not be orphaned, and an investor or board member should work hard to get those companies to the right outcome — whether it is sold or shut down quickly. Likewise, the venture capitalists are also obsessive with how they spend their time and believe a high proportion of time and effort should be spent preserving their capital in promising companies and helping them to succeed. These are all interesting points for an entrepreneur who is considering whether or not they should raise venture capital. On finding the right venture capitalists to work with, Wilson believes humility and failure, as it is for founders, is often the best teacher for investors. He says:

"Making bad investments is humbling, frustrating, annoying, time sucking, and most of all, a big part of the VC business. I look for VCs who have done it a lot, have done it with grace and respect, and continue to learn from it. They are the best VCs to work with."

Through Wilson's experience, investors and entrepreneurs can begin to better understand how investors are motivated and what outcome they are searching for.

CHAPTER 2
RAISING A VENTURE CAPITAL FUND: VCS AS ENTREPRENEURS

"The thing that drives me is that people are invested in us and I cannot let those people down. There is a world where I am hugely successful. Or, there is a world where this fails and I lose money, but one thing is for damn sure: in that scenario, it will not happen from a lack of effort."

Jacob Yormak, Story Ventures

Jacob Yormak, a former lawyer with a lucrative career ahead of him, set out to be an entrepreneur in 2016. During the two years that I followed Yormak's entrepreneurial journey for this book, he was transparent about his struggles, long nights, self-doubt, even while he established a respected reputation within the New York startup ecosystem. In an industry where public perception and personal branding is often overvalued, such transparency and honesty is hard to find. It is difficult to distinguish from Yormak's sentiments above that he was not embarking on the typical startup journey one would expect. Instead, Yormak was opting to launch his own venture fund with his brother, Brian Yormak, who also left a role at a top venture capital fund to build what would become Story Ventures. While much of venture capital is often portrayed as an elitist industry of affluent individuals who are disconnected from their entrepreneurial counterparts, the Yormaks' story, and other ones like theirs, reflect the reality of the industry.

As founders pitch to venture capitalists, many overlook the simple fact that venture capitalists, like Jacob and Brian, are invigorated by the radical and genius entrepreneurs they surround themselves with. Instead, they often view these men and women solely as gatekeepers of elusive capital who do not have skin in the game. In many cases, venture capitalists are entrepreneurs in their own right. During my conversations with veterans in the industry, many shared their entrepreneurial stories, often unprompted, of when they decided to leave the security of a well-paying job to launch venture funds to test their own theses. They candidly shared their failures and how those experiences helped them evolve as investors. It is clear that an investor's unique experience — even if it stems from a failed investment or startup experiment — makes them assets to the founders they would eventually invest in. Through my conversations, I learned that the majority of these investors ride the waves of the entrepreneurial cycle alongside founders themselves, yearning to share their own perspective and lessons learned with the next generation of entrepreneurs and venture capitalists. Ambitious venture capitalists launching their own funds are choosing a career path with an uncertain outcome. And because of that, the line that once divided venture capitalists and entrepreneurs has become blurred through the similarities they share. In one such anecdote, Jacob Yormak shared his perspective on establishing a presence as a first-time fund in a competitive venture market:

"Brand building is an important factor with the abundance of capital out there. It would be nice to be a top-tier fund and have quality inbound deals but we [Story Ventures] are years away from that and we need to hustle to find that deal flow. After we have done that, how do we win a deal and convince an entrepreneur to let us into a deal? If we do a great job with our existing founders, they will tell other good founders to work with us. Our brand as a fund is not exclusively to attract founders because it also determines how other investors, future LPs or service providers react to you. All of those parties are key to winning a deal. These pieces are all important to consider as we look to build a sustainable fund. It's not as easy as it appears from the outside."

A common perception of VCs is that they receive an abundance of "quality inbound deals". This is not the case. VCs themselves are responsible for generating deal flow and finding the entrepreneurs to invest in, just like founders have to find customers. This is yet another example of how the VC and founder share the experience of the entrepreneurial cycle.

Raising a Fund

The process of establishing a venture fund is similar to starting a seed-stage company. It requires a hopeful venture capitalist to craft a vision that will sell to investors in exchange for financing. Similar to starting a company, launching a venture fund is often irrational and holds a low probability of success. In order to provide perspective into how venture capital funds are formed and the drivers that motivate LPs to invest in this asset class, I spoke with both new and seasoned venture capitalists. The insights drawn from these conversations might serve to create a higher level of empathy between founders and investors. How did they raise their first funds? How do they sell their vision to investors and manage their expectations? For a change, the onus was off of the entrepreneur to answer questions around financing and now on the venture capitalists themselves.

Raising a fund is a process that is still largely opaque because LPs do not advertise their theses the way venture capitalists do, and they are not as readily available to deploy their capital. In raising a venture fund, there is no concept of a 'lead investor' as there is in a startup financing round which other smaller investors can rally around. Instead, it is a frantic process without a structure where GPs try to find the appropriate introductions to disparate family offices, pension funds or random, high net-worth individuals who will buy into that investor's belief despite the high degree of uncertainty in the investments they will make. As in entrepreneurship, success in venture capital is not manifested overnight but determined over a long-term horizon. Nicholas Chirls, a co-founder of Notation, humbly and cautiously describes this experience even after successfully raising his second fund and backing lucrative ventures out of his first fund:

"The venture capital business takes a very long time to get good at. You need decades to prove that you can consistently provide great returns as a VC. Until you've proven that over multiple funds, you can attribute much of one's success to luck. If we find the next Uber-like investment in this fund, it will be luck. If we can find similar returns in fund 1, fund 2, fund 3, fund 4, then we can say we know what we are doing. In this business, whether you're a VC or a founder, you're consistently humbled, and when you feel like you're killing it, something happens, and you're knocked on your ass again."

Indeed, it's that roller coaster story that so many founders often tell of their own experience. Many of the 'startup' venture capitalists of the early 2000s have now established themselves as mainstay players, but they're not unfamiliar with this struggle. Rick Heitzmann, a venerable venture investor and a co-founder of FirstMark Capital, likens the early days of launching his fund and the competition to get into deals to his time as an entrepreneur:

"As a startup VC shop, we were competing for mindshare, for deals, and for companies. When we were starting off, the most established venture capitalists would look down at us. They most definitely would not return our calls asking for their advice and oftentimes, when we would run into them at a conference, they would look at my partner and I like we were asking for a job. We had no initial credibility and it was very much, for several years, like running a startup. Some of the LPs, who we were able to eventually secure, we had solicited and pitched for eight years before they trusted us with their capital. It was like one of those old Wall Street movies where we would show up for a meeting and the manager of investments would then tell us they didn't have time to meet with us and would send his or her analyst to the lobby. The analyst would then say, 'I only have 5-6 minutes, do you want to buy me a coffee?' So, I, with no money, would now be buying this analyst a coffee and hoping he would put in a good word with his boss to invest in our fund. But this is normal if you're scaling a business. From the operating side or the investment manager side, it's very much the same hustle."

Ten years later, FirstMark Capital has had success in the venture market with investments in companies such as Airbnb, Pinterest, DraftKings, inVision, and Riot Games. With this reputation, it is able to quickly raise large funds to continue to build on that vision with the original hustle that Heitzmann alluded to. Through the slow grind that Jacob Yormak and Nicholas Chirls are now familiar with, Heitzmann and his partners have built a deep level of trust with their LPs. This trust has convinced LPs to commit over $1.5 billion to FirstMark Capital's different funds.

Establishing an Investment Case

Heitzmann told a compelling narrative to his LPs in 2008 when the New York City startup ecosystem was still collectively a handful of startups challenging the dominance of Silicon Valley. Heitzmann established FirstMark Capital in New York City to generate outsized returns with the vision that it would continue to grow in tandem with the ecosystem. According to Heitzmann, their investment approach needed to not be informed by the current macroeconomic environment of the financial crisis, but instead be more forward thinking:

"Launching right before the financial crisis, we hoped that our fund and our thesis would last more than one economic cycle and that we would have headroom to expand. We started FirstMark Capital on a few different themes. The first theme, which over 10 years ago was a contrarian view, was to focus our investment focus only on companies built in New York. The second piece of our thematic focus was to be industry-focused and experts in certain sectors. In our case consumer and enterprise software. This would give us a proprietary advantage in deal sourcing and be uniquely qualified to help our portfolio companies. We were focused on the early stages of development and looking for businesses that took advantage of open source, Amazon Web Services (AWS) or additional tools that helped people get traction quicker. Most importantly, we wanted to be a service business, when that was not common at the time. When we started FirstMark Capital, venture capital as an industry was viewed as an 'old boys club' sitting in an ivory tower deciding who would and wouldn't get money. They often invested in former colleagues or within their own networks. It was a hierarchical structure with many providing little value add. It was more of a reporting relationship than a collaborative relationship. Our belief was that we could work with better entrepreneurs if we flipped this model on its head."

This model has been fruitful for FirstMark Capital, its LPs, and the other venture funds that recognized the potential in the New York City startup eco-system and invested heavily in the early days. Heitzmann attracted New York City-based LPs with a strategy for the VC model: not only was FirstMark geo-graphically localized in New York, making Heitzmann himself uniquely privy to regional deal flow that national or Silicon Valley based investors weren't, but also, FirstMark specialized in select industries and business models, enabling them to approach deals with a propriety advantage that broad-stroke VCs at the time simply didn't have. It's that unique specialization that Story and Nota-tion Capital are mastering today.

Eventually other investors arrived at the New York City startup scene and began to capitalize on the growth in this market outside of traditional venture markets of Boston or Silicon Valley. Over a decade later, startup funds continue to emerge and find opportunity and returns by working alongside these veter-ans and establishing new focus areas. From 2012 to 2018, over 500 micro-VC funds were raised in the U.S. This indicates a growing number of investors who want access to the technology and startup scene.

While Heitzmann focused on geography as a narrative to his LPs, other funds look at funding lifecycles and find opportunities to invest in smaller amounts, as part of smaller rounds, to bring value to a different group of investors. As funds have ballooned in size, so too have the investment round sizes of companies. The larger funds do not want to invest the first $50,000-$250,000 into a company anymore because it is not worth their time to take hundreds of small bets. This has transformed the venture landscape to make space for new funds such as Story Ventures, Notation Capital, and Betaworks that are willing to make small bets. When thinking about their second fund, Peter Rojas and Matthew Hartman of Betaworks discusses how the landscape has changed to create an opportunity for new funds like theirs:

"The seed investing landscape has changed over the past decade. Because of increasing round sizes and valuations, writing $25,000-$35,000 checks does not cut it anymore. Seed rounds are now hundreds of thousands of dollars all the way up to $4 million. A $25,000 check into a round such as that would be a waste of time."

Operating with a model of making smaller investments, Nicholas Chirls realized that funds like Notation Capital would still be able to add value to founders despite the resources and capital that larger firms promised. That's the narrative Notation is uniquely providing LPs, as Chirls explains:

"We worked together for five years and developed a thesis around the New York market, which now had a critical mass of high-caliber technical and product talent. Many of these folks were leaving the bigger tech companies that were established here after 2008 and starting new things. At the same time, as the New York market matured, the seed VCs that had been historically funding experiments had now raised so much money that they spent more of their time writing bigger checks and migrating up the venture capital stack. So, who would fund that first $1 million? It's unrealistic to expect every person to have a wealthy 'friends and family' party round. We knew we could be helpful early as lead investors in rounds that are typically under $1 million to start, and we raised a small fund to do just that."

Limited Partner Perspective

A common frustration I heard from emerging venture capital fund managers is similar to the frustrations entrepreneurs have with venture capitalists. The concept of transparency is an issue that plagues all sides of this market as information is not always readily available. Some GPs claim their goal is to be more transparent about the companies they invest in, what stage of the company's lifecycle they will likely invest at, and what industries or business models are interesting to them. These same GPs, however, believe that LPs rarely do this about their own investments. As a result, it is often difficult for an emerging fund manager like Yormak or Chirls to identify LPs and understand their motivations. While the preceding anecdotes help to demystify what drives the GPs of a venture fund, the LP perspective is one that entrepreneurs should be aware of. William McQuillan, a partner with Frontline Ventures in Europe, discussed this further and the implications on their fund:

> "Limited Partners affect how fast you can invest, the checks you can write, the geographies you can invest in. People think the strategy is on the venture capitalist's website and is solely determined by the General Partners. That is only true up to a point. The strategy is heavily influenced by the investors in that fund and there are factors that aren't always clear. It is important to understand who the investors of your investor are, and the longevity or tolerance of those investors. Some investors are willing to wait much longer for a return and some are new to the venture game. If an entrepreneur asks, I'm willing to share that information but oftentimes they don't ask when they should."

With the goal of bringing further transparency to this market, I spoke with LPs from different entities, including investors from J.P. Morgan's growth fund, Cambridge Associates, Hearst, pension funds, and wealthy individuals to better understand their perspectives on venture capital as an asset class to invest in. Resoundingly and to little surprise, the primary motivation continues to be driven by financial returns, but the metrics they use to evaluate fund managers are similar to the frameworks that venture capitalists use to judge entrepreneurs. One LP from a Fortune 100 company who is making investments into venture funds off of its balance sheet stated that she had conducted over 15 background checks to make sure a fund manager had developed a positive reputation within the venture community. Other LPs place less importance on one monumental success in a portfolio of 10 companies and preferred seeing balanced returns across multiple companies in a portfolio to prove that the investor has not just been lucky with one outlier. When asked if LPs are interested in strategic investors who claim to have a thesis-driven approach behind investing, the LPs vehemently stated that they will back generalists who come from a successful operating background but prefer funds that have a strategic focus or insight on a specific vertical or business model.

David Lee, the managing director of Laconia Venture Asset Management (LVAM), has gained a unique insight into the LP perspective over his 20-year career. In 2017, Lee started a business advising family offices on a strategy to invest in emerging fund managers who were investing in the Seed to Series A stages. Today, he works with dozens of wealthy family offices to help source and evaluate venture funds for them. Lee breaks down the LP motivations into a few categories:

"One thing family offices as Limited Partners are often looking for is expertise they could not do in house because they are a certain size. When they are looking to invest $30-50 million over a 3-5 year period, they cannot internally hire a staff that would make sense. For family offices, venture capital is a small portion of their total assets, anywhere from 2% to 8% of their total assets. It's not like public equities or real estate that would take a ton of their time. So, they want outsourced expertise where they could still have investment decision control. Secondly, venture gives family offices insights into the future of the economy. If a family has established its wealth in real estate with shopping malls and had been exposed to venture over the past 10 years, they would have been exposed to next-generation e-commerce and would have seen how these behaviors are moving online and how they should adapt their businesses. Similarly, if a corporation is currently in transportation and logistics, and not aware of autonomous vehicles, the new fleet, and shipping companies, it is missing out on what could seriously impact its underlying business. It is often easier to invest a few million dollars into a transportation-focused fund or a consumer-focused fund for knowledge sharing. Finally, LPs, be it family offices, corporates, foundations, endowments or wealthy individuals, are being driven by the excitement around unicorns and the fast-growing nature of the startup ecosystem."

Lee's points around knowledge sharing and exposure to the startup ecosystem hold true across most LPs. In some cases, family offices or large corporate organizations who saw themselves at risk of being disrupted sought to diversify their exposure across funds that were actively invested in future technology and industry shifts. These funds, through knowledge sharing, provide LPs with a glimpse of this new world. Sharon Rutter, with the Empire Development Fund, New York State's investment vehicle which has invested in dozens of venture funds to boost New York State's economy, shares that Governor Cuomo sees venture capital as essential to building local economies in regions beyond New York City.

As for the qualities of a good GP, Lee thinks that the days of 'two older, experienced men deciding to launch a venture fund' is no longer compelling to LPs. Similar to venture capitalists and their future makers, LPs are searching for a compelling story on fund managers. Today, a partner must articulate a good story, have some investing track record, and also share a 'secret sauce that gives them a competitive edge at deal flow.' Lee discusses some of the funds that he has helped secure investments into:

"We've invested into funds that view themselves as contrarians, where they find deals that are outside of New York City or Silicon Valley. They have exposure to emerging hubs that other venture capitalists do not. We have invested in funds that are using a more data-driven approach to find investments by scraping the web for companies that meet certain metric thresholds. We have invested in founder-focused funds, where we believe the GPs have a unique ability to assess talented entrepreneurs. The range of funds that we can invest in is vast. There are deep domain expertise funds that focus solely on investments in artificial intelligence and machine learning companies or funds that focus only on virtual reality or fashion or consumer technology. As an LP, we need to see that the GP has a unique thesis on where these technologies or sectors are going and why their specific fund will capitalize on that trend. There is no one-size secret sauce to picking a 'genius' GP, but the minimum hurdle that we must be able to clear is that a partnership of general partners has a coherent investment thesis, a track record of working together, and some traction in an existing portfolio of work."

Measuring Performance

On measuring venture performance, the LPs alluded to the internal rate of return (IRR), the measure of profitability of a group of investments, being most important. However, there are other metrics used to measure a fund's performance, including metrics such as Distributions to Paid-in Capital (DPI) or Total Value to Paid-In Capital (TVPI). DPI is how much money a venture capital fund has returned to its LPs divided by the amount of money the LP invested into the fund. TVPI is the total value of the venture fund's holdings (realized and unrealized) divided by the capital that has been called by the fund. In breaking down these venture fund performance metrics, Rob Go, the founder of NextView Partners, writes about the implication to entrepreneurs:

"VCs have an incentive to make sure that successful companies raise more money from new outside investors at higher prices, as this allows them to increase the value of their own position in the company. This is great if you are interested in raising more capital but it can lead to raising too much money too fast at excessively high valuations if not kept in check. It's also part of the reason why VCs don't usually lead inside rounds unless they have to, because it's hard to justify increasing the value of their holdings if they are marking themselves up. Ironically, some of the best-performing funds are the ones that resist these incentives. They realize that raising more capital increases their effective post-money on their investment, and so are mindful of external capital unless it really has a multiplicative impact on the value of the company. And those that are able to lead multiple rounds also realize that intermediate holding values matter a lot less than how much of a winning company they own at exit. If you have a really big fund, and you really believe in a company, and you don't feel external pressure to mark up your investments, why would you let anyone else buy additional ownership of the company instead of buying more yourself? This is a fairly rational strategy, but one only a few funds tend to employ."

The metrics of venture capital funds and how they are measured is important and I have only briefly touched on the topic here. If you would like to learn more on this topic, I would recommend reading Rob Go's blog post on the topic or Brad Feld's book, *Venture Deals* which I have included in a resource list compiled at the end of the book.

CHAPTER 3
GENERAL PARTNERS AND THE JOB OF A VC

"If you can't invent the future, the next best thing is to fund it."

John Doerr, Kleiner Perkins Caufield & Byers

Trae Stephens was a senior in high school on September 11, 2001. Through the horrific events of that day, and in seeing the geopolitical climate transform around him over the next few years, Stephens chose to pursue a career in U.S. Intelligence to work on counterterrorism projects. He went to school for foreign service at Georgetown, a common feeder for jobs within the intelligence community, and majored in Arab studies. Upon graduating, Stephens worked at one of the large U.S. intelligence agencies. With respect for the work the agency had achieved historically, Stephens believed he could be a force for change in the government. With a growing interest in the accuracy and speed with which modern technology could analyze threats or offer insights, Stephens made it his goal to push the intelligence community to adopt more private sector improvements. In particular, Stephens pushed his leadership to license technology from a Silicon Valley-funded company known as Palantir to augment their intelligence work.

Instead, Stephens grew frustrated by the bureaucracy and his superiors' unwillingness to adopt new private sector technologies. The leadership refused to adapt and Palantir poached a frustrated Stephens to join their internal leverage team to try to change the intelligence community from the outside. Several years later, when the government was leveraging Palantir with credit to Stephens' work, Bloomberg media described what the organization had succeeded in doing:

"The company's engineers and products don't do any spying themselves; they're more like a spy's brain, collecting and analyzing information that's fed in from the hands, eyes, nose, and ears. The software combs through disparate data sources including financial documents, airline reservations, cell phone records, social media postings, and searches for connections that human analysts might miss. It then presents the linkages in colorful, easy-to-interpret graphics that look like spider webs. U.S. spies and special forces loved it immediately; they deployed Palantir to synthesize and sort the blizzard of battlefield intelligence. It helped planners avoid roadside bombs, track insurgents for assassination, even hunt down Osama bin Laden. The military success led to federal contracts on the civilian side. The U.S. Department of Health and Human Services uses Palantir to detect Medicare fraud. The FBI uses it in criminal probes. The Department of Homeland Security deploys it to screen air travelers and keep tabs on immigrants."

While the future of Palantir is still hotly debated, Stephens developed a unique understanding of a specific technology, the inner workings of the government, and how purchasing decisions were made by a bureaucracy as large as the United States Government. He had succeeded where so many other entrepreneurs had failed and began to advise other companies on how they too could navigate that sales process. Stephens' skills could have landed him many jobs back in intelligence, within the tech sector or within government, but a request from Palantir and PayPal co-founder Peter Thiel took him in a different direction.

In recent years, Thiel has become known for his support of President Donald Trump during the 2016 election. However, prior to that, Thiel was famous within the Silicon Valley community and beyond for his role as an innovator and astute investor in entrepreneurial geniuses including Elon Musk and Mark Zuckerberg. In 2005, Thiel launched Founders Fund to invest in revolutionary technologies. And it did. Founders Fund went on to invest in Spotify, Lyft, Knewton, Airbnb, Stripe, ZocDoc, Palantir, and SpaceX. If anyone had the ability to spot entrepreneurial genius, it was Peter Thiel and the investors he surrounded himself with, including his partner, and Stephens' mentor, Brian Singerman.

Trae Stephens and Peter Thiel grew close while Stephens was still at Palantir. Recognizing the insights Stephens had developed, Thiel approached him to join Founders Fund in its early days as a venture investor. Stephens' response was, "I don't know much about investing and I have no knowledge of finance," to which Thiel responded, "the best venture capitalists are not finance people."

The best venture capitalists are not finance people. The venture capitalists who shared their insights for this book were former journalists, medical doctors, military, government employees, entrepreneurs, professional athletes, bankers, lawyers, and teachers. Trae Stephens is one of the many investors who find themselves working in venture capital after operating in a diverse role for several years prior. They offer unique insights to companies and are the 'trailwise sidekicks' that entrepreneurs want in their corner. They want individuals who will support them as they embark through unchartered territory and bring an alternate perspective. While a role in venture capital was once the landing pad for semi-retired executives or successful entrepreneurs, venture capital has expanded, and individuals now arrive at this role from a slew of different professions much like Trae Stephens did with Founders Fund. The common qualifier is often an interest in technology or profound fascination with entrepreneurs. But the venture capitalists who thrive are those who approach the career from a unique perspective: from a role as an operator, a unique set of experiences in an industry, or as a former founder. The venture business is less about understanding financial models to quantify genius but instead relying on intuition that is developed over time.

Venture capital, as Andrew Parker of Spark Capital admits, is a mentorship-driven business. Parker, who shadowed Fred Wilson, a reputable investor with Union Square Ventures, before striking out on his own, believes it will be difficult for an investor to develop that intuition unless it is tested and refined by more experienced investors. After Stephens joined Founders Fund, Brian Singerman (an investor in companies such as Airbnb, Postmates, and Oscar

Health) became his informal mentor. He told Stephens: "I don't expect anything out of you in the first year. All I want you to do is to just take 1,000 meetings with different entrepreneurs. The only way you're going to get good at this is to meet with as many entrepreneurs who are willing to meet with you as possible. Take every meeting with every person at our fund and begin building your own network. Start building opinions about what things are good in the meetings and what things aren't. What do partners like about companies? What do they hate? What founders stand out to you? Why? Develop these opinions."

Like most entrants into venture capital, Stephens began his career through this approach. He took over 200 meetings in the first two months and quickly understood Peter Thiel's statement that venture capital is not a finance-based profession. Stephens expands on this:

"I started to realize that one of the key reasons that investments in the seed or series A companies happen is that it's not well suited for the finance thing. What I learned through those meetings and by watching Brian Singerman, was that this is not about finance at all. It is more about developing an intuition about the difference between a truly exceptional founder and a good founder. After taking my first 100 meetings and not understanding this, Brian called me into a meeting he was having with a founder that is now in our portfolio. He recognized genius in that founder and wanted to show me. It became so apparent how one founder can be different from hundreds of others that you'll meet in your career."

Developing this intuition is a critical skill for venture investors as they grow into their careers. Like most successful investors, Stephens' intuition has been shaped through a set of unique experiences in his past. When I asked Stephens if he believed his unique advantage as an investor was his non-finance background, Stephens responded:

"As far as my experience goes, I am confident that if I did not have the Palantir experience, I would be useless to Founders Fund. People have this bias where they think they can come out of college and be a VC intern and help with deal flow or evaluate deal flow. I think that's nonsense. I do not think I would be remotely valuable to a venture fund if I didn't have some meaningful operational experience. The only reason I have any insights into what works and what doesn't work is that I've lived through it and I've seen a company do a lot of things right and make many mistakes. I don't have any confidence I'd be good at this had it not been for Palantir. Does this go for all investors? No, but I think you need to have a blend. You need individuals who can go through the spreadsheet and figure out how well your business model is working, but the real gut intuition about a founder comes from unique experiences. There is an enormous information edge of knowing what works and doesn't work."

I'll discuss this 'information edge' more through a deeper dive on venture theses in the next chapter.

The allure that drives young professionals into a career in venture capital is that many of these people are enamored by entrepreneurship, are intellectually curious, and are often humbled by the entrepreneurs they are surrounded with. It is a career that is constantly changing. Spencer Lazar, an investor with General Catalyst, describes his affinity for his career in venture capital after pursuing a startup of his own:

"The idea of working with and being surrounded by entrepreneurial genius is something even a young person can fall in love with. The entrepreneurial geniuses who know how to affect insanely large numbers of people and change their lives is a really powerful thing. You can do that as a doctor or as a teacher but that's generally with fewer people at a time. For me, the Internet and technology was this new force factor for change in the world where young people could build things that would monumentally change billions of people's lives. You have to be a lot of things but you don't need to be old or seasoned to affect that change. Getting excited about being around those types of people is a big part of this job. The second part about this job that people have to be excited about is the investing piece. Some people don't get excited about capital allocation. You have to find the entrepreneurs who want to change the world in a small way for a ton of people but to do it in a capital efficient way. You have to want to do the work to price deals, size the markets, evaluate exit opportunities, and make only a few picks over a long career."

Measuring Performance

William McQuillan, a partner with Frontline Ventures, approaches his role as a venture capitalist with a similar humility and fascination to Lazar. He also recognizes that despite the excitement and allure of being around founders all the time, his instinct or intuition may often be off when he meets founders. He captures this understanding through a unique methodology to make him a better investor:

"Venture capital has a slow feedback cycle and it is extremely frustrating not knowing if you are good at your job or not. Forestry has quicker feedback cycles than venture capital. I started this practice of tracking my decisions on when I have said no to a company and why I said no. I track these companies with publicly available data on the total amount of capital each company has raised since we passed and divide it by the number of months since then. This allows me to compare companies on a level playing field. I group companies that we passed on in a few categories: weak founders, small market, competitive market, product or technology, price of round, and speed (the deal closed too quickly.) The weak teams raised the lowest follow-on capital, but this practice helps me gut-check which areas I'm right in and where I am wrong when evaluating companies. The analysis shows that we should not be investing in small markets, even if there is a great team. We should avoid investing in companies with highly competitive markets unless we think the team is incredible. I learned that my gut instincts on founders were pretty good and that I should trust this instinct more often. Finally, at the seed stage, product and technology are not good reasons for rejecting a company. This practice has already solidified my previously held views on weak founders or small markets, questioned my view on how I evaluate business models and products, and changed some of our internal thinking with how fast we can get to a decision."

Information Edge

Like that of an entrepreneur, the job of a venture capitalist is often lonely. It can be competitive from one partner to the next on who sources the best deals. Some investors I spoke with expressed their insecurities on whether or not, after two decades of being in venture capital, they had proven that they were truly capable venture investors. One such investor, a partner at a reputable fund, candidly speaks about the challenges of being a venture investor:

"Venture is a tough business to be in. The learning curve is long because you don't know for a long time if an investment was in fact, a good investment. It can be many years before you know if something was a good investment and you'll get a lot of false signals along the way because companies raise additional capital and increase valuations to be exorbitant but then ultimately go out of business. Terminal value is all that matters. When your feedback cycles are long, your learning curves are slow. People who have this job should treat it like it's the last job they'll have because if you do it for just a few years, you won't get much out of it."

An 'information edge' is something venture capitalists strive to create in order to remain competitive in this industry. The job of an investor is to make major investment decisions through a series of short meetings about a technology, company, or founder, all of which they have little knowledge about. Investors who develop theses in specific focus areas are at a unique advantage and focus on 'thesis-driven' investing. The venture capitalists themselves admit their fascination with colleagues who are able to quickly comprehend the intricacies of a business within a short period of time. Sitting at the forefront of innovation, investors often need to ramp up their knowledge quickly in order to compete. Ellie Wheeler of Greycroft details what acquiring this information edge has looked like for her over a decade of investing:

"Talking to people is more effective than individual, solitary research. Venture capitalists don't become deep experts; they become broad experts and focus on the big picture. The VC looks at a space, where the gaps are, where companies should be started if they don't see it. That's a model of research that can be adopted by incubators, startup studios and a model that some investors do well with. That's likely why you'll see some investors focused on thesis-driven investing because it is difficult to stay ahead of the curve on every business model, every industry, every founder type. I've also learned, in the number of years I've been doing this, that I have to remain nimble in my thinking and approach every new idea as its own despite what patterns I have seen in the past."

On this knowledge gap, most investors astutely recognize that their ability to match a founder's dedication and knowledge of an industry will be a nearly insurmountable feat. Instead, funds and venture investors form investment theses and approach genius through a framework.

CHAPTER 4
INVESTMENT THESES AND DEVELOPING AN INFORMATION EDGE

"The commitment to a thesis is part of the fiber of USV — a shared set of ideas creates a framework that allows us to operate with focus and work on what matters most to our team. But what that thesis is has evolved over time and will continue to evolve. It reflects both a changing world as well as the shifting interests of our partnership."

Rebecca Kaden, Union Square Ventures

Thesis Building

Theses are the bedrock of entrepreneurial endeavors. The most successful entrepreneurs observe systems in place around them, develop a set of forward-looking hypotheses about behaviors within that system, and identify a gap ripe for them to take advantage of. These gaps, which ultimately transform into businesses, persist across consumer behaviors, enterprise patterns, and general world movements. Vishal Vasishth, the former Chief Strategy Officer of Patagonia and co-founder of Obvious Ventures, recognizes in the entrepreneurs he invests in 'an amazing ability to develop a view of the world and fight for that new world without being stopped until their thesis is either proven right or wrong. An entrepreneur's thesis about how the world should operate fuels their conviction to persistently chip away to create change.

Venture capitalists take dozens of meetings each day with founders who all arrive at their doorstep from starkly different backgrounds and with unique visions and expertise. To better understand the intricacies of a company, to fully comprehend or push back on a founder's vision where unrealistic, investors look for systematic approaches to understand new industries and technologies quickly. In parallel to these entrepreneurs, venture investors operate in silos, developing their own robust theses on human, enterprise, and world behavior. Venture capitalists use their meetings with diverse founders to add to their thinking or to challenge their own reasoning or assumptions. As a result, their frameworks factor in the rapid disruptions enacted by the entrepreneurs around them. While an entrepreneurial thesis may be myopically focused on a problem and how a solution solves it, an investor accounts for the problem and examines the investment opportunities across a vast landscape. The investors match multiple entrepreneurial theses against their own to piece together a jigsaw puzzle

As Ellie Wheeler of Greycroft suggests, investors are compelled to adapt and be ahead of the knowledge curve with sectors of interest or technologies. If they are not, they are at risk of falling behind when the next best idea is introduced to them. This desire to surface new information and identify new patterns is tied to their ambition to prove that they, as investors, stand out from their peers because of their original thinking or hypotheses. Theses are the bedrock of entrepreneurial endeavors, but also act as a fundamental driver behind the strategic venture investment funds. In the absence of strong theses, investors can be easily swayed by the latest trend and fall victim to a herd mentality.

In the latter part of this book, investors from preeminent funds such as First Round Capital, Tribeca Venture Partners, Northzone Venture Partners, and others share their informed theses on sectors such as transportation, digital healthcare, financial technology, artificial intelligence, and the future of language, blockchain, genomics, and other interest areas. It's with this in-depth view into how investors form their theses that entrepreneurs can get a glimpse into how investors approach radical ideas and changing industries.

Software Eats the World

In 2011, in a contribution to the Wall Street Journal, venture investor Marc Andreessen outlined the thesis of the fund he co-founded, Andreessen Horowitz (known as a16z.) Most investment theses are grounded on the impact technology can potentially have on a sector and a16z's investments in Facebook, Airbnb, Box, GitHub, Lyft, and Slack were centered in the concept that "software eats the world." An excerpt from this WSJ piece details that strategy:

> "More and more major businesses and industries are being run on software and delivered as online services — from movies to agriculture to national defense. Many of the winners are Silicon Valley-style entrepreneurial technology companies that are invading and overturning established industry structures. Over the next 10 years, I expect many more industries to be disrupted by software, with new world-beating Silicon Valley companies doing the disruption in more cases than not. Why is this happening now? Six decades into the computer revolution, four decades since the invention of the microprocessor, and two decades into the rise of the modern Internet, all of the technology required to transform industries through software finally works and can be widely delivered at global scale. Over two billion people now use the broadband Internet, up from perhaps 50 million a decade ago, when I was at Netscape, the company I co-founded. In the next 10 years, I expect at least five billion people worldwide to own smartphones, giving every individual with such a phone instant access to the full power of the Internet, every moment of every day. On the back end, software programming tools and Internet-based services make it easy to launch new global software-powered startups in many industries — without the need to invest in new infrastructure and train new employees. In 2000, when my partner Ben Horowitz was CEO of the first cloud computing company, LoudCloud, the cost of a customer running a basic Internet application was approximately $150,000 a month. Running that same application today in Amazon's cloud costs about $1,500 a month. With lower start-up costs and a vastly expanded market for online services, the result is a global economy that for the first time will be fully digitally wired — the dream of every cyber-visionary of the early 1990s, finally delivered, a full generation later."

When this thesis was developed, the Internet was still a recent development in the history of the world. Even in 2019, however, PC and smartphone penetration is still bringing most of the world on to the Internet with access to modern tools, technologies, and access. The 'software eats the world' thesis expands to all industries, be it media or finance, and how software and the Internet will continue to change consumption patterns or behaviors as the global population comes online. Given this fairly broad approach, the partnership invests in categories that they believe will fall first to the forward-looking belief that "software eats the world" and then find the geniuses who can execute against that vision.

a16z witnessed this trend play out in media and information and invested opportunistically in companies such as BuzzFeed and Facebook. Chris Dixon, a partner at a16z invested $50 million in BuzzFeed in 2014. As the vanguard media companies were not keeping pace with these upstart technology companies, this bet proved to be a fruitful one to make. At the time of the investment, BuzzFeed had continued to change the way media was consumed. Dixon explains how the investment was in line with the a16z thesis:

> "Many of today's great media companies were built on top of emerging technologies. Examples include Time Inc. which was built on color printing, CBS which was built on radio, and Viacom which was built on cable TV. We're presently in the midst of a major technological shift in which, increasingly, news and entertainment are being distributed on social networks and consumed on mobile devices. We believe BuzzFeed will emerge from this period as a preeminent media company. We see BuzzFeed as a prime example of what we call a "full stack startup." BuzzFeed is a media company in the same sense that Tesla is a car company, Uber is a taxi company, or Netflix is a streaming movie company. We believe we're in the "deployment" phase of the Internet. The foundation has been laid. Tech is now spreading through every industry and every part of the world. The most interesting tech

companies aren't trying to sell software to other companies. They are trying to reshape industries from top to bottom."

Reshaping industries from top to bottom is how investors like Marc Andreessen like to invest. This persisting trend that dominates the world around them is a lens through which they guide their investment strategy.

As software 'ate' the financial sector, a16z invested in companies such as Branch International and Affirm. Looking to the future, a16z predicts this trend will occur in healthcare, government, and other sectors that will be impacted as the Internet continues to grow more entrenched across the global population. Given the broad focus of their thesis, that software will disrupt any and all industries, a16z looks to remain current. When asked by his colleague about pace and staying current, Ben Horowitz responded that investors must approach industries through the unifying approach of an investment thesis:

"Like a lot of things that are extremely complex, if you don't have some understanding of what's going on than it does get very complicated. One of the tenets when we started the firm was we were only going to invest in things that we understood. That meant things where software was a core intellectual property. If you look at what is happening across all of those [industries], they are different manifestations of software becoming a more powerful force in the world — the improvement in the underlying platforms; the improvement in the programming languages and connectivity. And so, whether it is software eating money or software eating entertainment, it all comes from the core root phenomenon of software."

a16z has successfully predicted many of these patterns through a deep understanding of software and technology, perhaps rooted in their experience as founders at the turn of the millennium when the Internet was spreading its tentacles into all areas of life. Yet, Andreessen and Horowitz tied their investment strategy to a specific horizontal platform in a slew of entrepreneurial endeavors.

As theses diverge and converge from fund to fund, tracking and staying abreast of them is a useful exercise for founders who are identifying the investment partners they hope to work with. The a16z foundational thesis has remained largely constant through the multiple funds the partnership has raised. As new partners join the firm, they bring new ideas and worldviews with them to extend this framework of thinking. Similarly, my conversations with investors at funds such as Union Square Ventures, Greycroft, Spark Capital, and Canaan Partners reveal unique insights into how theses evolve as partnerships expand, and how investment partners view the future of technology and its impact on sectors.

Evolving Theses

Union Square Ventures (USV) initially set out with a focus to invest in the 'application layer of the web.' Andy Weissman, a partner at USV, shared that their approach, as compared to Andreessen Horowitz's understanding that technology will continue to disrupt vertical industries, is focused on the network effects created as more people use software and are connected to one another online. Put simply: What exists when software does eat the world and now people interact in that new world? The USV approach is to look at disruption from a different angle and see how networks change as technology permeates our lives. The partnership believed that network effects, where the value of a service increases the more people use it, would play a central role in all web applications. Thesis 1.0 emerged: 'invest in large networks of engaged users, differentiated by user experience and defensible through network effects.' This investment thesis focused primarily on consumer businesses that could point to a highly engaged user base. USV's astute understanding of what drives networks across the web became the foundation for their investment decisions. These network effects lead to defensibility and scale. From this thesis, USV invested in valuable businesses such as Etsy, Twitter, Tumblr, Foursquare, and Kickstarter.

As existing networks became impenetrable, including those within and outside of USV's portfolio, the partnership evolved its thinking to focus its investments on the next layer of the web as it related to companies built around networks. Led by Andy Weissman, the partnership spent its second generation investing in networks and marketplaces that were vertically oriented within specific sectors — healthcare, education, finance, etc. — where a network could capitalize on a specific value proposition to an engaged group of users focused on a specific behavior. Within this second thesis, Weissman prescribed the fund invest in the technologies that power existing networks. Juxtaposed with its original thesis, USV began making investments in 'enablers of decentralized open technology and decentralized data which have the potential to counteract the centralizing force of the large Internet networks.' This included companies such as Coinbase.

In its third and most current generation, USV refined its original theses to invest in companies that 'broaden access.' Rebecca Kaden, a recent partner at USV, expanded on this thesis:

"In education, for example, Duolingo allows users to learn new languages around the world, on their phones and from their couches, for free. In healthcare, Nurx creates new ability for consumers to access medical care at dramatically reduced cost. Coinbase makes an emerging asset class accessible to mass markets. Twilio allows developers anywhere to easily access the world's voice and text communications infrastructure. We believe we are still at the beginning of the opportunity to broaden access with the most critical implications ahead of us. As a result, we decided to revise our thesis into a third version: 'USV backs trusted brands that broaden access to knowledge, capital, and well-being by leveraging networks, platforms, and protocols.' We think of knowledge, capital, and well-being as each encompassing multiple components. Knowledge includes education and learning, but also data-driven insights and access to new ideas. With capital, we include financial capital from financial services innovation, whether in the current system

or emerging financial platforms like crypto, but also human capi
technology infrastructure. And with well-being, we think about .
and wellness, but also entertainment, connection, community, ...u
fun. The goal of these businesses is to build trusted brands; products
and services that not only serve a purpose but integrate into the hearts
and minds of their customer in a way that is durable and important.
Trust comes from true alignment and convincing the customer that
their values and priorities are shared. The bar for this is higher than
ever but the best businesses will continually meet it."

Jigsaw Puzzle

Through the theses established by the reputable funds of a16z and Union
Square Ventures, the partners were able to specialize and identify trends and
patterns to invest from. They developed an information edge in a competitive
financing ecosystem and continued to refine it over decades. The process of
rapidly learning about diverse sectors and technologies and synthesizing that
learning to make quick investment decisions is a unique skill investors develop
that I sought to learn more about.

Peter Rojas, an investor with Betaworks and former founder of Gizmodo
and Engadget, shares his perspective on theses:

"Our job is similar to that of a critical theorist: take in information
and synthesize it into some analysis of a bigger framework. We
(Betaworks) think about things as systems. We have to be good at
understanding emergent systems and figuring out tactically where the
opportunities exist. If an industry is a cube with different layers in the
stack and different players in the market, an investor's thesis is a multi-
dimensional approach to understanding how an individual company
fits within that stack."

While most founders take a hyper-focused approach and examine how their
specific startup venture or technology fits into a larger competitive landscape

and industry, Jeremy Liew of LightSpeed Venture Partners calls his approach to investing a 'jigsaw puzzle' and says an investor's focus should be a higher-level, systems approach that transcends any one particular industry. Investors systematically work through this 'jigsaw puzzle' and identify how shifts within an industry present entrepreneurs with opportunity. Yet their approach is structured to focus on the full stack and see where each element meshes with the other. How will regulation play in one entrepreneur's favor over another? How will the past investments in this space dictate the future? Is the industry, overall, prepared for this shift? While entrepreneurs will undoubtedly be asking the same questions, an investor has the liberty to analyze the stack from a new perspective after meeting several companies approaching an identical problem from different angles, and to patiently wait for the market to mature. With each relationship and funding, entrepreneurs and investors continue to become better at understanding each other's motivations and a thorough understanding of thesis continues to mature.

Proving these theses true or false, with startup experiments, is something that will drive an investor's career, much as it does for an entrepreneur. Portfolio construction, or the investments made, reflect this. Ellie Wheeler of Greycroft describes thesis-driven investing as a time-bound approach. It takes five to 10 years to determine if a thesis proves to be true:

"Through the years, the common wisdom you hear in the industry is that you get a chance to figure out if your thesis is true for yourself and you tweak your investment model so that you either go further away from the common wisdom that is relevant or you actually find that it is true and holds true. Investing in people for example that exhibit certain qualities, investing in spaces that might be considered unsexy because you get higher leverage for each dollar invested, or patiently understanding an industry and waiting for the right opportunity to present itself when the market is mature enough are all important in our field. This requires incredible patience and rigor in order to find, as you put it, entrepreneurial genius that you are willing to take that once-in-a-decade bet on."

As Wheeler suggests, investment theses are not set in stone, nor should they be. They are continuously evolving and the venture funds behind them spend a significant amount of time informing their opinions about a space. In my own experience, I have worked with investors who will spend years on a specific technology, business model, geography, or stage, and meet with every company or expert in the space. As they gain a deeper knowledge about the landscape, they articulate where they believe the dollars will flow and how those dollars will exit the space as the industry ripens. Should this thesis not play out, the same investor will move to another sector and so on and so forth. Wheeler's thoughts on the topic, informed by her time at Lowercase Capital observing investors like Chris Sacca, and now proving out her own theses true at Greycroft with investments in companies like Plated, Blinkist and ELOQUII, remove the sense of randomness behind venture capital and introduce a more structural approach to how some of the best investors think about this topic. She describes this rigor and the mechanics behind developing theses:

"Investors have to remain flexible in their thinking and remain curious and willing to learn. That is the job. I've evolved my own thinking over time and a lot of that has to do with going through more repetitions. Meeting more and more founders, learning about more businesses and what works, seeing multiple lifecycles of the same company, or different companies informs your theses and builds a muscle memory to do it again with new areas. This information edge is important in our business."

The flexibility and curiosity Wheeler refers to is magnified by most investors I spoke with. As the pace of innovation accelerates and consumer trends and technologies go in and out of vogue, investors need to be at the precipice of each wave to catch it at the right point and ride it through subsequent cycles.

Naval Ravikant, an angel investor in companies such as Uber and Lyft, has said across multiple interviews that 'new companies always look really strange and they don't look very much like previous companies.' As a result, investors can often miss great investments because they were not flexible in their thinking. They will come to believe that there is a certain way of thinking and doing things to build successful companies and will miss exceptions to that rule. Spotify and Facebook are examples of companies that were not the first attempt in their category, but both turned into outsized returns. In his podcast, Ravikant references Sequoia Capital, a fund that invested in Uber, and expands on how investors remain flexible in their thinking:

"Before Uber came along, it was believed that the money was in all virtual goods and software, and not in handling real-world things like taxi dispatchers and dealing with unions. The conventional wisdom is always wrong. So as an investor, if you have a failed investment in one space, the worst thing you can do is write off that space and not make an investment again. For example, Sequoia Capital is one of the best investors on the planet. They were investors in Webvan, which was the failed grocery delivery service in the late '90s that blew up very badly. That they saw their own investment blow up, they lost a lot of money, they had egg on their face; they didn't care. They actually reevaluate every opportunity on its own merits and they know that a lot of these things are about timing. It might have been the right idea at the wrong time. And they also know that each great business looks weird, and there's no such thing as the perfect deal. So, there are lots and lots of venture capitalists who miss out on the great companies because they're looking for the perfect deal, and there is no such thing. So, I think anything that becomes conventional wisdom in this business gets blown up. "

In speaking with the successful entrepreneurs behind companies such as Pinterest, Betterment, and Learnvest, founders often take this landscape approach to building their company as opposed to being too myopic about their unique solution. To be a successful founder or investor, you have to be free of preconceived biases or concepts on how the world works and look for opportunity in areas that may appear strange or opaque at first.

Ilya Fushman, a partner with Kleiner Perkins (a venture fund founded by John Doerr that has invested in Amazon, AOL, Google, Spotify, and Twitter) has evolved as a venture capitalist through an investor role with Index Ventures followed by an operating role at Dropbox, when the company had less than 50 employees. Prior to these roles, Fushman earned a Ph.D. from Stanford University. In seeing the paths to which these partners have found themselves leading investments for venture capital funds, I became interested in how the theses or investment perspectives have evolved over a long career. Fushman elaborates on how he believes being thesis-informed is, at times, the optimal way to approach investing:

> "When you grow up in academia, you focus heavily on the problem and the solution and a lot less on the people. Over this whole journey, my biggest realization was that it is really all about the people. When you talk about being thesis-driven, I think about it as being *thesis-informed*. If you're truly thesis-driven, you have a bias. You're going to try to find the company that has the solution to the problem that you've identified, as opposed to finding the team in a space that you think is interesting and that has what it takes to build something that's big. That nuance is quite significant at the end of the day. When you get into early stage investing, the investments are 80-90% based on the team. Over time, it's still very much about the team, but you have more data to understand if the initial hypothesis on whether this market is playing out or not. You have more data around the product, the go-to-market, or whether the path the organization is taking is successful or not. You can be thesis driven at the later stages, but at the earlier stages you have to have a gut feel for people, which is what this book is getting at."

Over 15 years, Fushman has developed that 'gut instinct' on people within sectors he is interested in. Building on his experience as the head of business development for Dropbox, Fushman admits that when he first began his career, he had inherent biases and beliefs that were challenged by the people he worked with. These people, his fellow GPs at Kleiner Perkins, help keep Fushman's perspectives fresh and prevent any preconceived bias from blocking lucrative investment opportunities. With time as a venture capitalist's scarcest resource, it is often easy to dismiss new ideas that never worked before. Fushman says being thesis-informed and having the discipline to dig into new opportunities is important in his role as an early stage investor. Most often, it is a founder's unique perspective on an opportunity that is contrary to how the rest of the world thinks. It is this perspective that helps eliminate bias. Fushman shares an example of Nova Credit, a portfolio company of Kleiner Perkins that helps immigrants secure access to credit within the United States, that has helped to define this unique perspective:

"With Nova Credit, if you meet with the founder, Misha Episov, he's able to captivate your attention. But if you hear the pitch peripherally, you may write it off because of market size. The company is focused on credit for immigrants, but there are tens of millions of immigrants and not hundreds of millions, so how will this ever be a big business? But if you look underneath the hood and investigate, the number of times you need a credit report for an immigrant is 5-6x higher than what you need for someone who is native. So, your total market is much bigger than it seems. Misha understood this. It's easy to dismiss this off the back but here you need good judgement and be able to make a good call that is informed. Frankly, it comes back to people. You want to sit in the room, and you may be ready to dismiss the idea, but then the founder gets you incredibly inspired by the entrepreneur and you dismiss some of the biases. I do think there are some businesses that are not venture-fundable — commodities, such as solar businesses, that can't have premium pricing in the market and then need a lot of capital to hit scale. Those two things together are very hard from a venture perspective."

Multiple Points of Disruption

When discussing why investors made a bet on companies such as Uber, Pinterest, Twitch, or League of Legends, Rick Heitzmann of FirstMark Capital alludes to the 'jigsaw puzzle' approach mentioned earlier, as several pieces aligned perfectly to make these companies attractive investments. Heitzmann evaluates investment opportunities as the culmination of converging consumer behaviors, advancements in technology, or incumbents not evolving to meet a customer need, occurring simultaneously to present a founder with an opportunity. Heitzmann describes how his thesis evolves and how he analyses opportunities when investing:

"It is necessary to change and evolve a thesis as it plays out. You see different industries being disrupted at different times. As a VC, you're constantly looking for the beginning of a disruption. With Riot Games, there was high enough penetration of broadband where users could play social video games digitally. Secondly, there was high enough delivery on that broadband that you could deliver a high-quality game broadly. People were open to digital commerce so you could pay for a game over the computer where the market could move to an item-based, microtransaction economy versus a pay-up-front economy. There were enough gamers out there that could absorb a broad-based game. There were multiple points of disruption, therefore innovation. Online gaming was not as broad, but that market has evolved to where people not only play as online gamers but are now competitive, which has led to our investments in Riot's League of Legends. We look for themes like this to play out and if it is big enough, in our eyes, we see it pull other things downstream."

With two other examples, Heitzmann discusses how the idea of multiple points of disruption have played out in different sectors and why investors were willing to make those bets:

"Look at Pinterest as an example. The world is moving mobile, the world has become increasingly visual as people are now consuming more content on a small screen and also commerce trends have shifted to a more visual approach. The world was increasingly becoming more social through this lens as well, so curation is important. All of these multiple points came together to point to Pinterest. Outside of my portfolio, but a perfect example of how multiple points of disruption play out, is Uber. The penetration of smartphones was such that every person driving a cab, or a car is equipped with a smartphone and they now act as a beacon. Everyone who is looking for a cab, for the most part, has a smartphone in large metropolitan cities. Yet, the taxi and limousine commissions were not driving innovation around that. The GPS system across these devices is enough that we know where those people or cabs always are. There is an ability to pay through mobile and to track people through mobile. All of these abilities and points of disruption came together to point to Uber."

Heitzmann refers to the introduction of mobile technologies as the catalyst behind companies such as Pinterest and Uber. Mobile, as a platform, was a fundamental piece within the jigsaw puzzle that Heitzmann analyzed from the perspective of market penetration, processing power, and consumer behavior.

Similar to a16z's approach to software or Heitzmann's approach to mobile, other seed funds such as Eniac Ventures and Betaworks inform their theses through an approach driven by platforms. As opportunities have slimmed with an abundance of capital, they have gone more specific than 'software' and developed more vertically-aligned interest areas. As smartphone penetration increased, most investors have developed opinions on the capability of smartphones and where opportunities would arise as a result of penetration, until these opportunities tapped out. They formed their theses around a platform and examined opportunities related to that specific interface. Mobile phones, VR/AR headsets, Google Glasses, Apple Watch, Apple Airpods are all new platforms that may change the way the puzzle is built. Peter Rojas, Matthew Hartman, and John Borthwick, who collectively established Betaworks' venture fund, suggest that this interface-layer of investing will hold true for its next set of investments, but across new areas such as synthetic media or at the intersection of live experiences and digital media:

> "To find opportunity, we begin by looking at interfaces. We look at the platforms or interfaces that are driving change in areas or behaviors now and we believe, in 2018, that those interfaces are voice computing, augmented reality, virtual reality, computer vision, conversational interfaces (chatbots), eSports or game streaming. These are broad areas but reflect the idea that we want to be more forward looking as opposed to looking at established behaviors. We will look at legacy tech if something fundamentally has changed in that space. While audio has been around a long time, we're investing in audio now because of smartphones and speakers in pockets or the tech that Apple has rolled out with Airpods. So, we invested in five companies within the audio space who we believe will take advantage of these changes."

Obvious Ventures & Values-Driven Investing

Obvious Ventures is a recent fund (when compared to a16z, Founders Fund, Sequoia, USV, and the likes) to the Silicon Valley VC scene, but they bring a radical approach to investing that its LPs appreciate. The fund was co-founded by Ev Williams, a co-founder of Twitter and founder of Medium, and Vishal Vasishth, the former Chief Strategy Officer of Patagonia. When they set out to develop the thesis of this fund, Williams told Vasishth:

> "When I was pitching my startup ventures to investors, I often talked about the metrics, the total addressable market, the customer, the user

metrics and rattled those off because it's what I thought they cared about. We rarely, if ever, spoke about the values behind why we were building what we were about to build together. Why we thought it was better for the world. Investors do think about those things. I think about those things. But that conversation never comes up. Yet, if the values break down while building the company, the entire operation is a disaster. The values breakdown between an investor and a founder is where the true misalignment begins. That should be our thesis, to be value-driven."

Williams and Vasishth thought through their investment thesis to make them timeless but to also redirect capitalism: to make the world better through technology and innovation, while still returning capital to their investors. The resulting areas of focus for Obvious Ventures became sustainable systems, health and food, healthcare, and people power. A growing number of limited partners and venture capitalists are partnering to determine if capitalism can be used to make the world better through technology and innovation. These funds are still driven to invest in profitable businesses that return money to its investors, but a simultaneous goal is to create a positive impact. Obvious Ventures has looked at resource-intensive industries and invested in businesses focused on renewable energy and the electrification of transportation away from fossil fuels. Obvious Ventures has also invested in businesses that improve the holistic health of humans through healthy eating and nutrition. In that vein, Obvious Ventures invested in Beyond Meat, a company that returned a large financial return to the fund's investors when the company went public on the New York Stock Exchange. While Obvious Ventures' investment categories are seemingly broad, Vasishth explains the group's thinking by outlining the investments that resonated with them:

"Strategically, our investment theses are intended to be timeless and forever in service of that goal. Obvious was built on a conviction that technology is transforming every sector of the global economy, and those doing so through a world-positive lens will be moving humanity forward. If we can invest in these entrepreneurs and these theses, it makes business sense while concurrently solving our world's biggest problems."

Venture capital that invests in companies with impact can be used to achieve the same kinds of returns for investors as a traditional venture capitalist can. Rethink Impact, a venture capital fund launched by Jenny Abramson, the former CEO of LiveSafe (a tech security company focused on preventing school shootings and sexual assaults), raised over $110 million to invest in female-led technology companies focused on improving education, healthcare, the environment, and economic inequality. Abramson says that often times, the diligence in a company focused on impact is more rigorous than in other scenarios:

"During diligence, we layer on the impact piece on top of the financial model and we look at both as intertwined. We ask if the quest for impact is deeply embedded in the company. We ask if the company is solving a challenge in a way that is sustainable. The major part of that sustainability is that it has to be a strong financial business where business success actually fuels the impact and vice versa."

Funds such as Obvious Ventures, a16z, Union Square Ventures, Notation Capital, Betaworks, Greycroft, and FirstMark Capital make their investment theses known to entrepreneurs so that the founders who share their worldview will reach out to them to build that partnership. While USV or a16z have been fairly consistent in their approach, some venture funds actively describe their changing investment thesis each year. They are public about their investment interests and it is up to the entrepreneur to do the work to identify which investors will be the right fit for them and vice versa. One of the more prominent investors to do this is Mary Meeker, a former partner with Kleiner Perkins Caufield & Byers, who launched a $1 billion growth equity fund called Bond in 2019.

Meeker issues an "Internet Trends Report" in which she documents the ideas, industries, and changes she is interested in. Collaborative Fund, once focused on consumer ventures, is now looking to behavioral trends of Generation Y and Z and will often publish their perspective on these trends. Peter Rojas of Betaworks is clear about their forward-looking approach and recognizes that some themes will remain embedded in their DNA as a venture fund:

> "Betaworks is at the intersection of media, technology, and communications. Going back to the early 2000s, the frontiers of these industries revolved around social, mobile, and real-time data. Those elements came together and changed the way media was organized or monetized. Social changed the way media is curated and engaged with. Now that those behaviors are well established, when we look for investments in social and mobile, we want to see some emerging behavior or element that is changing and now creates an opportunity. When we get pitched the next mobile photo sharing app, we're not going to take a very serious look at it."

Bouncing Around the Echo Chamber

The counter point that many entrepreneurs, including myself, have felt about the theses that drive venture capital is that it forms an echo chamber. One investor may write a blog post or publicly proclaim that (picking a random sector for the purpose of making a point) *"Voice Interfaces are Dead!"* and all investors may follow this person's train of thought and refuse to fund or meet with founders despite the solution they offer. This has happened in every cycle to different groups of entrepreneurs. It happens to entrepreneurs within media companies pushing advertising business models against investors who claim that Facebook and Google have taken the pie away from them. It happens to education entrepreneurs and investors refusing to believe that there will be a big enough exit within the education sector or that it is too hard to sell into schools and to teachers. This opposition began to take hold, as of 2018, with direct-to-consumer commerce companies and the belief that most of these companies could not survive post-venture dollars or offer a differentiated enough solution to justify a high return on investment. Theses can often be subject to "group-think" but as all investors will tell you, the investors who follow the pack like lemmings rarely survive, nor offer value to a company when it's needed. When I asked Ellie Wheeler how she prevents herself from forming a negative perception of an industry just because it hasn't worked in the past, she recognized the importance of remaining fresh in her approach, despite having a successful career in venture capital for over a decade. Wheeler says:

"Sometimes seeing the same kind of company in a space over 50 times and knowing that it won't work will make me pass again on the 51st time. Investors won't invest in a space until they are confident that something has fundamentally changed about that market — maybe it's a business model shift, maybe it's that an incumbent has switched their strategy, maybe it's something novel in the go-to-market strategy, maybe it's something within the problem that the market did not fully understand. If there are a ton of failures in a space, it colors the water but there is usually an underlying cause behind these failures. There is a tech reason or a go-to-market reason, but a founder's job is to tell us why the market is now ripe and now ready, where it was not in the past. We have had those experiences in the past, where we think something must exist, based on a thesis, but the rest of the characteristics around the market — competition, regulatory, or another dynamic — were not ready. Sometimes there is a change in the market, but that's where if an investor is following the herd or not an expert on the space, they'll miss the opportunity. You need to stay flexible in your thinking and you need founders to challenge you in your thinking."

Venture capital veteran Andy Weissman, a GP with USV, acknowledges the echo chamber and remains nimble in his thinking. He says that, as with entrepreneurs, being lucky is important to venture investors in determining whether their theses play out as they had hoped:

"I think there is an incredibly healthy and underappreciated amount of luck that comes into what we [venture capitalists] do. There is some skill, but there is an enormous amount of luck. There is so much randomness at the early stage that it is really hard to predict what will work. Theses help to move strategy forward and if you have a point of view about the world and you are constantly unpacking that point of view you get closer to the companies in order to be lucky. We evaluate hundreds of opportunities and are helping to build dozens of companies at a time. Through that experience, you refine your point of view and every now and again, a company comes in front of you that fits that point of view that you've been developing. Maybe it's Tumblr, maybe it's Kickstarter. There will be 10 companies that don't work out but over the course of a portfolio, you can find success by being informed."

SECTION 2
PATTERNS OF GENIUS

CHAPTER 5
IN PURSUIT OF GENIUS

"Smart people are a dime a dozen, and many of them don't amount to much."

Walter Isaacson

Genius is reserved for non-conformists who push the boundaries of their fields through creativity and exceptional talent. This is rarely defined solely through a measure of IQ, because geniuses need more than raw intellect to achieve the extraordinary. They often pursue paths of great resistance to redefine our basic understanding of the world around us. Genius manifested itself through the creativity of Spielberg, the athleticism of Serena Williams, the scientific reasoning of Stephen Hawking, the imagination of Rowling, and the political feats achieved by Barack Obama. By studying extraordinary stories of humans such as these, Malcolm Gladwell deconstructed the relationship between intellectual aptitude and success in The Outliers. In a contemporary work with a similar conclusion, The Originals, Adam Grant writes that outliers and geniuses are not only the ones with exceptional ideas, but those who take the necessary action to will them into existence. Grant argues that being born smart is not enough of a precursor for genius and adds that 'child prodigies rarely amount to much' because they never establish an appetite for failure.

Like Grant and Gladwell, Walter Isaacson has studied history's geniuses — Benjamin Franklin, Albert Einstein, Leonardo Da Vinci, the creators of the modern Internet. Isaacson also studied a modern genius, Steve Jobs, and suggests that his 'success dramatizes an interesting distinction between intelligence and genius' in which his defining characteristic as a genius was his heightened sense of intuition. Jobs' imaginative leaps on human behavior were not developed through analytical rigor, but instead sparked by his 'experiential wisdom' which in turn, shaped his intuition. Isaacson writes:

"So, was Mr. Jobs smart? Not conventionally. Instead, he was a genius... Trained in Zen Buddhism, Mr. Jobs came to value experiential wisdom over empirical analysis. He didn't study data or crunch numbers but like a pathfinder, he could sniff the winds and sense what lay ahead. He told me he began to appreciate the power of intuition, in contrast to what he called "western rational thought," when he wandered around India after dropping out of college. 'The people in the Indian countryside don't use their intellect like we do,' he said. 'They use their intuition instead... Intuition is a very powerful thing, more powerful than intellect, in my opinion. That's had a big impact on my work.'..."

Genius, according to those who have documented it, goes beyond IQ or raw intellect. It is developed through creativity, intuition, and a heightened resilience to achieve the extraordinary.

Finding Genius

Gladwell, Grant, and Isaacson approach genius after it is has already been exhibited for the world to see or after the geniuses have willed their creations into existence. They tell stories of human excellence for the world to hear and learn from. However, a few groups of people — teachers, athletic scouts, grantors — define their living on spotting genius before qualities of grandeur have even manifested themselves. Venture capital is one such field, founded on attempts to find genius before an entrepreneur has proven to be an original or an outlier. There are patterns that set entrepreneurial geniuses apart and this group of individuals hopes to capitalize on those patterns.

A successful venture capitalist thrives on being able to find genius in its rawest form, using little data or insight, multiple times over their career. As Nicholas Chirls of Notation Capital says, 'finding a genius once or twice is lucky, doing it repeatedly is true validation that you're equipped to do this.' Venture capitalists will succeed or fail on their ability to make quick judgments, with limited information, based on trends they have observed in the past, and as Isaacson observed of Steve Jobs, through intuition over intellect.

Fred Wilson, the founder of Union Square Ventures (USV), reiterated this claim that an investor's ability to use intuition and recognize patterns is what will define their career. Wilson is a career venture capitalist whose fund's partnership has made select investments in entrepreneurs it believes to possess entrepreneurial genius — Jack Dorsey of Twitter, Patrick Collison of Stripe, David Karp of Tumblr, Mark Pincus of Zynga. The USV thesis has been refined over decades of backing successful entrepreneurs. So too has the intuition of its partners — an intuition that is difficult to capture or mimic, but something I hoped to better understand.

Fred Wilson believes 'that someone is either born an entrepreneur or they're not.' Wilson expresses an openness to being challenged on this belief given that the 'judgments' he will make on people and entrepreneurs will be some of the most important decisions he will make as a venture investor. Based on a career that has spanned over 25 years, Wilson wrote in his blog (AVC) of the inherent qualities that to him, define entrepreneurial genius:

- A desire to accept risk and ambiguity, and the ability to live with them
- An ability to construct a vision and sell it to many others
- A confidence bordering on arrogance
- A stubborn belief in one's self
- A magnet for talent

Fred's comments guided my conversations with dozens of other investors who have led investments in companies such as SpaceX, Facebook, PayPal, Tesla, Airbnb, Lyft, Uber, Twitter, Pinterest, and others. These investors are part of the best venture funds both in the U.S. and internationally and include men and women from diverse backgrounds and experiences. The questions remained the same, but the answers varied. Does entrepreneurship fall within the age-old debate of nature versus nurture? Did these men and women who invested in founders agree with the qualities and patterns presented by Wilson to describe genius entrepreneurs?

Investors such as Keith Rabois, Paul Graham, and Ben Horowitz largely agree that genius begins to manifest itself earlier in life through anecdotes of unique tenacity and competitiveness. Rabois argues that the founders he has worked with, or invested in, across arguably some of the most successful technology companies — including YouTube, Twitter, Opendoor, Yelp, LinkedIn, and PayPal — would definitely score high on an IQ test because their minds must see connections and patterns that others do not. Yet IQ alone, according to Rabois, is not the trait that drives successful founders. High IQ is a common foundation on which the characteristics set forth by Wilson begin to reveal themselves.

The Antifragile: Accepting Risk and Ambiguity

The antagonist to Wilson's entrepreneurial genius is the individual who is obsessive and rigidly focused on the structured path of conformity. These are not the outliers or the originals, but the ordinary. Even with high IQ some of these men and women choose to pursue stability or wealth. They can be incredible additions to a team in the early years of a company and add value to a growing organization, but the founders themselves must be accustomed to a healthy level of uncertainty and be able to ride the ups and downs of starting a business with poise. FirstMark Capital's Rick Heitzmann, an investor in companies such as Airbnb, StubHub, Pinterest, Riot Games, Upwork, and others, elaborates on this:

> "The biggest thing that frustrates me about entrepreneurs is that every quarter, I sit with founders who want to be entrepreneurs that have potentially groundbreaking business ideas, but they say, 'I currently have a certain quality of life and do not want to leave my job. If you give me funding, I will leave my job and work on this full time.' You can start a company while you're working another job and often times that

may be smarter, but in order to secure financing there is a requirement of commitment. There are far too many tourist entrepreneurs ("wantrepreneurs") who do not want to take much risk. They want to make excuses and hedge themselves from failing. It is hard to back that type of entrepreneur."

Heitzmann says he has made mistakes in the past by investing in these types of individuals and has refined his questions and intuition about founders to test their endurance. Ellie Wheeler of Greycroft shares that 'tourist founders' have become a trend in recent years:

"Because the technology media covers success and financing events, there are still too many people who don't understand how hard it is to go at being a founder alone. There are those people that are tourists — they see starting a company as hot, they see it as a get-rich-quick scheme, typically they use a lot of lingo. They don't have the unique insight or experience but they're coming at it because it's a shiny new object and they don't have staying power. It becomes very obvious when you've seen it thousands of times."

The 'overnight success' story where smart people believe they can cash out from an entrepreneurial endeavor within months of starting is a common, but misplaced, expectation. Success to these entrepreneurs is defined as the path of least resistance, and in the event the company faces the slightest rejection, the founder pulls the escape cord and jumps to the next opportunity. Entrepreneurship requires staying power and venture capitalists invest in those founders who have the staying power for that seven year, or more, holding period. It is on the founder to demonstrate this level of commitment and according to Heitzmann, it is on him to 'develop a sense of intuition as to which types of founders will demonstrate a healthy appetite for uncertainty, but not chaos.'

In *Antifragile: Things that Gain from Disorder*, Nassim Taleb discusses how some individuals endure through uncertainty. Taleb writes that there are some people who can be more intelligent than others in a structured environment. They can exhibit that IQ that Rabois and Wilson mention in environments built on repetition where there are clear indicators of success. Traditional schooling, he writes, has a 'selection bias as it favors those quicker in such an environment, and like anything competitive, at the expense of performance outside of it.' Taleb explores structured environments versus ambiguity, and there are parallels to the entrepreneurs described by venture capitalists. He explains:

"Although I was not yet familiar with gyms, my idea of knowledge was as follows. People who build their strength using these modern expensive gym machines can lift extremely large weights, show great numbers, and develop impressive-looking muscles, but fail to lift a stone; they get completely hammered in a street fight by someone trained in more disorderly settings. Their strength is domain-specific and their domain doesn't exist outside of ludic, extremely organized constructs. In fact, as with over-specialized athletes, their strength is the result of a deformity. I thought it was the same with people who were selected for training to get high grades in a small number rather than follow their curiosity: try taking them slightly away from what they studied and watch their decomposition, loss of confidence, and denial... I've debated many economists who claim to specialize in risk and probability: when one takes them slightly outside their narrow focus, but within the discipline of probability, they fall apart, with the disconsolate face of a gym rat in front of a gangster hit man."

It is difficult to break away from organized constructs. Despite Silicon Valley's best efforts to upend the status quo, most children and young adults operate on structured educational paths that train our minds to choose the defined path set in front of us in order to succeed.

According to some of history's greatest biographers of extraordinary individuals (Taleb, Isaacson, Grant, Gladwell), venture capitalists behind the geniuses who founded Tesla and Apple, and the founders who shared their stories for *Disruptors*, shying away from conformity or structure and having the experience of enduring hardships is what wakes up a person's inner-genius. It is through unstructured paths and experiential wisdom where intuition begins to form, as Jobs experienced through unique, differentiated experiences. Similarly, an entrepreneur's tenacity and ability to live with ambiguity or risk does not magically appear when they decide to start a company. According to Rabois, tenacity appears earlier in the founder's life and is something an investor should dig for:

> "People like Max Levchin (PayPal, Affirm), Peter Thiel (PayPal, Founders Fund), Reid Hoffman (LinkedIn), Joe Gebbia (Airbnb), Brian Chesky (Airbnb), Chad Hurley (YouTube), Jack Dorsey (Twitter, Square) are all entirely different founders with different skill sets. It is hard to say that a singular definition for genius can be attributed to all these people. The one common thread between them, however, is something Paul Graham (Y-Combinator) talks extensively about: being relentlessly resourceful — a modified version of tenacity. These founders, when I've worked with them, have this unrelenting energy, a feeling like they'll never be defeated. I believe people are not born with tenacity but by a certain age, it has been built into them. There are examples in your background of where you've used heroic energy and refused to lose. My goal as an investor is to learn about those. I'll do calls with old colleagues, classmates, teachers, coaches to hear about those. That tenacity does not suddenly show up when you're 25 years old. You either just don't accept excuses and prevail, or you accept excuses. I can tell fairly quickly who is who."

Genius founders are amongst the world's most impatient, unsatisfied people — with themselves, with markets, with the status quo. It's not always that the world has put them in positions of conflict, but instead, they themselves seek out conflict or discomfort. They have always put themselves into challenging situations — competitive sports, academics, coding competitions

— and may have competed in some extracurricular activity. They thrive amidst discomfort, stress, and challenge, and have always had that since they were eight years old until the time investors meet them. Someone's tenacity is one of the top things investors like Rabois is looking for when they are making an investment.

The risk and ambiguity of entrepreneurship met with the tenacity of disruptive founders has been personified through stories of founders such as Vin Vacanti of Yipit who endured 13 failed prototypes before landing on a profitable data-driven enterprise. Then there's Nihal Mehta who declared bankruptcy at 22 after a startup failure prior to founding Local Response and going on to launch Eniac Ventures. And Rabois tells of Joe Gebbia and Brian Chesky of Airbnb. Gebbia described the most ambiguous point of a startup to be the 'trough of sorrow' where an entrepreneur is tested most. After the initial excitement of Airbnb's vision petered out, the founders of Airbnb went through an 18-month period of being completely broke and owing over $15,000 on their credit cards. A series of rejections from venture investors set them back further. As the founders altered their product and approach to the market, they endured through this trough and found innovative ways to stay afloat. Gebbia says that most entrepreneurs fail during this point because they cannot, or are unwilling, to endure the uncertainty. Rabois recounted a quote in which Gebbia said:

> "I think most people fail when they've hit the trough of sorrow. If you can get through the trough of sorrow, you can get through all the adversities of starting a company. The trough of sorrow makes or breaks people. The key to success is finding your way out of the trough of sorrow, where an entrepreneur's true mettle is tested."

Josh Wolfe of Lux Capital, a venture fund that has built its reputation on investing in moonshot ideas and businesses, shares a similar perspective on founders and the adversity they face. In an interview with Term Sheet, Wolfe said:

"In a founder, we love when there is something to prove. The best founders that we back have an indistinguishable flame that usually comes from some sort of adversity... there's something that made them feel like an outsider. And there's this indistinguishable drive that they want to prove other people wrong. It's interesting because success, achievement, and wealth never put that fire out. I think it's this broader secret to societal progress if you can spot these rebels who are fueled by the passion that comes from some dysfunction that happened early.... I find that people who are born into circumstances where they had silver spoons, everything was handed to them, or they come from great wealth, more often than not, don't have the same kind of drive."

How can entrepreneurs grow and thrive through 'volatility, randomness, disorders, risk, and uncertainty'? The Antifragile entrepreneur is one who will bend, but not break. As Josh Nussbaum of Compound sees it, an antifragile entrepreneur is 'one that thinks about their business decisions in a way that will allow them to make mistakes, but not cost them, or their investors, the entire company' or create the 'chaos' that Heitzmann alluded to. The genius entrepreneur is antifragile because they have demonstrated a willingness and persistence to thrive through the ups and downs of entrepreneurship and the uncertainty of the process, while having a calming effect on the vision and mission of their organization. Taylor Greene, a partner with Collaborative Fund, explains how he approaches entrepreneurs and their tolerance for risk:

"I'm trying to find entrepreneurs who walk the line between risk-loving behavior and reckless behavior. Entrepreneurs that take calculated risks are the best entrepreneurs and if I can hear those stories, it compels me to invest. It will never be the perfect calculation. They have just enough imperfect information to make a decision to move forward and they know when to move forward and move it in a different direction. They're scientists with a hypothesis to prove it out or prove it wrong.

It's a series of decision points and you're looking for the people with that mentality."

Wolfe expands on this by talking about the 'risk fallacy':

"I actually believe there is a narrative fallacy that people are totally wrong in thinking that entrepreneurs are these great risk-takers. I believe that the very best entrepreneurs are risk-killers. They're thinking, "How do I achieve what I want by eliminating every risk along the way?" The best leaders of companies are able to imagine failure and prevent it from happening."

Given that uncertainty is inevitable with running any startup experiment, genius founders possess a high degree of adaptability. Ilya Fushman, a partner with Kleiner Perkins and an investor in Slack, recognizes that many of the great businesses of our generation, including Slack, are the products of pivots where founders adapted quickly given new learnings or challenges. Fushman argues that genius founders are constantly adapting to changing teams, markets, and concepts, furthering the idea that the best founders are those who thrive in unstructured environments.

Adaptability, according to Fushman, is often something that the most pedigreed founders lack. Fushman elaborates on this with a contrarian view from the rest of the venture capital industry:

"It is easy to invest in companies with central casting. Central casting being the pedigreed Ivy League, followed by a great business school, with some consulting or financial industry time, and then they've decided to build a company. But a lot of them are not good investments because those people also often don't have that risk tolerance. We want to invest in the underdog founder who has consistently adapted to new conditions and defined their own definition of success or made their own path."

Future Makers

"Mediocre VCs want to see that your company has traction. The top VCs want you to show them you can invent the future."

Suhail Doshi, Founder of Mixpanel

The New Yorker, 2015

Spark Capital, an early stage venture fund established in Boston in 2005 with a growing presence in New York and San Francisco, boasts early investments in companies such as Twitter, Oculus, Tumblr, Wayfair, Slack, Warby Parker, and Cruise Automation. Cruise Automation, an early bet on autonomous driving, sold to General Motors for $1 billion just six months after Spark Capital made its initial investment, and has been behind GM's innovation for autonomous vehicles. Oculus was sold to Facebook for $2 billion in 2014, and Twitter and Wayfair, two 'startup' ventures Spark backed at inception, have had initial public offerings valuing the companies at $14 billion and $3 billion, respectively. Collectively, the geniuses existing within Spark's portfolio of companies are shaping the future of industries. Spark's prior successes paved the way for it to raise its fifth investment fund of $450 million to continue investing along the same themes as it did when it began.

Andrew Parker, a general partner with Spark Capital, began his career in New York City at Union Square Ventures, under the mentorship of Fred Wilson. With Spark, Parker has led investments in companies such as Kik, Upworthy, and Tumblr. Tumblr, founded by David Karp, sold to Yahoo for $1.1 billion in 2013. When asked about these investment decisions, Parker explained that when he is sitting across from a founder, the first thing he is looking for to identify 'genius' is an ability to be a 'future maker'. While Wilson described a similar quality as someone who is able to construct a vision and sell it to others, Parker takes this thinking one step further:

"I sit across from entrepreneurs all day. Sitting across from a compelling entrepreneur is like feeling swept up in a feeling that I'm sitting across from a future Wozniak of the world, or maybe they are already that type of person. I want to see a future maker. A future maker is someone that sees a vision for how they expect the world to look seven to 10 years from now and has an incredibly compelling picture of that world, how they plan to make that impact and how you (the investor), in a small way, can help them get there. If by the end of that conversation, you feel like you want to just quit your job and go work for them, you know that you are in the company of 'genius'."

Tactically, when acting as a 'future maker,' Rick Heitzmann believes that it is important for entrepreneurs to identify and present multiple points of simultaneous disruption that can predicate groundbreaking innovation. As an example, Heitzmann discussed the success of Uber as an innovation resulting from several minor disruptions and shifts occurring simultaneously and a subsequent, future innovation that would take place as a result of those changes. These converging factors included smartphone penetration (especially with taxi drivers), advancements in GPS technology, and the taxi and limousine commission in large cities not evolving fast enough to keep pace with growing urban populations. Heitzmann explained that genius founders are able to explain their vision for the future in those terms, of diverging forces and interests converging around one unique founder's vision for the future, rather than being hyper-focused on the problem that they are hoping to solve in its current state. This type of thinking demonstrates that even if the specific solution or manifestation of a product is not apparent yet, there may be shared vision between the investor and the entrepreneur for a future where a product can take shape by monitoring user behavior.

Heitzmann admits that he would generally fund a team that he believes to possess these qualities even if their specific perspective on a solution does not have the typical investible product-market fit just yet. In that vein, Heitzmann and the FirstMark team have invested in serial entrepreneurs and trust that together, the investors and the founders would work together to build the proper product for that shared vision of the future. Genius, in Heitzmann's eyes, is a founder who can eloquently sell him on a future where a product must exist, but while also articulating the exact strategy that will bring those forces together.

Conviction vs. Arrogance

Startup founders are often described as trailblazing disruptors who refuse to accept traditional rules or norms. While this description was once a positive indicator, some investors stepped back from this unapologetic approach. In a time where startup founders are likened to celebrities and scandals involving their often unchecked exuberance are widely reported on, the nefarious practices at companies such as Uber, Theranos, and Zenefits come under greater scrutiny. The investors I spoke with pointed to a tempered humility, rather than boundless confidence, when identifying the founders they prefer to partner with. They alluded to the chaos caused by the exuberance of the architects of the 2008 financial crisis and likened this same arrogance to some founders and investors they encounter today who have not lived through a downturn in a venture cycle. Elizabeth Holmes of Theranos defrauded seasoned investors such as Rupert Murdoch and DFJ (Twilio, Twitter, Skype) to the tune of $1.2 billion in invested capital. Journalist Caroline Polisi reported on Holmes' hubris:

> "Whether it's confidence or hubris or just unbridled ambition, many truly believe that their company will be the next big thing, that they can pay off their debts as long as they can close the next deal, and that all will be forgiven once their investors are rich. By all indications, Holmes ardently believed that her company would change the world. And her promises to investors were consistent with the media image she was simultaneously cultivating for her company: that it was on the forefront of revolutionizing the diagnostics industry, breaking into new territory to drive change and quite possibly eradicate epidemics as we know them. Except, according to the SEC, she was lying to investors along the way."

Starting a company does require a founder to be bold and willing to bend existing frameworks, but unchecked arrogance has led to a mass destruction in capital in recent years. With Zenefits, an insurance marketplace that had achieved a valuation upward of $4.2 billion before tumbling down after a series of internal scandals, CEO Parker Conrad was accused of having an arrogance that took him away from understanding the happenings in the corners of his company. After being replaced, Zenefits' new CEO wrote to his employees and inferred that the hack-first-and-ask-questions-later philosophy does not work once a company matures past the startup stages.

Throughout 2018, this behavior appeared again at Facebook as the executive team comprised of Mark Zuckerberg and Sheryl Sandberg deflected blame from themselves to 'rogue behavior' within their organization. Silicon Valley's 'change the world at all costs' culture is filled with fraudsters and arrogant egomaniacs who ignore the minute details of running a company. Investors have refined their intuition to stress test for these founders. Brian Laung Aeoah, the son of an education entrepreneur from Uganda and now a partner at KEC Ventures, says the genius of an entrepreneur is to be able to set vision and be a high-level thinker, but to have the willingness and humility to pay attention to the details:

"There are founders that are great at the big picture things but can't get into the details or just don't want to. What I'm generally looking for is someone who can do both. Someone who can talk about the $13 trillion market potential, but can then tell me what their strategic plan is for the next 12 months and how they'll reach the customers who are going to buy their product. They can tell me what these customers look like, talk like, where they live, and what they do in their free time. Sure, the $13 trillion market is appealing, but if we don't make it into the next 12 months, it's going to be irrelevant. The second thing I want to know about is the vision. Everyone will have some kind of an answer to this question but may not have given it enough thought. One big vision answer will be very vague and lacking details, another one will have the details. That's how you know that this is probably someone that can do both. You obviously want to figure out that they know who the customer is today, how to sell to them, what the pain points are, why those people are buying."

Humility is what guides entrepreneurs to spot opportunity and their genius begins to appear through a unique set of experiences. Josh Nussbaum expands on Aeoah's thoughts:

"Genius does exist, but not in the traditional sense portrayed in 'The Social Network' that made everyone think they can become the next Mark Zuckerberg. It's not only the internal factors — your aptitude, your intellect, your persistence — but it's also a combination of the external factors that shape you. I'm always most curious why entrepreneurs ended up on a certain path and why did they see an opportunity over anyone else? After seeing the opportunity, why and how did they choose to execute on that? How did they have the foresight or experience to see roadblocks, hire the right people, be lean enough and open enough? One of the archetypes of the founders I gravitate to is that it's their second or third or fourth company. Maybe they weren't successful with the first three but does that mean they're not genius? No. I'd rather bet on them because they know their mistakes. They know which bets to make or not make. They handle their cash well because they wait to see signs of a product market fit and then double down. They're less arrogant than that to assume everything they do will be correct."

Beth Ferreira, a venture partner with Rick Heitzmann at FirstMark Capital, transitioned into venture capital after gaining extensive operational experience at venture-backed startups like Etsy and Fab. Ferreira left a lucrative career in finance, when that was considered the hottest ticket after graduating from business school, to learn to become an operator. Having done this with two successful startups, she has a unique edge over her peers. Ferreira is able to absorb a founder's vision but presses them on the details. Genius, to Ferreira, lies in a founder's humility and understanding of the minutia of an industry and not in the lofty statements that cover a pitch deck. With an acute understanding of the internal operations at startups that have raised venture capital, Ferreira believes that some founders are given 'too much stock' for their genius for being high-level thinkers — they're given significant venture financing but are not encouraged by their investors to continue to push the limits of what is possible. Ferreira says that a founder's unchecked arrogance can often be blamed on a board of negligent venture investors who do not push the founder in the way their fiduciary duty requires:

> "It requires a heightened sense of awareness and humility to be a founder that is consistently praised in the press, and often times in board meetings by venture investors, to be fully grounded in what needs to be done. There is a lot of unsexy work from an organizational and operational standpoint. This means something different at every company and in some cases it's dealing with supply chain issues, understanding network effects, working with or building fulfillment centers, managing customer complaints."

To start a company, a founder is constantly ignoring feedback and focusing on what they believe is right. By definition, going after a big opportunity either implies that it is not obvious to everyone else or other people have tried it before and now believe it is impossible. For Ilya Fushman of Kleiner Perkins, it is important for a founder to be able to bend their risk curve over time and open their aperture for listening and learning. This is a trait he believes was best exhibited by Drew Houston of Dropbox who ignored discouraging feedback when critics of his vision could not define the market opportunity. Fushman explains:

> "You have to be deeply opinionated about building a product in the beginning, but over time as your product user base grows, your users

actually have a better sense of what they need. They can't articulate it necessarily but they really will tell you if you ask them the right way of how you should build and change and evolve your product. You have to go from being opinionated and ignoring feedback about a product to eventually taking feedback as an input to your process and change your trajectory. That takes humility."

Magnets for Talent

"Creativity is a collaborative process. Innovation comes from teams more often than from the lightbulb moments of lone geniuses. This was true of every era of creative ferment. The Scientific Revolution, the Enlightenment, and the Industrial Revolution all had their institutions for collaborative work and their networks for sharing ideas."

Walter Isaacson, *The Innovators*

Walter Isaacson deviated from his typical approach of celebrating individual genius for his book, *The Innovators,* in which he discusses the collaborative efforts of individuals, across generations, in building the Internet and staging the digital revolution. After honoring hundreds of individuals who would have otherwise gone unnoticed in the history of the Internet, Isaacson credited the concept of collective genius. As future makers and storytellers set a vision and build with humility, they must recognize their shortcomings and surround themselves with the people who can fill those holes or blind spots. Historically, true change and execution has been brought about through a pairing of visionaries with people who can execute on that vision.

Brian Laung Aeoah chooses to invest in entrepreneurs who exhibit a hunger to succeed, while also recognizing their shortcomings and being able to plug those holes before they adversely affect their companies. He shares:

"I'll use my mom as an example. While I was growing up, she tried a few different businesses and eventually started a school. She is passionate about, and great at getting children to fall in love with learning. They do extremely well when they're with her, and then they go to other schools and continue to outperform their peers. She enjoys it and is also very persistent. That is why she is successful. Her persistence and her passion. Even though she has that knack, and it has enabled the school to grow, she is the first to admit that more formal training in accounting, management, or strategy would have been helpful and might have enabled her to accomplish even more than she has. Maybe the genius some founders have that others don't is in the awareness to recognize when one lacks certain skills or knowledge, and then surrounding oneself with people who fill those gaps. They can focus on becoming phenomenal at what they do, and then empower others to execute based on their specific expertise and the team's goals and mission. That's one of the things I noticed about the two turnarounds I was managing between 2008 and 2013; this distinction can separate startups that succeed from those that fail. I think it's a mix of both. It boils down to self-awareness and recognizing where you need help as a leader."

Venture capitalists are searching for inspiring leaders who can rally teams around them to cover for the founder's shortcomings. As Ferreira, Nussbaum, and Aoaeh suggest, founders must intrinsically have a self-awareness to know what areas of a business will struggle because they are not equipped to handle those entirely on their own. Starting a business requires support across acquiring customers, predicting legal hurdles, optimizing the user experience through design, and nurturing engineering talent, and a founder's job to build the right team is critical. Josh Nussbaum delves into this further:

"The ability to hire, and an understanding of what hiring or recruiting means is super important to me. Knowing that this founder or CEO will know how to build a team is critical. Their job is to continuously hire themselves out of their own job and set strategy. When I meet someone that is fundraising, I get a good sense of whether they'll be able to assemble a world-class team around them. By the way they communicate, tell their story, connect with someone and generate excitement, I can tell if they'll be able to scale a team. I ask detailed questions around their hiring plan: who will they hire first? What is the roadmap? What channels will they use to hire those people?"

The phrase "founder first" has become a common buzzword plastered across websites of most venture funds. They seek to portray an entrepreneur-friendly venture firm. Yet, many of the investors I spoke with articulated why promising founders, regardless of business concept, oftentimes help de-risk the investment process for an investor. That being said, they were more concerned with solo founders and grew excited about teams of founders working together towards a common mission. Jonathan Teo of Binary Capital, an investor in Snapchat, articulated his thoughts around forming teams, and the fabric that draws teams together to solve some of the world's pressing technological problems:

"I'd rather invest in a stellar team once I've understood what brings them together. I'm okay if they are operating in a new, untested space if I can understand the background of what has brought them together. Is it a shared experience and now a breakthrough idea that they are rallying around? I would much rather invest in two non-technical co-founders who are brought together because of a strong desire for something they want to solve but need built. This is more attractive than two hackers that have been brought together just to build something generally without much charisma or passion."

Think Differently

Genius entrepreneurs are built to withstand risk and ambiguity, are humble enough to recognize their shortcomings, and act as beacons for others to rally around towards a shared vision. They are storytellers who develop a passion for change and possess the persistence to see that change come true. Like the artists, athletes, and inventors mentioned at the beginning of this section, entrepreneurs are wholly committed to their pursuit of genius; the successful founders are eccentric, focused, and have a disposition far removed from most people. Fred Wilson prescribed some of those qualities of entrepreneurial genius over a decade ago and many of those qualities have been reinforced by the dozens of partners behind successful venture funds. Ilya Fushman believes genius appears when all of these qualities collectively exist in a founder. The absence of even one often leads to a startup failing.

Peter Thiel, a co-founder of PayPal, went on to become a venture capitalist through his fund, Founders Fund. This fund has invested in the companies that have shaped the startup revolution, such as Airbnb, Spotify, Stripe, Facebook, Flexport, ZocDoc, Twilio, Oscar Health, and SpaceX. According to Trae Stephens of Founders Fund, Thiel established the fund around the thought that human beings tend to be followers and generally want to do the things that others want them to do. We want our friends to tell us that we're working on something interesting and crave validation that we are doing the right or important things. Thiel believes that humanity's need for validation is often what leads people into structured paths where they waste away their genius and don't think differently about their purpose or mission to solve interesting problems. Thiel believes that the most interesting thing about the founders he has worked with is that they were individuals who did not seek that peer validation. In fact, their businesses were initially deeply unpopular and unsexy, but the founders were committed to building them over 15-20 years.

CHAPTER 6
FUTURE MAKERS AND STORYTELLERS

Future makers, as Andrew Parker calls genius entrepreneurs with an ability for storytelling, show us how our lives and surroundings can be improved. They masterfully paint a picture that expands our imagination of what is possible. Through broad strokes, these geniuses tell humanity stories of how the world should operate and how they'll work tirelessly to get us there. This bold future includes a world with autonomous vehicles, the highest quality of healthcare, new forms of human behavior and interaction, and a superior quality of living for those who have too often been marginalized. Oftentimes, these future makers are leveraging innovation and technology to realize this vision. And because of their ability to tell a good story, it is human nature for the masses to support them in their mission.

Entrepreneurs such as Elon Musk and Richard Branson tell the world a story of intergalactic, commercial travel and continue to make monumental accomplishments in achieving that story. While few people believed them when they told it, Bryan Chesky and Joe Gebbia imagined a world, with Airbnb, in which strangers would open their homes to other strangers. Adam Neumann of WeWork told creators and creatives alike a story of how people should 'work' and live, and he helped bring that future to life. Compelling stories are a founder's strongest asset in their war chest, and if told the right way, possess an infectious energy to attract investors, employees, and customers to bring a vision to reality.

charity: water, a non-profit headquartered out of New York City, has become a stand-out organization in the technology and social impact communities for its ability to capture, craft, and convey a meaningful story. The organization has moved millions of people and investors globally to support a cause by consistently delivering on its promise of creating a better world for people without access to a basic and elemental human need: clean water. charity: water's meaningful campaigns can move audiences to tears, but also inspire hope to spur them to take action around the solutions being implemented by the non-profit. While charity: water's mission is to provide clean and safe drinking water in developing countries — a bold vision that countless nonprofits have worked toward — its founder, Scott Harrison, has a unique entrepreneurial talent for storytelling that has led the organization to compounding success, where others have failed. Through its novel business model, brilliant media campaigns, and grassroots support, the organization has been supported by everyone from CEOs like Jack Dorsey and Sean Parker, to venture capitalists like John Doerr of Kleiner Perkins and Chris Sacca of Lowercase Capital. Scott Harrison embodies the entrepreneurial traits of a 'future-maker' introduced by Fred Wilson and Andrew Parker in previous chapters.

In 2014, I met Scott Harrison and documented his inspiring story for *Disruptors*. I subsequently left my job on Wall Street and went on to work for charity: water for several years to help realize Harrison's vision. While there, I learned that charity: water's persisting success, where most non-profits in the U.S. fail, has been largely due to its ability to be an organization of storytellers. In meetings, the underlying thread behind new initiatives, projects, and ideas rested in our ability to tell a good story that was uplifting and focused less on the problem, and more on the solution we hoped to enable. Each asset we put out into the world was a story of its end user: the beneficiaries celebrating access to clean water or the donors in cities across the U.S. campaigning their communities to support similar communities in another country. No story went untold, including the story of a child in the middle of America who donated her $8.50 in savings to the clean water crisis and inspired a national campaign of donors donating in her name.

While charity: water is not venture-backable in the traditional sense and Scott Harrison is not the typical founder seeking venture financing, the metrics and performance of the organization mirror the story of a high-growth startup.

charity: water raised over $70 million in 2018 to support over a million beneficiaries across 26 countries such as Ethiopia, India, and Kenya. Since being founded in 2007, over 29,000 water projects have been funded, providing over 8 million people worldwide with clean water. Like a venture-backed company, charity: water's board demands high-growth to prove that the dollars they have invested in the non-profit are creating a meaningful impact. The organization works with technology organizations such as Google, Facebook, and YouTube to ensure that the impact is scalable. The team leverages the latest technology across motion sensors, virtual reality, tracking, and audience engagement to bring their goals to reality. While many of charity: water's supporters are compassionate donors from across the country, a series of well-established entrepreneurs and investors donate to the non-profit's operational budget through multi-year donations. This funding is used to support the fight for clean water in developing countries through a unique operational model furthered by Harrison — a model in which 100% of donations go towards funding clean water projects.

Crafting the Story

The story of charity: water is a growth curve that goes up and to the right, but the story of its founder is choppy and erratic. Scott Harrison is a reformed nightclub promoter who spent his twenties abusing alcohol and drugs and living lavishly in the present. Harrison's redemptive story from a drug-induced, nightclub promoter who found meaning through a crisis he witnessed firsthand is one that investors have rallied around. He is the hero, working towards a solution, who they want to win and back. Reid Hoffman, the founder of LinkedIn, a current partner with Greylock (a venture capital fund behind investments in companies such as Airbnb, Facebook, Instagram, Tumblr, and Workday), and the host of a popular podcast called Masters of Scale, interviewed Harrison to better understand this ability to tell a story. Hoffman reiterates the point made by most investors throughout this book that a founder's ability to tell a compelling story ranks among the highest traits of a genius founder. A story, according to Hoffman, has three parts: a character or a founder, the trouble in their lives, and their path to a solution for that problem. All great companies have problem-solution structures, and Harrison's is no different. About the compelling founders who tell good stories, Hoffman says:

> "A good storyteller draws you in, a better one puts you in their shoes, a great one makes you feel the pain from every jagged rock, stone, and piece of gravel they clamber across while also filling you with the hope of redemption. Scott Harrison is amongst the greatest I know... I believe great companies are built on great stories, and great stories are transparently honest."

As with most stories shared by charity: water, Harrison opens up about his troubled past. He recounts how his childhood and personal journey relate to his current mission. What were the forces that drove him to make certain decisions? What makes him compelling to invest in or be the person to change the face of this monumental crisis facing humanity? After leaving a decadent lifestyle behind, Harrison volunteered as a photojournalist in Liberia where he came face-to-face with what happens to humans without access to clean water. Children drank from dark, muddy water infested with insects, mothers and young girls walked miles every morning to fetch water instead of going to school, and individuals in these countries suffered from ailments — tumors, diarrhea, dysentery — all caused by bacteria in dirty water. Harrison documented this, believing that visual storytelling, for most problems, is more effective, as it allows your stakeholders to buy into what you want to solve. Harrison says that by simply *telling* a story of a tumor on a child, you may spark empathy, but readers cannot relate to it. Harrison says an image evokes feelings and tells a more powerful story:

> "I'm a visual learner and visual communicator. For me, it is show don't tell. I was given the role of a photojournalist. I had 15,000 people on my club emailing lists. Open rates were 100% back then. The only thing I knew to do was to share these images that I had captured in Liberia and

hope people would be keen to learn more about this problem. I knew photos would move people the way words could not. The pervasive health problems in the developing world link back to the lack of access to clean water and I could show them the issue through their mobile devices or computers."

In the elements of a successful story prescribed by Hoffman, Scott Harrison had found his problem. In the months to come however, the concept of a non-profit did not resonate with donors immediately. There was distrust, as donors saw non-profits as a black hole for funding, with misappropriated funds shuffled to internal salaries or wasteful spending. Most genius founders will encounter this fork in the road and be tested on how to proceed. For many, the lack of enthusiasm for the non-profit can be a crushing moment of despair; but Harrison saw an opportunity to bring transparency to an industry that had none. Why were Americans, who were known to be some of the most philanthropic people, cynical of non-profits? Harrison realized the issue was that non-profits weren't successfully telling stories with transparency in a way to build trust with the customer.

Harrison made this transparency a cornerstone of charity: water. He showed donors, through GPS, which wells their money had built and allowed them to find them on a map. Eventually, charity: water would also be transparent if wells had broken down and needed repair. The 100% model for donations lifted the veil for donors and allowed them to wholly fund the cause they cared about. This transparency and storytelling won over early charity: water supporters and the founder of Beebo, Michael Birch, who committed $1 million when the organization was struggling to survive in the early days. Since that point, charity: water has grown its impact to provide millions of people with clean water across 26 countries. Today, 129 families including those of operators and venture investors like Jonny Ive, Daniel Ek, Jack Dorsey, John Doerr, Chris Sacca, and others, support charity: water's operations account. And 10 years later, storytelling remains a key element to the non-profit's growing success.

The final element that Hoffman details as essential to a good story is that of the solution. Hoffman says:

"People respond passionately to solutions, not problems. Problems can inspire outrage and guilt but they also trigger compassion fatigue. Solutions inspire hope and motivation. Solutions are an invitation to work together to make a difference and the key is to get people to say yes to that invitation... That is where the power of inspirational storytelling comes in. It creates a loop that feeds into people's desires to share and they open their networks to the cause and the inspirational story."

Giving people a taste of what it feels like to provide one person with clean water through a story of redemption from dirty water to clean water, charity: water gives humanity a taste of what the world would be like if all people were given access to clean water. This positive messaging is similar to that of the future makers discussed earlier in this book.

Pitching

The future makers featured in the first section of this book are storytellers who demonstrate their genius by gripping an investor's attention around a vision for the future in which their startup will not only exist, but be undeniably valuable. A founder's vision for the future should be powerful enough to recruit high-quality talent to take a risk with them instead of pursuing other lucrative roles. The fundamental differences in vision between investors and entrepreneurs begin to appear during the pitch for a startup opportunity. In his podcast, Hoffman has weighed in:

"As a leader, you need to be a master storyteller. You need to craft a compelling narrative that engages your employees and customers, builds a community, and infuses people with purpose. You have to be willing to tell the same story to bring new people into your tribe of believers. You also have to recognize when it's time for the story to evolve. But more important than this, you have to avoid the trap of stretching the truth. As a founder or idea sparker, you're competing with a cacophony of other stories, some of your less scrupulous rivals may tell stories that sound more like fiction than fact. Fiction is fine when your aim is simply to spin a yarn but when you want to build a real connection with your audience you need to make honesty the cornerstone of your story."

As revealed through Scott Harrison's journey, storytelling requires convincing someone across the table of facts you already know. Secondly, it is about convincing them that your story, your vision for the world, and your cause are more worthwhile of their time or money than another story or future being offered by another founder. This requires confidence to present the facts based on deep knowledge of a problem or issue, presenting a convincing argument, and sparking empathy or passion about this new future. Josh Nussbaum of Compound discusses this in the context of investments he is making in industries he's less knowledgeable about:

"A good storyteller, as a CEO who is fundraising, has an intuitive sense of the market, based on something they've done before. They have an intuition and want to share that prediction with us. We have conviction because based on their ability to share this intuition and vision, they are able to recruit people. They have a lens or a sense of where the industry is headed. For example, with a founder operating in healthcare, or a similarly regulated industry, the compelling founders have a sense of where regulation might be headed. They know their barriers and have compelling answers to all our questions. Having a strategic answer on where the industry is going and being able to articulate that is most valuable."

Beyond conveying the problem that drives them and the solution they are chasing, founders should place an emphasis on the story that their users are telling them. The concept of 'theses' in this book have thus far been presented from the investor perspective — a detailed perspective on industries and landscapes or deep-dives into technological or platform shifts that drive change. Genius founders, however, present their stories through a different lens: a problem-solution lens with a heavy emphasis on the people — the users — they are building for. Rick Heitzmann discusses his thesis around investing in companies such as DraftKings, Uber, and Pinterest and the difference between how founders who exhibit genius pitch their value proposition versus how investors interpret the vision:

"Founders mainly focus on the problem side. A genius founder, in my experience, tends to be product focused and user focused. They have such a deep understanding of the user experience and journey and are loyal to that. When they share that vision with me, they will tell the story from a user perspective. They will discuss each individual user and what made them tick or what problem it solved for them or where they dropped off from usage. They will obsess over their users and we want to see them do that. As investors, we see it as a mirror image and will place their user experience into how we see trends or theses play out more dynamically or across an entire industry."

Heitzmann elaborates on the experience of having the founders of Pinterest pitch their story to FirstMark Capital:

"The founders were focusing on acquiring users that wanted to share the things they like with their friends and with the world. They knew that users want to see what other people think about those things or those collections. It's similar to why humans scrapbook. We save collections when we're moving into a new apartment with furniture or scrapbook for a wedding and then show these things off to our friends or families. They saw this user behavior in the offline world and wanted to translate it to the digital world. They believed that users are excited by social endorsement when someone likes their stuff or wants to buy it. So they took this behavior online and said people can now do this by phone when they're sitting on the train or on the bus. I met with the Pinterest founders several times before investing and every time we met, they talked about how their users were taking this offline behavior and bringing it online. It was impossible not to invest at that point. It was radically clear that these founders would figure it out and they told a very clear user story."

As a founder, the skill of storytelling is one that is not only important during the first conversation with an investor, as evidenced by the relationship between FirstMark Capital and Pinterest or as seen with Scott Harrison and charity: water. Jeremy Liew of Lightspeed Venture Partners believes that storytelling is also one of the most underrated skills needed to raise capital. He says:

"Given enough runway, a lot of smart people can build a company. Companies are often just not given that chance because the founder is not a compelling presenter or storyteller. We work with our portfolio companies so often on crafting their story at each step of the way so they continue to evolve as their company moves forward. The worst thing as an investor or as a founder is seeing that often there are competitive companies in your market with a worse-off product, growth metrics, revenue traction, timing, etc., but they're able to raise more and get to the Series A financing before you can because the founder is just a damn good storyteller."

As I noted earlier, there will often be storytellers in your market who will not be transparent or who will be less than honest with their numbers, but often the customers or investors are able to see through that. It is imperative to craft a story that is transparent, genuine, and meaningful. Beth Ferreira of

FirstMark Capital emphasizes this trait of transparency between founders and investors:

> "It seems obvious but the biggest thing I want to see in a pitch is the truth. How do I get comfortable with what you are building and what is the path for it to grow? If you can be transparent about problems you are facing, it makes it easier for me to have the full picture and the full story before seeking investment approval. Anyone can be good at sales and beautiful decks."

In addition to hearing a story for the future, investors such as Taylor Greene of Collaborative Fund and Keith Rabois of Khosla Ventures are eager to hear the story that has brought a founder to their current predicament. What is driving them to want to build and create this future? For Scott Harrison, it was his experiences in Liberia. Greene uses preliminary meetings to understand a founder's personal story and his questions become more psychographic in nature to understand what makes a founder tick, what motivates them, and why they have chosen the irrational endeavor of starting a business. Greene expands on this in describing his experiences with the founders of companies such as Casper and Warby Parker:

> "It's important to gauge an entrepreneur's inspiration to start a company and I often look for that in their own personal stories — where they grew up, what decisions they made, and why. The questions become less about the business model but more psychographic in nature to get to the bottom of what makes someone tick, what motivates them, why they are doing this... a series of questions to understand their personal journey."

CHAPTER 7
EXECUTION: GENIUS AND THE INEVITABLE MARCH OF TECHNOLOGY

"In the annals of ingenuity, new ideas are only part of the equation. Genius requires execution."

Walter Isaacson

The startup stories shared by the founders featured in *Disruptors* portray a humbling reality of the execution risk involved with building a venture-scalable startup. Feelings of success and accomplishment are often fleeting, as new challenges threaten the survival of an early-stage business. In my current role as a venture capitalist, every day I meet with founders who reveal the firehose of challenges they face across market development, customer acquisition, team and culture building, legal battles, regulatory concerns, and other areas they must manage to keep their company afloat. Statistics show that most founders fail but the few who succeed are the ones able to manage the execution of an entrepreneurial vision, while embodying the definition of 'genius' I've been exploring. The intricacies of running a startup are nuanced and go far beyond the broad strokes of painting a masterful vision to attract financing. Attracting venture capital is only a small part of the battle.

Quarterback wisdom from VCs and entrepreneurs on building a startup is valid only to a point, as each entrepreneurial endeavor is a unique experiment in itself, with its own challenges and lack of a repeatable structure. The path is fraught with failure and an entrepreneur's ability to innovate around challenges, or exhibit traits of 'genius' through execution, is the differentiating factor to success. When it comes to entrepreneurship, execution separates the average founders with great ideas from the geniuses who are able to build enterprises with true, lasting value.

Investors such as Keith Rabois, Marc Andreessen, Andy Weissman, Ellie Wheeler, Rick Heitzmann, Rebecca Kaden, and Beth Ferreira can play the important role of supportive board members as they have seen the pattern of executing on a vision from different lenses during their careers. If a VC's job is to help the founder through the tight spots because they are the trail-wise sidekicks, what have they learned strategically on execution? In this next section, I'll provide a glimpse into the learnings on what it takes to build a scalable startup.

Running Lean or Growing Fat

A popular startup methodology touted by entrepreneurial gurus is the Lean Startup, pioneered by individuals including Steve Blank and Eric Riess. Riess' book, The Lean Startup, is a how-to manual to go from 'idea' to startup. It's sold millions of copies around the world. And conferences, workshops, books, podcasts, and university entrepreneurial departments have been built around its methodology focused on customer discovery, validation, and rapid iteration to create the product customers want. Rebecca Kaden of Union Square Ventures is one such believer in this methodology and says that founders, especially those building consumer ventures, should 'continuously be testing their ideas and hypotheses before putting substantial capital to work.'

As featured on its landing page, the Lean Startup methodology solves for a trap most founders fall into through a process of customer discovery:

"[The Lean Startup] is a principled approach to new product development. Too many startups begin with an idea for a product that they think people want. They then spend months, sometimes years, perfecting that product without ever showing the product, even in a very rudimentary form, to the prospective customer. When they fail to reach broad uptake from customers, it is often because they never spoke to prospective customers and determined whether or not the product was interesting. When customers ultimately communicate, through their indifference, that they don't care about the idea, the startup fails... The Lean Startup methodology has as a premise that every startup is a grand experiment that attempts to answer a question. The question is not 'Can this product be built?' Instead, the questions are 'Should this product be built?' and 'Can we build a sustainable business around this set of products and services?'

The Lean Startup methodology is designed to lead a founder to their first product. Through a series of customer interviews, the founder will establish their early adopters, add employees to run new experiments or iterations, and eventually, with enough data, build and launch a product that they know customers want. The method is data-informed and built on a premise of a 'build-measure-learn' feedback loop. Founders identify a problem and develop what Riess calls a minimum viable product (MVP) to begin their process of learning as quickly as possible. This MVP is basic, requires little engineering and is often a mock-up of what a potential product could look like. The MVP, however, should be informative and provide a better understanding of the problem and the eventual solution to the problem. Another interesting strategy furthered by the Lean Startup methodology, which is also sometimes used by investors to identify if a founder truly understands their industry, is the method called the "Five Whys." Founders ask questions to study and solve problems along the way and get deep at the root of a problem.

The Lean Startup is designed to train entrepreneurs to validate ideas and concepts through a process of customer validation. If measuring and learning is occurring correctly, a founder will be able to better understand if their product is working or if a pivot or 'structural course correction' is necessary to test new hypotheses. While there is clear merit to this thinking in the minds of millions of entrepreneurs and advisors, Keith Rabois, a founder and early employee of LinkedIn, Twitter, and OpenDoor, and an investor in Yelp, Lyft, and Airbnb, holds the deeply unpopular belief that the 'Lean Startup methodology is a guaranteed method of failure and mediocrity.' His criticism is specifically around the MVP and that an unfinished product cannot provide enough evidence. Secondly, he believes that it is a founder's job to move customers in a certain direction, not the other way around. When it comes to executing on a vision, there are few who would go against the Lean Startup methodology, but according to Rabois, entrepreneurs such as Jack Dorsey and Elon Musk would never follow these principles. While Rabois is in the minority of folks who distance themselves from the popular methodology, it's worth considering the contrarian view he shared when we chatted for this book:

> "Lean Startup is a bankrupt philosophy for mediocre people with mediocre vision and ambition. These founders aren't being bold. Instead, they minimize the chance of short-term failure and that is all they come to focus on rather than building something truly great. In doing so, it takes away the opportunity for upside. Startups are not bottoms-up driven exercises. The job of a founder is to paint a picture of a better world and then deliver that, not to go around asking people what they want because those people have no idea yet. The Lean Startup suggests you discover and find success, instead of executing on a vision. More people need to emulate Apple. You ship a finished product and nothing less. As Jack Dorsey at Square says, 'the customers are not your guinea pigs.' People who treat customers like guinea pigs have poor net promoter scores and you only have a few chances to earn their respect and loyalty. You can't keep going back to the customers and saying 'oh, this is just a test or a question.' At some point, you need to show you deserve their dollars because you are the visionary."

This contrarian view reveals that the distinction is more about believing and investing in founders who have conviction in their vision and who don't wait for the validation of customers. Separately, the lean startup methodology, a more patient approach to entrepreneurship, is at odds with the venture capital mindset of growing at all costs. This point made my Rabois is perhaps one of the largest distinctions between entrepreneurs who want to build businesses funded by venture capital and those who wish to build businesses without venture capital. Without venture capital, growth is often not an entrepreneur's primary concern. Instead, they often aim to create a stable business that quickly achieves profitability. The commonly held mentality in the startup ecosystem, fueled by venture capitalists, is to win an entire market through sheer force by raising an abundance of capital to outspend and outhire the competition. Some venture capitalists, as demonstrated by Rabois' comments above, do not believe in operating 'lean.' Instead, they believe that in order to win a market, founders need to raise hundreds of millions of dollars to reshape their industry and take bold risks. The investors I spoke with were split on this methodology: to build a company by operating lean and raising capital only when necessary, versus raising as much capital as possible and breaking down doors until you succeed.

Ben Horowitz of a16z is against wasteful spending, especially of venture dollars, but like Rabois, he believes that operating lean will never allow a startup to reach that multi-billion valuation. He wrote in his blog:

> "Running lean is not an end. For that matter, neither is running fat. Both are tactics that you use to win the market and not run out of cash before you do so. By making 'running lean' an end, you may lose your opportunity to win the market, either because you fail to fund the R&D necessary to find product/market fit or you let a competitor out-execute you in taking the market. Sometimes running fat is the right thing to do."

In a blog post, Horowitz referenced his own experience building Loud-Cloud in the early 2000s and raising well over $300 million to execute on the company's vision. In the post, Horowitz noted that a startup must find product/market fit before running out of cash and is constantly balancing those two scenarios. A good founder must work to establish a product that thousands of enterprises or millions of customers want to buy, but also raise enough cash and manage it wisely. Of these two priorities, Horowitz says that 'taking the market' is more important than running out of cash because of what he calls, 'startup purgatory.' He writes:

"Startup purgatory occurs when you don't go bankrupt, but you fail to build the number one product in the space. You have enough money with your conservative burn rate to last for many years. You may even be cash-flow positive. However, you have zero chance of becoming a high-growth company. You have zero chance of being anything but a very small technology business. From the entrepreneur's point of view, this can be worse than startup hell since you are stuck with the small company. You recruited all the employees, you raised all the money, and you made all the promises. You either see it through or leave — without your good reputation. No one wants to work for an entrepreneur who quits his or her own company. This is startup purgatory, where you work just as hard, reap none of the rewards, and watch all your best people leave you. It sucks to be you. The bottom line: spending a little or spending a lot is a means, not an end. Choose the right strategy to win the market or you may end up going straight to purgatory."

Horowitz writes that entrepreneurs should know the virtues of the lean startup — lightweight sales and light engineering — but that they cannot expect to 'save their way to winning the market.' Horowitz believes that founders should always consider raising enough capital to wipe out their competition. Founders I meet with are often torn about when and how much capital they should raise. Horowitz and Rabois, based on these comments, are arguing for founders to raise as much capital as they can whenever they can, in order to win the market. I present these conflicting views to show the different theories of capital management and execution as shared by some of the shrewdest VC investors. With the support of the board they put in place, founders must decide on their own where they believe capital should be deployed.

As a final thought on this point, Fred Wilson of Union Square Ventures takes a more centrist philosophy on the concept of 'running fat' versus the

Lean Startup methodologies. In response to Horowitz's "Fat Startup" blog post, Wilson says that most people cannot raise that type of capital because they do not have the pedigree that Horowitz has; investors are willing to trust that he will be a good steward of that level of capital. This is true for most entrepreneurs who have been successful with prior endeavors. Individuals such as Andrew Mason of Groupon, Jack Dorsey of Twitter when he was raising for Square, and Elon Musk for any of the companies he has started have not struggled to raise capital thanks to their prior successes. Wilson says:

"Ben [Horowitz] does a service to point out that raising a lot of cash and making a large investment in the business is a big positive. But in my opinion you only want to do that once you are 100% sure and have ample evidence that your product has hit its stride, you've got yourself in the place you want to be in your market, and you can raise the capital without taking much dilution. If all of those boxes are checked yes, then go for it. But please spend it wisely."

Frank Rimalovski, a former VC who now manages New York University's Entrepreneurial Institute, teaches aspiring entrepreneurs about managing capital wisely and identifying tangible customer problems, before they set out to launch businesses. Rimalovski says that the cost of launching a product has gone down tremendously and believes that founders who think they will launch a perfect product on the first try are operating in a fairy tale. Rimalovski echoes the principles taught in the Lean Startup:

"I think there is a trap of thinking you need a ton of capital to start a business. That's a myth propagated by venture capitalists. I think it's all fiction when founders think they'll use all this up-front capital, launch a product, and slice the market like a hot knife through butter. I don't think that ever works. No product will ever be perfect. You will always be iterating on your product and trying to make it better. If you have an idea you're excited about, before you start writing your first line of code, just start talking about it. Get feedback from the potential target market / customer. Is this really a pain point? Is it differentiated? What are other companies in this space thinking about? You'll be surprised how little progress you have to make in order to start a conversation with your market. Progress with your business will start only when you start getting market feedback."

This debate on building startups with the 'winner take all' mentality is something that is clearly adopted by companies such as Facebook, Google, and Twitter, which strive to acquire customers, regardless of the cost. The kinks in this strategy began to surface in recent years with a third perspective in the lean startup debate. The mantra of 'move fast and break things' was concepted early in Facebook's history; but in 2018, that radical statement was portrayed in the press as "Facebook moved fast and broke democracy." The 'grow at all costs' mentality — without customer validation or regard for what the customer believes to be correct — is one that has Hemant Taneja, a partner at General Catalyst, questions. He calls for re-thinking how startups should be built as we go into this next generation of venture capital and technological disruption. In this new era, where technologies around artificial intelligence, data security, gene editing, and quantum computing become realities, founders who execute with more capital have more responsibility to humanity. The unfortunate lesson of Elizabeth Holmes and Theranos is living proof of what happens when the philosophy of raising abundant capital to achieve a dream without proper execution goes awry. Taneja says there needs to be a more measured approach to execution. In "The 'Era of Move Fast and Break Things' is Over" published in Harvard Business Review, Taneja wrote:

"More often than not, venture capitalists promote a "winner-take-all" mindset, pushing expansion at the cost of impact on initial customer targets. This is increasingly untenable: the speed with which more narrowly-cast solutions can supplant incumbents means that subpar services will be replaced. The market will punish premature growth, to say nothing of the ethical issues inherent in hooking customers into half-baked solutions in healthcare, financial services, or other critical industries. We should not ignore the moral implications of the old "land and expand" business aphorism. Today when I talk with entrepreneurs about how quickly they can grow, I want to see them recognize that creating a "virtuous" product may require them to grow more slowly than they might otherwise."

Building with core values in mind and keeping those central to a startup operation become essential as one of many metric areas categories that should be measured as a startup grows into a larger organization.

Measuring What Matters: Metrics and Milestones

According to Matthew Hartman, a partner with Betaworks, once an early-stage business has established 'why' it will raise capital and 'how' it chooses to spend it, the company must measure and track the milestones for their business. This relates to the concept of 'testing ideas and measuring the experiments' prior to betting the future of the company on a new product set or business model. While this is fairly obvious, a common challenge investors such as Hartman have noticed is that early-stage founders often try to measure multiple performance indicators; but only a few of them are actually relevant to their company's growth. An abundance of metrics and teams tracking towards different goals creates confusion around strategic planning and execution. The key to a founder executing properly is figuring out the core metric that drives a business forward and the value the company is creating. Everything a founder does should relate back to that metric, Hartman explains:

"Where I often see founders mess up early is that they track key performance indicators (KPIs) for one thing like 'page views' or 'time on page' but their business model is based on something entirely different. For example, the business may be built around a software product that is being sold to publishers and charged on a per-seat basis, but the CEO is measuring page views as a measure of success. That is not his or her function or what the company should be tracking towards to know if they are doing well on a monthly or quarterly basis. The way you generate revenue is different; the function of engagement may be page views or head count, but that's not what is driving a return. That's the thing everyone has to be honest about."

Hartman went on to expand on how Betaworks evaluates consumer engagement and explained it in terms of Facebook. While Facebook has dominated consumer attention, their business, or other social media businesses, are not built on charging the customer. Instead, the business model is to sell the users' attention and engagement to advertisers. Advertisers are not buying space from a social network based on a cost-per-click or cost-per-mile basis, but instead on how long the average customer spends on the platform, making their views and engagement more valuable. Social media companies are monetizing as media companies and the successful ones run by focused founders have been clear about what they need to measure and why. Mobile game companies is another category of businesses that have had to be strategic with what metrics they measure in order to ensure longer term success. Mobile game companies are often targeting their users to buy in-application power-ups or in-app purchases. Still, some game company founders report on how much time people are playing their games; according to Hartman, this should not be the metric that these founders work toward. Hartman believes that genius founders know what metrics to optimize for when building a company and are able to identify unique ways to improve their operations with those metrics in mind.

Hartman is one of many investors focused on measuring and evaluating the appropriate indicators of success for a startup. For a founder, being diligent about these metrics and ensuring that every part of the business is moving the needle forward on the priority KPIs helps focus a company's vision and execution. VCs will ask their portfolio companies for quarterly financial reporting (as one would expect), but are equally interested in the KPIs that drive a business forward. In fact, early on in a startup's journey, these metrics are all an investor has to determine the value of a company, and the positive correlation of these metrics often leads to investment, or lack thereof. Rick Heitzmann of FirstMark Capital shares his experience with founders who are not disciplined enough to justify getting to a Series A or a Series B financing round:

> "Tracking milestones for your business is important, not only for your investors and your board members but also for yourself as the CEO. This is even more important when you are trying to raise capital. As a venture investor, it's frustrating when we see founders who could care less about the benchmarks about their businesses and still expect us to invest in them. I often meet founders I like that are still early in the process, but I tell them what milestones to hit over the next six to nine months that would make the business compelling to an investor. Six months later, they reach back out and tell me they're ready to raise, but they've forgotten the metrics we spoke about and haven't even moved the needle at all in any direction. I appreciate when a founder turns to me and says, 'I know we have a meeting set up but I haven't done the things we discussed yet, let's postpone.' I know thousands of entrepreneurs on the other side of this equation who are showing they've got grit and are working to the next milestone. If you're an entrepreneur looking for money you should look at the VC's criteria and ask yourself if you as a founder are meeting those criteria."

While investors can be opaque about many of the elements around a successful fundraise process, the venture capital industry has done a good job of documenting the common metrics that are important to meet in a certain industry before speaking with investors. Entrepreneurs should do the work to look at these milestones on what a company must hit to raise a Series A or a Series B round of financing. Beth Ferreira uses these metrics and milestones as a way to get to know founders better over time. She says:

"If I pass on a business that is early in development, I will be transparent with founders and tell them to come back to me when they have a certain volume of sales or a specific number of paying customers and if they do, I'll seriously consider investing. I'll share my concerns and ask them to report back on how they have worked against those concerns. In that process they get to know me as well and that's how we build a relationship..."

Taylor Greene of Collaborative Fund shares anecdotes of founders who have leaned into measuring what matters with consumer businesses. To Greene, it is that focus that separates companies in the minds of customers, investors, and board members. These founders have executed on a vision and helped transform their businesses into multi-million or multi-billion enterprises. Greene uses Philip Krim, the founder of Casper — the popular sleep-product company that got its start by selling pillows and mattresses directly to consumers — to illustrate this perspective:

"The entrepreneurs that are patient and take calculated risks are the ones that stick around the longest. It's not a perfect calculation but they have just enough imperfect information and metrics to make a decision to move forward. They know where to invest more in their businesses and where to pull back. They know when to move forward and move it in a different direction. It's a series of decision points and you're looking for the people with that mentality. For example, Philip Krim of Casper has known the mattress business his entire life. When he was 18 years old, Krim created an online mattress business out of his dorm room that was earning significant revenue. He developed an incredible amount of domain expertise, which he then carried over to Casper. He knew the industry in-and-out but he also knew where the larger incumbents were not investing their time and energy. Philip understood paid search before other people in the mattress industry. He was buying ads against branded terms and doing it better than

Tempurpedic. With consumer businesses there will always be paid marketing, so one point of differentiation will be about arbitrage. You need a good product to afford the acquisition costs to allow you to scale and you need to obsessively track these metrics of your business over time to understand what the levers are that you can pull. The channels of Facebook, Instagram, Snapchat exist today, and the new ones of tomorrow will be about where are people going next to hear about your product; but if you don't have a scalable, organic, repeatable customer acquisition channel that people are talking about, you're not going to make it. The best businesses have that, and they layer in the marketing to accelerate the growth. Retail e-commerce companies have been successful because they started six years ago when no one knew how to do Facebook acquisition. Now, you have a level playing field and investors used to look for a successful Kickstarter or some signal of some organic benefit."

Rebecca Kaden of Union Square Ventures builds on Greene's point and shares how consumer companies that have raised venture capital should think of customer acquisition in light of raising venture capital dollars. Venture capital often makes founders feel like they will always be able to 'buy' customers by spending on expensive marketing campaigns or running promotions. This irresponsible spending is not sustainable. Kaden urges founders to work towards building businesses with strong unit economics even while competing against huge incumbents with larger budgets:

"We don't believe that businesses that pay to acquire customer after customer are good venture businesses. They cost too much capital and you don't get enough leverage for those dollars. You don't hit the inflection points if you have to pay customer after customer. I think paid acquisition can be a weapon, it can be fuel for the beginning of a funnel, it can speed up funnels later on, it can create arbitrage opportunities. I'm a believer that you need to find consumer businesses that have passionate communities, that are acquiring through word-of-mouth. If you don't have strong, non-digital paid channels, it'll be a long, hard slog. The founder's strategy and ability to scale a core advantage is a key success metric with the consumer companies we've invested in. Allbirds demonstrated strong referral and retention metrics. Investors are attracted to a rabid fan base that forms a community with a high level of emotional engagement with the brand."

Kaden also referenced Stash (the popular financial mobile app targeting millennials), Glossier, Dia & Co., and Everlane for their ability to build a brand beyond the product by creating and leveraging a strong sense of community. Before investing in a consumer company, Kaden looks for this cult-like following where consumers wear and evangelize the brand proudly. In these cases, Kaden recognizes that a larger competitor with a more robust acquisition channel or capital flow will have a hard time replicating that organic enthusiasm and tribal fandom.

Metrics that drive a business forward can be humbling to early staff members and dictate whether a pivot is necessary. Respecting what the metrics indicate about the progress of a business keep a founder honest on whether or not they should continue to pursue an endeavor that is not meaningfully moving the needle towards their vision of the future. Beth Ferreira, previously with companies including Fab and Etsy and now an investor with FirstMark Capital, details her perspective on this:

"I can't emphasize it enough, but you need to be very real about metrics and the metrics that are important in your vertical. Every founder thinks they're the exception. If you only have 10,000 users at the end of year one, you might be screwed. Unless you are having a real conversation about changing the business or you've stumbled on some key learning or insight and are now taking a different path, it may make sense to not continue on. In the market, you hear a lot about pivots that were successful with companies like Slack and Flickr, but it's really hard to execute on those pivots and continue to convince people to back you — especially when you've pitched your investors / employees / partners on one set of metrics and goals and now you're changing your tune completely."

While much of this book has focused largely on lessons learned from investors backing consumer-focused companies such as Uber, Snapchat, or Airbnb, there are lessons to be learned from the anecdotes of software companies that sell into large enterprises. Software-as-a-service (SaaS) companies, given the size, structure, and approval process of the clients that they generally sell into, measure their progress through different metrics than consumer companies. SaaS companies track metrics such as total contract value per customer or the number of new customers in a period of time. Investors will often ask the founders of these companies to share details about the company's ability to expand their product offering across all lines of business or total revenue once they have already won a customer. Given that these contracts typically span several years, annual recurring revenue (ARR) is a common metric that investors track to assess growth. Ajay Agarwal, an investor with Bain Capital Ventures, shares insight on these types of companies:

"The simple metric I look at when evaluating a SaaS company is 'burn rate', which is how much money is a company spending during a certain period of time. I look at burn rate against where the company wants to be in terms of ARR within a certain period of time. How much are they spending in 18-months to hit an ARR target and is that scalable? I look at burn rate as a metric even when evaluating product milestones or key hires. I believe that this metric is one mechanism to drive alignment and focus. It's a metric the founders can understand because it translates directly to their solution and their survival. If you run out of money, you don't have a company. So what rate of cash burn can we maintain in order to hit a few key objectives or business goals? That's the important metric-based question a SaaS founder needs to ask themselves. The brilliance of entrepreneurship is achieving great things in a resource constrained way."

The concept of resource constraints shared by Agarwal was one I found particularly interesting and a concept that other investors indirectly addressed. The constraint of not having resources is one that often unleashes innovation because it creates drives focus. It is what forces a founder to identify the white space where the bigger competitors are not actively using their own abundant resources — money, time, employees, or experience — to compete. Being resource constrained forces founders to think of novel ways to go to market or attract talent. Agarwal believes that being resource constrained, measured through burn rate, helps founders remain innovative as they look at how they're spending a sparse resource like cash while hoping to achieve massive outcomes.

As a company scales, these metrics continue to become core to a startup's story. Early on, it is possible for a founder to pitch a grandiose vision of the future to attract supporters, but several years in, the metrics of the company begin to become the only relevant story.

Building Competitive Defensibility & Reacting to Regulation

Companies such as Facebook, Amazon, and Apple have entirely diversified their core offering. Facebook is no longer just a social network for Ivy League college students but is now using its trove of user data to enter into workplace tools, healthcare, augmented and virtual reality, mobile messaging, and gaming. Amazon is not just an online book retailer, but instead offers cloud services to all up-and-coming entrepreneurs, is experimenting with robotics and drones, and continues to launch new and innovative businesses targeted at consumers around video and audio. Apple is not just a personal computer or music player. As of 2019, Apple had acquired creator tools and AI companies, entered into music and video streaming services, and (according to rumors) will be entering into the automobile market. Companies like these possess an abundance of cash with which they can enter new industries through acquisitions seemingly overnight. By leveraging technology, they continue to quickly expand far beyond their original mandate of business and enter into new categories or industries. This is a constant threat for wide-eyed entrepreneurs on a shoestring budget.

Entrepreneurs are often faced with the critical dilemma around competition: What will happen if a large player like a Facebook, Amazon or Google decides to offer a similar product or value proposition? By asking questions around competition, investors hope to gauge an entrepreneur's understanding of the market landscape and where the competitive threats exist.

Venture capitalists invest in businesses with defensibility against these threats. To build a sustainable and profitable business, the most successful entrepreneurs build deeply entrenched defensive moats around their company. Warren Buffet is quoted for having said 'in business, I look for economic castles protected by unbreachable moats.' These competitive moats protect startups from other industry players looking to steal market share. These moats include network effects, strong brand loyalty, an impenetrable data set, intellectual property, or a high cost to switch off your service or product. These moats may also exist due to a unique advantage created by a changing regulatory landscape. Heitzmann discusses FirstMark Capital's perspective on moats, explaining how founders can establish superiority through their operations or market segments while larger, slow-moving players are stalled by being less willing to take risks that can disrupt their core revenue streams:

> "In the 1990s the question was: what happens if Microsoft comes into your category and takes over? In the 2000s the competitive threat was if Google entered your market. 2000s to 2020s will be Facebook, Google, Amazon. Most of the big companies can do whatever they want and can get involved and take over your market. As a founder, you need to figure out why they won't and communicate that. While they are slow to move in your direction, you should begin obsessing over those competitive moats and how you can build them around your business to protect it from bigger players, but also from smaller upstarts as you continue to grow bigger. As investors, we tend to

suspend belief around the large incumbents entering your space unless it's something abundantly clear. We invested in a company called HopSkipDrive when most people passed because they said Uber or Lyft will eventually offer the same service. For Stubhub, investors that passed said eBay will go into the secondary market for ticketing. The founders of Stubhub convinced us that eBay was focused on other key categories. Stubhub developed a moat by guaranteeing tickets and building a supply chain around their offering. In many cases, you'll see the incumbent of a large industry so wrapped up in their own business model that they are unable to change their whole system of operation. Delivery, pricing, accessibility make these models possible when the larger competitors can't do it. A founder should show us what their real, tangible competitive advantage is and the innovation around why the larger plays can't or won't be a problem."

As of writing this book, HopSkipDrive is a successful venture-backed startup focused on the ride-sharing economy. With HopSkipDrive, parents can hire trusted drivers to drop off and pick up their children from school. Uber and Lyft, to Heitzmann's point, could have been seen as insurmountable threats, but HopSkipDrive has carved out a niche for itself. During the pitch, the founders of HopSkipDrive demonstrated that larger competitors often have different strategic interests and are not willing to spend capital or resources on a new strategy, despite it being a large opportunity. The founders of HopSkipDrive claimed that Uber and Lyft were not focused on building a sticky emotional customer experience and were instead preoccupied with acquiring new markets. Embedded in Heitzmann's perspective is advice on pitching a startup: it's imperative to have knowledge about where competitors are focusing their resources, and how your startup is differentiated from that. Investors want to know that the founders have a good understanding of the landscape and what forces may impede their vision or execution over the next 18-24 months, or even on a longer-term horizon.

During our conversations, Josh Nussbaum of Compound discussed the importance of understanding a competitive moat and not mistaking the wrong things as being defensive enough:

"I see two common mistakes founders make. The first is to overstate their defensibility when it is not really defensible. This often happens with consumer companies who claim they have a direct communication line to their customers. It's a different world today. It's tricky to fall into a trap of looking at a past company and saying we'll run the playbook the same way, when the company was established 30-40 years ago, in a different time, with a different consumer behavior on how they bought or engaged with products. Now everyone is a media company through Twitter or Facebook. No one controls the messaging, so search engine optimization (SEO) or customer acquisition through social media is not a competitive moat. The second mistake is investing and spending money to do things to build this defensibility when there is no sign or signal that there is anything there to invest in yet."

Given its expansive strategy to enter into new markets each year, Amazon is one company entrepreneurs universally fear. Rebecca Kaden of USV says she shares a healthy dose of fear, awe, and respect for what Amazon has established and how it continues to land and expand into new industries. Kaden says it is "naive to think new startups can take them on" — a perspective which informs how she approaches startup opportunities:

"Amazon hasn't won because of structural product advantage but by an execution advantage. They just do more things better. We speak at USV about a kill zone, where startups are advantaged or where they are not. We talk about a Facebook, Amazon, Google kill zone and we talk about early companies going up against them. At the beginning, you [a founder] are so structurally disadvantaged because of scale, capital, and data, so I don't want to invest in companies that say they will take down Amazon because they're so disadvantaged. Still, I think there are areas where founders can challenge a company such as Amazon. With commerce, my view is that Amazon is obviously dominant, but it is solving for a tactical piece of the commerce puzzle. They're the best at speed and value. Amazon is a central repository where I can go when I know what I want. From my perspective, as I've learned with many of the upstart direct-to-consumer brands we've funded, there are more emotions involved with transactions, especially online, and Amazon is not doing well with the experience, entertainment or discovery piece of commerce. It's hard to re-shape the emotional pie of the customer experience, and that's where I see opportunity."

Kaden discussed a recent investment she made in a company called Shop-Shops, a cross-border commerce platform based on live streaming. Through this platform, hosts go to retail stores that are already struggling to maintain their businesses against Amazon, and the fashion-forward hosts live stream their shopping experience to a group of engaged communities and users. A massive number of international users are watching these hosts for entertainment and are also purchasing products in real time from these retailers. This is not a marketplace or a direct competitor to Amazon, but rather an alternate approach to shopping — one based on emotion. At the time of making this investment, Kaden shared that the founders understood this difference and were successful in conveying how they planned to build their market beyond Amazon's core focus.

On defensibility and competitive moats, a common overlooked differentiator is regulation. Trae Stephens, formerly of Palantir, and now with Founders Fund, believes that while regulation can be a massive hindrance to building a business, if a founder is able to navigate it and identify ways to work with the government, this can eventually turn into a tremendous regulatory moat. In his opinion, most businesses and founders do not have the competency to deal with regulation or the government in the appropriate way. He explains:

"Most Silicon Valley businesses do not have any idea of how to deal with regulation. How potentially game-changing founders interact with the government — at the local or national level — is strategically important to the health of a business. Airbnb, one of Founder Fund's portfolio companies, is one of the best companies at building a regulatory infrastructure and understanding the importance of working with municipalities. They have their own government affairs department and have invested in developing a positive brand image in every community they enter into. They work with regulators and invest in building the right way. Airbnb operates differently than Uber, a company that has not done that. This has affected Uber on a regulatory front, and they have to convince all these government regulators that they're not evil. Because of that difference, you see cities putting taxes and restrictions in place around Uber. Outside of working with government, companies like Tesla and SpaceX have made progress by not being overly reliant on working with integrators or lobbying congress for change. Instead, they are building standalone vertical businesses and becoming private sector solutions where the government has failed."

When evaluating an investment opportunity against regulatory risk, VCs often determine a company's potential value if regulation changes in its favor. Based on his investments, Heitzmann further explains regulatory moats:

"Three of our portfolio companies, DraftKings, Ro and Airbnb, are facing increased regulation and regulation will never move as fast as technology. In an accelerated technology market, regulation lags. The debate happens as a public conversation, in real time, about whether a company is a benefit to society and consumers or not. If it is, the company will do well with consumers and succeed. Airbnb has done a very good job in getting consumer buy-in in those conversations. Uber has started to work well with regulators. Especially in Miami and Los Angeles, Uber has worked within the parameters. Understanding that they are going up against the taxi and limousine commission, Uber has proven regulators wrong about congestion by using real data, not theoretical data. The purpose of these companies that are on the fringe is to figure out where they compromise."

Investors who are vested in the success of companies that 'are on the fringe' of regulation work closely with entrepreneurs and regulators to better understand if the externalities of a company are negative or positive. If negative, regulators quantify the damage and oftentimes those debates play out through public discourse that influences regulation. As investors look at these risk factors and see the opportunity for a company to grow massive if it does figure out the regulatory hurdles, Heitzmann says these bets are a no-brainer:

"Was there a risk the seed investors in Uber wouldn't get to a Series A? Hell yes, but if you overcome that risk, is the return significant enough where Uber will be one of the best investments ever? Yes. And you should make those investments every time because that is where the option value exists."

Ajay Agarwal believes that it is often the founders of these companies that offer the biggest competitive moat. While it is not always important in the case of a founder of a consumer company to be a deep subject matter expert, Agarwal believes that the founders of SaaS companies need to be domain experts and 'deep product thinkers' in order to offer a competitive product. SaaS companies need deeply entrenched, defensible moats as their customers are often paying millions of dollars across multi-year contracts in search of a solution that can solve a core problem faced by a large institution. Agarwal tests for this ability during his diligence process by having a discourse with the founder on their vision for the product and how it evolves over time to remain valuable to organizations. Agarwal expands on his investment thesis for enterprise SaaS companies:

"Being a deep product thinker doesn't mean that you're necessarily technical, but it means that you have a deep understanding of the problem you're trying to solve for the customer, the product you're building and where that product can go. Genius founders have the ability to articulate all of that in one to two sentences so anyone can understand it, but they can also go as deep into the problem or enterprise as you need them to go. With our investment in Kiva Systems, the autonomous robot and mobile shelving company focused on e-commerce that was eventually acquired by Amazon, the founder spoke about the dimensions of an assembly-line robot down to the tenth-of-an-inch. He explained that a half inch affected the turning radius of a robot and therefore, affected the size of the aisles and as a result, the cubic density of warehouse. He knew, that in this domain, because of his experience, that storage density was the biggest problem large enterprises in e-commerce were facing. He could explain at a high level why e-commerce was taking off, why they needed flexible fulfillment solutions, and why Kiva Systems could be the most innovative software company for e-commerce companies. I was giddy when I met the founder. He was the most amazing person I had met because he just knew everything about the industry."

Copy What Works

While disruptive innovation and creative genius can often appear to be random strokes of brilliance, the VCs featured in this book have made it clear that there is deep-seated knowledge and insights behind this randomness. With *Disruptors*, I found that many entrepreneurs have an uncanny ability to take their learning from one situation and connect it to an entirely different environment. In one such instance, Wayne Mackey, a neuroscientist with New York University studied the reaction times of police officers and helped create digital modules to improve their cognitive abilities. While selling this module to municipalities and police departments, Mackey recognized a long sales cycle and began to offer the module to them for free as he set his eyes on an entirely different market. As an avid player of video gamers, Mackey saw a parallel use case for this training module in the rapidly growing electronic sports market. Like professional athletes training their muscles, Esports athletes were searching for training tools to make them more accurate or faster in the games they played. I spoke with Mackey as he launched a startup, called State Space Labs, to service this space. I was fascinated by his ability to draw connections between multiple industries and areas of discipline to create a compelling business.

Many of the successful people I've interviewed for *Disruptors* and *Finding Genius* possess this trait to find morsels of wisdom from one industry and find new opportunities to adapt those learnings elsewhere. The VCs, often unprompted, boasted about the number of books they read because it helped them to be better investors. Within these books are anecdotes or experiences that they adopt to their personal life and business ventures. They are able to derive patterns from history, biographies, and stories on how businesses should be run or lessons on how consumers behave. Keith Rabois shared that he re-reads High Upward Management every year and calls it the 'bible of starting a startup.' He admits to borrowing learnings from that book when investing in companies and executing with the founders of those same companies. As an operator, Rabois disclosed how his ability to borrow ideas and supplant them into new situations helped create billions of dollars of value at companies such as LinkedIn and Square:

> "At LinkedIn, I borrowed an idea from Yelp, where I had been serving on the board. With Yelp, restaurants were fairly long-tail searches on Google, so restaurant owners were able to create compelling content that was unique to them to optimize for their businesses on the search engine. Yelp profited off of this and the search indexing of a restaurant led to more reviews. I realized that the same way Yelp had succeeded to do this for restaurants, LinkedIn should be able to do that for people. Both humans and restaurants are long-tail searches on the Internet. No company had ever indexed people on the Internet before, so I came up with the idea that we could create a public profile of these users

and then optimize the search engines for this. A user's LinkedIn profile would now be the first result on Google, which would lead to LinkedIn adoption or growth. Now, 12 years later, that has worked. LinkedIn will now always out-compete other social companies like Facebook on indexing public profiles. That simple lesson from Yelp led to an increase of 33% in usage. It became a mainstream value proposition that didn't really exist before. By accident, we innovated by borrowing an idea from Yelp. I can take one idea and adopt it to another; the more you read the more you're able to do that."

SECTION 3
THE VENTURE CAPITAL & ENTREPENEUR PARTNERSHIP

CHAPTER 8
ALIGNMENT AND TERMS

A venture capitalist's primary responsibility is to the LPs of their fund and the company they have invested in. And while it's ideal for a founder and investor to be aligned, the entrepreneurs themselves are not a venture investor's primary responsibility. There is a common misperception that venture capitalists work for the entrepreneur and as a result, founders are often bewildered when their investors behave differently. Once an investment is made, an investor will do what it takes to preserve the equity value of the underlying company. It is not only in the investor's interest; it is their fiduciary duty.

A high-profile example of this unfolded in 2017 around the popular ride-sharing company, Uber. An early investor, Benchmark Capital, sued Uber's founder, Travis Kalanick, for breach of contractual obligations and fiduciary duty. Benchmark made a $12 million investment in Uber and Travis Kalanick early in the company's lifecycle. At the time of the investment, Bill Gurley, a partner at Benchmark, likened Kalanick to Jeff Bezos of Amazon. In an interview with Forbes, Gurley said about Kalanick: 'It's great that people have instincts about product, but you also have to have instincts about business. Travis loves product, loves innovation, he loves technology, but he loves running a business also.' As of 2017, Benchmark's investment of $12 million was worth well over $7 billion and had the potential to return even more to their investors in the likely scenario of a liquidation event. Benchmark's responsibility was to ensure that nothing got in the way of the company's ongoing success, even Kalanick himself.

The previously indomitable relationship between Benchmark Capital and Travis Kalanick weakened as claims surfaced from 2014 to 2016 of sexual harassment, accusations of corporate theft, and a deceitful program called "Greyball" — a software program that allowed Uber to avoid law enforcement officials in cities and operate illegally without detection — tainted Uber under Kalanick's leadership. Uber's equity value, created by its users, had not completely recovered from a "#DeleteUber" social media campaign sparked by protestors the prior year. During this campaign to punish Uber for its practices, more than 200,000 people had deleted their Uber accounts, accounting for nearly 5% of the company's market share. That same week, Lyft passed Uber in the Apple App Store for the first time. Uber was rapidly losing its darling image in Silicon Valley and Kalanick provided his investors with little consolation that he would stabilize the ship to preserve their equity holdings.

With concerns around a devaluation and the future of Uber at stake, five major investors demanded Kalanick resign from the company with Gurley led the charge. Uber, which had raised more than $14 billion from investors since it was founded, had a growing and diverse base of investors other than the ones who signed a letter calling for Kalanick's resignation. Uber's investors also include TPG Capital, the Public Investment Fund of Saudi Arabia, and Blackrock. If Uber were to be marked down in valuation, investors could lose billions of dollars.

The investors succeeded in making this management change, exhibiting their responsibility to a company over the CEO or founder. At the end of 2017, before the dust had even settled around the Kalanick lawsuit, Uber's board hired Dara Khosrowshahi to fill the role of CEO at Uber. Khosrowshahi is an experienced CEO who served as the CEO of Expedia Group and as a member of the board of directors for Hotels.com and The New York Times Company. Regardless of Kalanick's actions, or lack thereof, Khosrowshahi represented what some investors look for in CEOs of companies that have matured beyond the startup stage. Some investors believe that a startup CEO should transition control over time to a more seasoned CEO once the company has achieved product/market fit. Some would argue this is what Apple did when it fired Steve Jobs, or what Groupon's board did when it fired Andrew Mason.

Ben Horowitz of a16z writes in the company blog that his fund 'goes against the conventional wisdom' and prefers to support the original founder regardless of the ups and downs of that relationship. In that same post, he went on to list over two dozen successful companies including IBM, Oracle, Dell, Amazon, Apple, Adobe, Salesforce, and other disruptive enterprises that achieved scale and maximized impact under the direction of the original founder. However, the larger debate centers around alignment between founders and their investors, and the lengths investors will go to protect their investments in a company.

Founder & Investor Alignment

'Alignment' is a theme that came up frequently in my conversations with entrepreneurs and investors alike. Jeremy Liew of LightSpeed Venture Partners, an early investor in Snapchat, claims that the misalignment between an investor and an entrepreneur in mission, values, or motivations can be catastrophic to an early-stage company. On a values level, perhaps this is what played out at Uber. With earlier stage companies however, investors claim that misalignment is often the result of founders not knowing how an investor's job works or what they are looking for from a company, despite being overtly clear about it.

Brett Martin is a former entrepreneur turned venture capitalist who willingly talks about the failure of his startup, Sonar. While he has documented the many reasons behind this failure, he attributes misalignment with his investors as one of the major reasons behind the demise of the company that, from his perspective, still had tremendous potential to grow. Brett says the job of picking your investors is important and as a novice entrepreneur, he did not fully understand the impact that a misaligned cap table might have on the company. Martin describes the relationship with one of Sonar's equity holders:

"The decoupling of responsibility from control created ambiguity and confusion, tension, and frustration for all parties. From day-to-day decisions such as negotiating an employment contract to company-defining ones such as when to sell the firm, alignment was a constant challenge. Occasionally, we were simply at odds. Avoid bad relationships like the plague but when you inevitably find yourself in a difficult partnership, don't waste precious energy wailing against it. Make it work or move on quickly."

Now, several years later and as an investor on the other side of the table, Martin says he has empathy for investors because they are often transparent about their goals at the beginning of a funding relationship. Entrepreneurs, at times, can have tunnel vision when raising money and often accept capital even if it may not be the best for the company in the long run. Brett says:

"The reality is that VCs and entrepreneurs are simply structurally misaligned: VCs have a portfolio strategy whereas entrepreneurs are 'all in.' Different strategies create different incentives. My point is that everyone should be aware of and acknowledge these fundamental differences. Doing so will make it easier to understand the other sides perspective and actions. Alignment is not just having a good rapport with your investors but understanding how they are set up structurally. Being misaligned is catastrophic. If they're partners in your business, operational or financial, having them misaligned with you will make your life hell and be a distraction/annoyance at the least, and rip your company apart at the worst. As an entrepreneur, you'll hear about the portfolio nature of investors. When you're an entrepreneur, you're so 'tunnel vision' and thinking about your company/business and that's the center of the universe to you. They're often not in the same place and the quicker the entrepreneur understands that, the better."

While in the case of Uber, the stakes were higher than normal and the breaches of trust were largely unethical, it exemplifies a misalignment that may have taken shape in the early days of the venture, with few people willing to challenge Kalanick. With Martin — and founders who have found them-selves in his shoes — the misalignment comes from a naivete of how venture capitalists are motivated or incentivized, how decisions are made and what theses drive those decisions, and how venture funds are structurally set up to maximize returns for a group of investors. All of these elements are largely unknown to the founders themselves. For the purpose of transparency, it is important to look at where alignment begins to fall apart and how entrepreneurs can prevent this from happening. How can genius truly thrive and work well with venture capital?

Venture capital in itself has become a sexy asset class that some entrepreneurs believe to be the most important validation of their businesses. This is a complete fallacy. This notion is due in part to the stardom achieved by some VCs and the importance placed on large financing rounds in the popular press. Nicholas Chirls of Notation expands on this:

"...many venture capitalists have turned into mini celebrities. Chris Sacca is on television. Ashton Kutcher, Kevin Durant, Leonardo DiCaprio are now investing in startups. Fred Wilson has become a legend amongst people within the startup ecosystem and beyond. A lot of these people tend to be great people to be involved in a company, but to some degree, there is a perception that if you can raise money from these folks, you've somehow made it already. You can talk to any of these same investors, and they'll tell you that most startups will fail regardless of whether or not they raised venture capital. Venture capital is an expensive and highly dilutive source of capital. There are cheaper forms of capital, but as a founder, those sources of capital are largely unknown because they don't market themselves the same ways VCs do. Venture capitalists market themselves really well so that they are visible, that they become the first choice of capital, but there's a huge over-reliance on venture as a capital source."

Yes, entrepreneurs should be aware of other sources of capital that exist and that venture capitalists, focused on greater valuations, may not be the best partner for a founder who is looking to establish a company with gradual growth. Moreover, it's time for entrepreneurs to take venture capital and the venture capitalists themselves off the pedestal, as what dictates the success of the startup. In the next chapter, where I cover the future of venture capital and new forms of financing, I elaborate on some of these other capital streams and how venture capital continues to become a commodity.

While I've touched on valuations several times throughout this book, it can be difficult to quantify or accurately describe the pressure that comes after raising venture capital, and the impact it has on the psyche of a founder and executive team. I meet with founders who fearfully discuss their takeaways from investor calls and the pressure their investors put on them to spend more money. The venture capital model is built on this model of spending capital quickly in order to fuel growth. Venture capitalists want to hear that the founders they have invested in are taking calculated risks and bets on areas of the company that have shown promise. They want to see the founders spending capital, and not saving it. That is the purpose — that this is a brief, pressurized experiment to see if a business can take off by throwing capital at the problem. Less sophisticated investors will often chastise founders for not spending their capital, even if the metrics of the business are not improving or the founders need to take a step back to reassess where to invest.

I spoke with a founder who recounted this pressure. She felt that she was not being given sage advice from her investors who were pushing her to raise another round of financing, even though she did not need the capital. Many times, this kind of scenario comes down to a valuation, where the investors are looking for the next step-up in a company's valuation so that they can a) put more of their own capital to work; b) report back to their LPs that their companies are continuing to become more valuable; and c) help the founder realize a greater valuation on the company, even if it is not yet justified. This is an issue I frequently see come to a head, and it often leads to an alignment issue not only with a founder and their investors but also with their early founding team.

Beth Ferreira of FirstMark Capital brings extensive operating experience to her role as an investor. Prior to joining the venture capital community, Ferreira was COO of Fab, an e-commerce company that at its height was valued at over

$1 billion, but ultimately was rumored to be valued at $15 million. Ferreira also ran operations at Etsy. Given her experience at both of these venture-backed companies that saw swings in their valuation, Ferreira discusses how venture capital and valuations often become a slippery slope to maintain:

> "Companies can fail because of their investment strategy. It's really hard to get off the fund raising train when you've raised your first round of capital ahead of your traction at an outsized size or value. I got to Fab when we had $10 million in invested capital and within six weeks of my arrival, we raised another $50 million. At the time of that financing round, the business was working but when we tried to accelerate that with more capital, it was too early to do that, and things started to break. We had a big valuation, a lot of capital invested, and the conversations internally and externally turned to how the management team is going to live up to that valuation. The company began to make decisions that were premature or a stretch for the business to execute."

As I learned from these conversations, the founding teams in these situations stop protecting what has been built, and instead begin pushing the envelope and making gambles going forward. Ferreira talked about how this played out at Fab:

> "With Fab, we had a business that was 70% optimized in the US with lots of momentum and positive indicators on how we could get to of owning outsized market share in the US. We were doing things right compared to competitors. Then we raised a ton of capital ahead of our traction, and started to look to manufacture growth, expanded into more categories and entered Europe prematurely. This was the result of pressure that management just told everyone the company was going to be a $1 billion company in five years and now need to find a way to get there."

These are important areas that both venture investors and founders must understand to get aligned early on and identify what outcomes are most important for each side of the equation. Venture capital, in its chase for Uber-like returns, places an expectation on a company to grow at an accelerated pace. In an effort to demonstrate outsized returns for their investors, a venture capitalist has duties that go beyond the founder and will do what it takes to find those returns.

Founder-Friendly VCs and Establishing a Board of Directors

In 2019, venture capital funds now tout the term 'founder-friendly' on their websites to advertise that the terms of their financing and their diligence or management method will be in support of the founder. While this is certainly an ideal, and a goal that venture funds strive towards (as measured by a higher NPS), it is a tough balance: it can be difficult to manage the relationship with a founder and be 'founder-friendly,' while also managing the fiduciary duty to the LPs. Rick Heitzmann of FirstMark Capital discusses this dynamic that, in his words, leads to the lack of diligence on an investor's part and making investments without doing the necessary research:

> "In the last cycle where companies were being funded that very clearly should not have been funded, 'founder-friendly' was the thing most VCs wanted to be called. These VCs viewed 'founder-friendly' as not asking entrepreneurs the tough questions which ended up being a huge disservice to the LPs and the entrepreneurs themselves. Great entrepreneurs want to be tested with the hard questions and want an investor and Board member that it will to challenge them in a constructive way. In addition, entrepreneurs have to understand that my job is to service them and that they're my customers, but also, I have a fiduciary duty to my LPs who are investing with college endowments, the pensions of policemen and women and driving medial research, because they want to earn a return on this money — often times with a double bottom line impact. They're not doing this to make friends with

entrepreneurs. We have the fiduciary duty to drive high returns and that return is by not only doing good things but also sometimes doing hard things. We want to be known as fair."

The board of directors of venture-backed companies becomes a founder's strongest weapon in making strategic decisions. And it's important that entrepreneurs use this group of experienced individuals as confidantes to move a company forward. Ilya Fushman of Kleiner Perkins believes that like the role of a founder, the role of a board member is continuously evolving as a company scales. Fushman says that he observes where the company is in its lifecycle and in the early days, he sits in the back seat when the founder has strong conviction on product or vision. During this time, he helps founders think critically about what is ahead of them and helps founders add to the team or build processes, but really he just lets the founder drive the company forward. Over time, Fushman thinks the board should help the management team think about what the next level of scale or opportunity requires and begin offering more input. Beth Ferreira expands on this evolving process:

"The relationship between a venture investor and an entrepreneur should be an open conversation and the investor should act as a sounding board for the founder. The founder should be comfortable that this person can operate as a consigliere in the best or worst situations. A founder should be comfortable with it being their first time and can turn to their investment partners to figure out how to be prepared, or how to think about the world and where their product can or should be iterated on. They should have scenarios laid out in front of them by the investors with the upside to each avenue or scenario and what the value proposition is to the founder. If as an investor, I'm not doing that, I'm doing a disservice to the founders."

In contrast to his roles as an early executive at many of the well-known technology ventures, Keith Rabois discusses how his role evolves as a board member:

"My role as an early employee was very different than it is now that I am a board member. It evolves. Part of it is a bit like playing psychologist where you can give the founders and executive team someone to talk to and to clarify their own thinking and vision. The law school version of this would be a Socratic dialogue. Fundamentally, the role of a board member is about asking the founders and the management team questions that allow the founding team to better understand their own thinking by responding to their questions. It's a cartoonish mirror: you hold up a mirror to the company to play back what you're hearing in an exaggerated way, by exaggerating to the founding team what you are hearing — what the team wants, what they don't want, and what is being lost in translation. It's a combination of mirror and psychologist, staying out of their way, helping to clarify thoughts and vision, and removing roadblocks to their success where possible."

The board, according to Ellie Wheeler of Greycroft, is also responsible for helping the company mature at each stage by coaching the founder and bringing in the right talent to support them as the company scales. As many of the investors noted, much of the venture capital business from a board member perspective is a matter of seeing patterns play out repeatedly from one company to the next. Access to talent remains a consistent and evolving challenge. The amazing hire that was brought in to scale the company for the first 180 days may not be the right person for the next 500 days or beyond. Keeping a structural understanding of the business and what the founder needs at each stage is a key area of support board members provide. Wheeler says:

"On the lifecycle side, the team you start with isn't the one you end with. Typically, as the company scales, something breaks or is in the process of breaking before it's recognized. As a board, from an experience standpoint, we should recognize problems that may not exist now but are looming in the distance, and help the founder get ahead of those things — through talent acquisition or organizational design. The brute force required to start a seed company worked, but now we need to build an engine to scale. That is a common role for board members in any sector. For example, with SaaS businesses, what gets a company from $0 to $3 million in Annual Recurring Revenue (ARR) will likely be founder-driven sales. The company may have a handful of sales folks and an early VP of sales who had relationships and won deals narrowly. But as you scale, the company needs to get to $20 million or $60 million of ARR, so that machine looks very different. The board should be there to help the founder understand the different phases of the business, what kind of people you need around the team to bolster them, and those are the conversations you're going to have with any kind of business in any sector."

As an early-stage investor, Wheeler is also focused on the journey of the early leadership team. She says:

"I always am looking to understand if the leadership team can make the entire journey through the company. I want the original founders to make that journey, but you need to be a different leader in the early days when you know everyone in the organization, are involved in every decision, and are still in charge of every department. The business evolves and to be a part of the business where you don't know everyone or aren't involved in those decisions is a big change for some founders and something, they need to be aware of."

Keith Rabois of Founders Fund, who has been an early employee at multiple successful startups, shares his thoughts about how board members can complement leadership early in a startup's lifecycle:

"My role has always been the same as the complement to the founder. Different founders have different skills or traits. Some are product-driven founders, some are technical-driven founders, some are sales-driven founders. Some are atrocious managers of people and some are great managers. I've learned that my role is to always be the complement to that. I try to figure out what the person likes to do and is good at and provide support in other ways. I worked for Reid Hoffman, Jack Dorsey, Peter Thiel, Vinod Khosla, Max Levchin and they're all different so they all require a different complement. It's not so easy. You need to be fairly broad, with a horizontal skillset. You need to be very sharp so you can keep up with these brilliant people. They have no patience and speak succinctly so you have to fill in the dots to accomplish their vision. It has to be a derivative viewpoint about your role. It's not your vision, it's theirs. You have to have that humility that you're working to accomplish their vision. My job is to make sure the vision doesn't get screwed up because a lot can go wrong, and I want to help deliver the missing pieces. The missing pieces vary from company to company; some understand technology, some do not, some are good recruiters, some are not. To do the role well, you have to block and tackle their vision, identify the gaps from the skillset of the current team and inject yourself in the most acute areas of need. At Square, unlike at LinkedIn, the revenue model was obvious, and we didn't need someone to conjure up a business model."

Transparency at the board level is another quality that entrepreneurs should strive for with their boards and their investors. Jonathan Teo, formerly of Binary Capital, made investments in companies such as Snapchat and Grubhub. His approach to investing was to build the relationship and learn about the problems of a venture prior to making an investment. He explains:

"Typical in the venture community, the first board meeting is where all the bad stuff comes out. We want to build a relationship with the founder where we do our diligence and back work and get to know the founder for as long as possible; where they turn to us as a confidante and feel comfortable sharing the problems with us, long before we invest. We want to be deep in the weeds of the company and figure out how to move forward now that we know all the bad stuff and know what to be aware of. Doing it this way, we've found much less conflict and that we're actually more aligned."

The relationship between an investor and a founder is not always a story of kindred partnership. Yes, those do exist but they're not the norm. The reality is that, if not aligned properly, this is a partnership that can end in disaster. It can end in legal disputes similar to the ones recently documented around Uber's founder and CEO, Travis Kalanick, and his investors from Benchmark capital. The high-profile venture-backed startups with an absolute disregard for investor capital culminated with Theranos and its founder, Elizabeth Holmes, who deceived her investors into financing the company to the tune of $900 million against the bold claim that she could revolutionize blood testing. In other and more private anecdotes shared by the venture investors I spoke with, some distanced themselves from companies they knew to be toxic or rampant with fraud or abuse. At times when they were needed the most, investors walked away from companies after making an investment when they felt the company could no longer generate the returns it needed to. Perhaps, in most of these cases, the venture investors themselves were not the trail-wise sidekicks, but instead profiteers watching from safety miles away.

While these anecdotes will be used to besmirch the name of venture capitalists who are truly founder-friendly, it is important to note that entrepreneurs are not free of blame in many of these cases. Entrepreneurs paint a picture of the world to rally venture support and in the process often gloss over important details, exaggerate projections, and in some cases, fabricate stories to win venture financing. As an ecosystem, venture capital and startups are being held to a higher degree of discipline and transparency through the reporting of the media. It is important for the media, as well, to do a better job of capturing the honest realities of entrepreneurship; along with the massive financings and lofty valuations, they must also cover — and celebrate — the struggles entrepreneurs face and the partnerships they forge with venture capitalists to use technology for the betterment of society.

CHAPTER 9
THE FUTURE OF VENTURE CAPITAL

"Venture capital is no longer the 'cottage industry' it was when it started. I think there are a lot of people in venture now that have never seen a bad cycle or a downturn. There are fund managers that have only invested during this decade-long boom. Any rational being realizes that things won't always go up. It is easy to invest money, it's hard to find ways to get it out."

Ellie Wheeler, Greycroft

The rise of venture capital from the 1950s has been swift and fierce. From the trail-wise sidekicks who supported private investments for entrepreneurs returning from World War II to backing geniuses such as Mark Zuckerberg, Steve Jobs, Elon Musk, and Jack Dorsey, venture capital has established a place for itself in the entrepreneurial ecosystem. In its evolution since, venture capital is more transparent and more accessible than ever before. The industry, in some ways, has begun to transcend the 'old boys club' of a few funds wound together in a tightly-knit, impenetrable investment network. Through supporting innovation and the entrepreneurial spirit, the venture capital industry has lived up to the promise of spurring the American economy. As entrepreneurial culture continues to become the bedrock of most modern societies, the international demand for venture capital funding continues to grow.

In 2019, venture capitalists who pride themselves on being disruptive to old and stodgy industries approach the venture industry from a critical perspective. Encouraged by greater competition, they are testing the limits of their own funds with the hope of generating higher returns for their investors and becoming more efficient stewards of venture capital. More importantly however, in 2019, the venture capital conversation is centered around equality within the ecosystem and the power these investors yield. The anecdotes and lessons shared throughout this book reveal that the venture capital model is not identical from one fund to the next. The definition of 'entrepreneurial genius' also varies from one investor to the next. In this discourse, entrepreneurial ideas and diversity find the room to thrive. Like entrepreneurship, there is no single 'correct' path to finding great investments in venture capital. Knowing this, venture capitalists are compelled to experiment and innovate or go extinct.

During the time I was writing this book, there have been several pertinent trends and catalysts driving the venture industry forward: the commoditization of capital, the technological impact of blockchain and artificial intelligence, the removal of inherent bias from the investment decision process, the paths to liquidity, and the elevation of the geographic and demographic makeup of venture capital and its constituents. I explored some of these concepts with the venture capitalists I interviewed.

Commoditization of Venture Capital & Genius Dilution

As additional sources of capital — corporate venture funds (Salesforce, Microsoft, Intel, Nvidia, Google, BP, Boeing), sovereign wealth funds (Singapore, China, Abu Dhabi, Saudi Arabia), incubators and accelerators (TechStars, Y-Combinator, 500 Startups) — enter the ecosystem, the competition from one venture fund to another has led to a commoditization of the asset class. Venture capital funds that once operated with small teams and manageable funds are raising mega-funds as more LPs want to join the entrepreneurial boom. As more capital enters the ecosystem, investors compete for a smaller share of 'genius' founders. These genius entrepreneurs are in a position to demand more value, outside of working capital, from their investors. Simply said, entrepreneurs have more power now than ever before. They can raise capital from a host of different service providers and choose the provider with the best rate. Beth Ferreira of FirstMark Capital discusses this shift:

"Venture capital is becoming more and more commoditized. Until you have established yourself and your fund, as a venture investor that delivers value and has built a brand, the only thing an investment fund should focus on is how they partner with companies and develop a reputation to win deals. That's where having something different, something value-add as an investor, is important. I'm very focused on delivering demonstrable value quickly because it most importantly delivers on our promise to entrepreneurs and it demonstrates to the market, we are great partners."

Ferreira, in alluding to a16z, Sequoia, and Union Square Ventures, credits funds that have established themselves for investing in geniuses time and time again. Yet, in the venture capital industry, this self-fulfilling prophecy is important as the best entrepreneurs want to flock to the funds that have previously created 'unicorns', or billion-dollar valuation companies. In order to stand out, venture funds showcase the logos of companies that are high performers in order to attract more deal flow. Other venture funds launch their own publications, podcasts, or hire public relations firms to elevate their image and reputation. This is all done to 'get into the right deals.' Taylor Greene of Collaborative Fund echoes Ferreira's sentiment, simplifying a VC's job in this new competitive market into a few words:

"People often forget, but truly the only thing that matters in venture capital is deal flow, deal flow, deal flow."

In order to find this deal flow, venture capital funds are evolving in unique ways.

Platform Services

Beth Ferreira began her venture career at William Morris Endeavor — a talent agency that represents the likes of Denzel Washington, Larry King, Kanye West, and Taylor Swift — when the organization decided to make equity investments, similar to venture capital, in startups that were strategic to its core business. In doing so, William Morris Endeavor's venture arm had at its disposal celebrities who could promote consumer products or startups to their fan bases. They did exactly this with Masterclass, a popular video subscription service where experts teach an audience about their craft. Through Masterclass, Malcolm Gladwell teaches subscribers how to write, Stephen Curry shows his viewers the method behind his spectacular three-point shot, and Serena Williams teaches aspiring tennis players how to hit a powerful forehand down the line to defeat an opponent. William Morris Endeavor's unique differentiator is access to talent, and this becomes the 'platform service' for the venture fund. William Morris Endeavor, Hearst, Salesforce, Google Ventures, Nvidia Ventures, Intel Capital, and JetBlue Ventures all promise some corporate-related value-add to its founders. The concept of a service offering that extends beyond capital, also known as platform services, is not restricted to corporate venture groups. Instead, this practice was pioneered by traditional VC funds, more specifically a16z.

As of 2019, a16z has several dozen professionals working at the investment fund, but only a small percentage of those are investors in search of genius. The rest of the team supports portfolio companies with recruiting, marketing, finance and accounting, data analysis, and other operating tasks as part of the relationship. Venture funds have institutional knowledge on how best to scale a company and can infiltrate companies at every level to propagate that knowledge. Platform services are one of many ways venture investors are evolving against the backdrop of increased competition. Lindsey Gray, a partner who manages platform services for Two Sigma Ventures, explains how the data-focused fund differentiates itself to seed-stage companies that are being chased by a highly competitive venture industry:

"The strategy behind platform services, as a term, is to focus and be specific on how your venture fund can be helpful. A lot of funds are now focused on 'platform' but the strategy falls apart when they are not focused on something unique to them or their ethos. The two things that Two Sigma has, that most venture funds do not, are related to our parent company. Our platform strategy is based on the history that Two Sigma started 15 years ago as an engineering and data science startup. The founders had to figure out how to hire the best engineers and data scientists, and then train them to be managers. How do you grow people into leaders who joined here when they were 22, but are now managing an organization of 500 people? In an engineering and data science environment we help our portfolio companies with those specific issues — product, engineering, data science, and organizational development, and the reason we do that is because we have a resource that other venture funds do not."

Gray expanded on the traits of genius laid out by Fred Wilson and elaborated that for some funds, platform services also means helping founders develop those areas of risk management, storytelling, recruiting, and execution. Given that all founders face the shared challenge of recruiting, venture funds have actively hired talent partners who are responsible for filling the talent gap within a high-growth company, so that the founders themselves can continue to focus on execution. In other cases, venture funds are hiring public relations firms to tell the company's story, or they are having their own staff execute on customer acquisition or product development. In all of these cases however, according to Gray, the trick is to teach the founders to manage these areas on their own:

"The flaw in platform services, if not executed properly, is that venture funds are not teaching the founders to fish for themselves and the founding teams become reliant. This may not have to happen in the beginning when there is a firehose of issues but by the Series A, a founder should not be reliant on their investor for figuring out what the talent or execution gaps are in their company."

As the pendulum swings and entrepreneurs gain more optionality on sources of capital, they are able to select the investors who can truly add value to their vision. As discussed earlier, this may also manifest itself as investors who have deeply-held theses or beliefs about certain systems that can complement a founder's view of the world. There are anecdotes of founders walking out of venture funds that did not display enough diversity within their own teams. And in some cases, as companies become more valuable, founders can also retain control of their company even as they accept cash from investors who are desperate to join a high-flying startup. The cyclical nature of venture capital, however, implies that while the economy is doing well and venture funds are able to compete for entrepreneurial talent, in a downturn the opposite often happens; entrepreneurs can get caught in the middle of building a company and not be able to raise follow-on financing to execute on the vision on which they originally set out to achieve.

New Modes of Investing

As venture funds increase in size, they have two potential strategies. One is to expand their investment focus to all sectors, increase their partnership to manage this capital, and truly take bets across every sector. Another strategy funds employ is to take more small bets at the earlier stages of a founder's journey and then continue to invest heavily if the company succeeds past the first stage. Seed funds once invested at the earliest stages of a company by making an investment solely on a vision but have now moved further up the investment stack and want more proof points prior to investing. As a result, to fill that gap, a new type of fund has emerged called "pre-seed funds," which step in to write checks for $25,000-$100,000 as initial capital to provide the entrepreneur with the support needed to quickly test business models or ideas. This is one shift that has occurred as more capital enters the venture ecosystem.

Simultaneously, over the past decade, technology and the Internet have opened up new fundraising avenues.

Digital Investing and Coin Offerings

Ironically, despite the abundance of venture capital in the ecosystem, entrepreneurs still face a series of challenges in raising venture capital. The model is inefficient, largely network-driven, and a lack of transparency exists where founders have an overwhelming knowledge gap to cover. Likewise, many venture funds are putting more capital behind the same few companies rather than giving all founders an equitable chance.

This problem drove Naval Ravikant to build AngelList. Ravikant is an angel investor in Postmates, Uber, and Twitter. He is also the founder of Epinions, Venture Hacks, and as of 2010, AngelList. Ravikant believes that the venture industry operates by arbitraging information. The prevailing sentiment in Silicon Valley is that venture capitalists compete to find a hot deal, before the deal is competitive, and that their competitive advantage is often solely due to the networks that they are part of. Outsiders are unable to invest in promising companies and the venture investors with the most established brands and networks gain access. Ravikant is a believer that as capital becomes commoditized in the future, large, brand name venture capital funds will be inconsequential. He believes in an unbundling of large corporations and funds where people will have more independence and have their own brands, instead of being centralized around one institution.

While angel investing and investing out of a small venture capital fund, Ravikant recognized that in an age where the flow of information was often free, venture capital deals should not be so exclusive. His vision was for a platform that distributed and monitored deal flow and also allowed ordinary individuals to invest in earlier stage companies. This marketplace solution, if executed correctly, would also make it easier for founders to quickly raise capital without having to go on a long roadshow. AngelList has evolved into an online-funding marketplace that connects investors with early-stage ventures. Collectively, as of 2019, AngelList has reportedly executed over 1,200 deals through the platform and raised hundreds of millions of dollars for early-stage founders. Still, the venture community is hesitant to acknowledge its success. The large funds claim that investors on AngelList lack sophistication or a true ability to support or identify genius founders. Ravikant is betting against that. He believes that venture capitalists should operate like software companies or service providers that are transparent about their pricing and their business models.

AngelList is one of many digital means that founders are now using to raise capital online. Other platforms, including Kickstarter, SeedInvest, and Funders Club, aim to democratize fundraising and make the process more transparent and efficient. The change, however, has been slow. The vast majority of entrepreneurs I spoke with use these platforms to raise initial seed capital but often want the reputation of a large venture fund or the value-add platform services provided by funds such as Two Sigma Ventures and a16z. While traditional venture capital still dominates the financing market for entrepreneurs, one thing is for certain: AngelList and other platforms working to make the fundraising process easier for the entrepreneur have begun to crack the walls that VC funds have been hiding behind that purposefully make entrepreneurs jump through hoops to reach them and test their mettle.

Blockchain & ICOs

In his disruption of the traditional venture models, Ravikant has been a vocal proponent of how blockchain technology can enable founders to raise capital for their businesses. This movement began in 2013 and grew in popularity in 2018. Through Initial Coin Offerings (ICOs), entrepreneurs skipped the venture capital process all together and raised financing for their startups by offering tokens or coins to the public. ICOs were intended to be like IPOs in that it was a mass-market offering without the hurdles (e.g. paperwork, regulatory filings, roadshows, bankers, and other product approvals) of an IPO. In 2017, ICOs allowed founders to raise money by selling tokens or 'coins' as an investment in their blockchain project's vision. Individuals invested in the digital rights to a venture, which provided access to goods or services provided by that project, and the value of the token/coin fluctuated based on the performance of that company.

While the concept is compelling to founders and offers an easier pathway to funding, most ICOs in 2018-2019 were fraudulent or junk. Still, these businesses raised millions of dollars overnight from both sophisticated investors and often unsuspecting individuals who hoped to cash in on a gold rush. For example, a developer launched a token called the XMAS token, which promised to bring gratitude and appreciation to the cryptocurrency (digital currencies) community. Other developers launched coins called "Useless Ethereum Token" as a joke, "Jesus Coin" as a religious token, or "DentaCoin" for the dental community. Investors poured into this asset class as two popular coins — Bitcoin and Ethereum — skyrocketed in value and minted hundreds of millionaires within under a year. In 2018, over $8 billion was raised in ICOs for over 1,200 'companies.'

But the fortune and party for other investors was fleeting. The United States Securities Exchange Commission was slow to regulate the new technology and coin offerings. Thousands of household investors lost fortunes by speculatively betting on these non-traditional investments as the value of the coins tumbled in value. The value of Bitcoin and Ethereum (as well as XMAS Coin and Jesus Coin) dropped by over 75% between 2018-2019. These coin offerings demonstrated startup hysteria in its worst form. Inexperienced individuals who believed that 'luck' plays a big role in venture capital thought that they too could join the gold rush offered by early-stage companies.

Proponents of the technology were quick to remind the world that the frothiness and speculation is commonplace during the early days of any major technological breakthrough. The breakthrough in this case is the financing shift that occurred through ICOs and the premise that new ideas can be funded online.

After the bubble burst, Ravikant and other proponents of ICOs say that blockchain technology is building free open systems and creating financing mechanism where owning a token is enough to support a company. With ICOs, companies no longer need to register with the SEC, and they can be freely traded around the world. This system threatens capitalists who work with companies over a 3-10 year period until they achieve an IPO. With ICOs, entrepreneurs can raise a small amount of venture funding and work towards an ICO as the next step instead of raising Series A, B, or C financing. This squeezes venture capital and forces it to operate in a small segment of the market as opposed to owning the entire financing chain of a company. While this may be exciting progress, ICOs often offered coins at absurd valuations and protections were not built from investors losing all of their money. In 2019, the reputation of ICOs became so toxic that most investors were staying away until the industry had more regulation and systems in place. Neil Devani, an investor in Silicon Valley, wrote in his blog about the emergence of cryptocurrency and what it could mean for venture capital:

"[Blockchain] has opened startup investing to a global capital market bringing unprecedented liquidity, drawing from a now inflated set of currencies. The increased demand and liquidity premium has resulted in companies that can't raise a $2 million round from VCs raising $20 million from crypto investors, with returns expected from speculation versus revenue or profit. Losses have mounted as Bitcoin trades at a ~80% discount to its all-time highs, but the appeal of liquidity in an otherwise illiquid asset (startup equity) and investing from an inflated asset will remain strong. As the hype and easy money fade, future investment will depend more on the performance of existing investments. In 2013, there were 39 unicorns (tech startups valued at $1B or more), with four more created annually. Five years later there are 146 unicorns and we're adding about 15 annually. That said, unicorns are arguably overvalued by almost 50% on average. It's hard to envision all of these companies growing into or exiting at these values."

Inherent Bias & Leveling the Venture Playing Field

A fundamental area that entrepreneurs and venture capitalists continue to explore in 2019 is the extent of human bias in venture capital. Examined from another perspective: are humans capable of evaluating true genius or can this be a data-driven exercise? Early stages of investing are inherently characterized by a lack of data and proof points, so many investments are made on conviction or loosely-held theses. Investors who backed companies like Lyft or Airbnb in the early days say that in the absence of traction, they trusted their gut instinct that those founders would go on to succeed. Artificial intelligence (AI) cannot quantify or program gut instinct. Rational computers would almost always shoot down startup endeavors given the irrationality of these experiments and the low likelihood of success. Does the human element of optimism or conviction to shoot for the stars make venture capital as compelling as it is? I will leave the overall debate on AI versus human investment for another time, and here, put an emphasis instead on human-centered investing — specifically, the responsibility investors have to create equanimity within the startup ecosystem.

The individuals who manage the capital behind the entrepreneurs who will re-shape the future share a moral obligation to humanity. In order to create and support businesses and enterprises that represent the values that all humans hold important, it's critical that all minorities, socioeconomic groups, and genders be represented in this future environment of venture capital. And it comes down to this: the responsibility for a level playing field falls squarely on the shoulders of early-stage venture capitalists who are deciding who is given a fair shot at shaping this future, and who is not. Currently, this is not the case — far from it. While the venture capital industry tends to pride itself on being progressive, it's reared its ugly head time and again by excluding large swaths of people from the opportunity to showcase their genius.

In 2019, the extent of the diversity problem in venture capital and technology cannot be overstated. As Rebecca Kaden of Union Square Ventures puts it:

> "The venture market is not efficient. If you look at the statistics of the number of women or minorities that have raised venture capital as a percentage of the total number of entrepreneurs that have received venture capital, you can't honestly say that every founder that deserves venture capital is getting venture capital."

Despite what some of the investors I spoke with claimed about why this problem exists and why they believe that venture capital is in fact efficient, I fundamentally agree with Kaden's point. The venture market is not efficient. It leaves large groups of individuals and geographies marginalized. Women-only teams historically raised about 2% of all venture capital while all-male teams raised about 80% of it. According to CB Insights, in 2016, less than 1% of venture capital funded founders who were black. Considering these statistics, 'genius' has been defined from a very myopic perspective, skewed in favor of certain groups of individuals. One cause is selection bias. Most partners at venture capital funds have historically been white males and oftentimes, even if unwittingly, have associated with founders who resemble their own professional, socioeconomic, or educational backgrounds. Defining genius based on how they have been trained their entire lives, these VCs have a bias that has created serious inequality in the venture and technology ecosystem. The National Venture Capital Association (NVCA) reported that, in 2016, 11% of venture capital firm investment partners were women. In terms of ethnicity, 13% were Asian; 2% Hispanic; and 0% black. Melinda Gates, an advocate to change this disproportion, wrote in a ReCode post:

> "While the average investment in companies led by men jumped 12 percent, to $10.9 million, the average investment in companies led by women dropped 26 percent, to $4.5 million... The people who are running these VC funds aren't necessarily setting out to be exclusive or discriminatory. But even so, there is a lot of evidence that unconscious biases are impacting the way female founders are received. Consider, for example, the finding that investors tend to describe young male entrepreneurs as "promising," and young female entrepreneurs as "inexperienced." Or that the managing partner of one of Silicon Valley's leading VC firms admitted that one of the things he looks for when deciding whether to invest is an entrepreneur who fits the Gates, Bezos, Andreessen or Google model — which is to say, "white male nerds who've dropped out of Harvard or Stanford."

In 2018 and 2019, this conversation finally became front and center. AllRaise, a nonprofit launched by 34 female women partners at prominent venture capital funds, aimed to transform the industry by mentoring and creating additional opportunities for female founders and investors. AllRaise has facilitated networking opportunities between female founders and female venture capitalists, it has encouraged the broader community to support diversity at their own funds, and more importantly, it has forced this conversation to happen on center stage. Simultaneously, Arlan Hamilton, the founder of Backstage Capital, has exhibited the traits of 'genius' venture capitalists search for — an unwillingness to fail, a tolerance for criticism, recruiting acumen, and a proficiency for storytelling — as she has risen from poverty to launch a venture capital fund focused exclusively on funding minority and female founders. Hamilton's story is inspiring and reveals that founders like herself are often discounted because they did not have a similar background to the investors who controlled the majority of venture capital. Other funds, such as Female Founders Fund (Sutian Dong, who wrote the prologue for this book, is a partner with Female Founders Fund) and Unshackled Ventures, have also done their part in driving this shift.

This change can be enforced by Limited Partners who fund venture capitalists committed to creating this more efficient startup market. Jenny Abramson, the Founder and Managing Partner of Rethink Impact, an impact-focused venture capital fund dedicated to investing in women, discusses the importance of finding a diverse LP base that respects the investments she makes:

"Our LP base is ~50% women. If you think about most venture dollars in this country, they come from the coasts (primarily from New York and California). Our LP dollars are coming from 32 different states, from people on both sides of the aisle, and from foundations and other sources. We think that when you get this notion of women investing in women who are investing in women, you start to turn the tables on the gender gap in the startup industry. If you follow the expected transfer of wealth in the coming years, I believe you're going to start to see even more shifts in the dynamic. Millennials, as they inherit wealth and make investment decisions, will also cause shifts, both on the impact side and on the gender side. Both groups care deeply about investing with impact, even more so than previous generations."

I find the trends in venture capital to be particularly disturbing, but I remain optimistic that the efforts by female investors like Beth Ferreira, Jenny Abramson, Arlan Hamilton, and Rebecca Kaden will continue to level the playing field for entrepreneurs. Led by the example of these individuals, this issue is being rectified by both men and women across the venture capital industry.

In writing this book, I set out to capture a diverse set of perspectives to define 'genius,' and in doing so, I was fortunate to connect with investors who represent the gender, socioeconomic, racial, and geographic diversity that I anticipate venture capital will eventually come to represent. Each of these investors has agreed to share their insights in an even more transparent way; they've each written a chapter with their own investment thesis, which I will share in the next section.

Geographical Distribution

Venture capital should play a vital role and support the entrepreneurial ecosystem in emerging economies. Unfortunately, venture capital dollars have historically not been evenly distributed across the US or internationally. As venture capital came to prominence, the first funds settled in Boston to be in close proximity to prominent academic institutions and the talent that was drawn to them. Over time, the venture capital industry consolidated in Silicon Valley, which still dominates much of the mindshare of the venture ecosystem. New York and Philadelphia have risen as contenders with massive companies being built out of these cities including companies like Glossier and Pinterest.

As the cost of building a company goes down and access to talent becomes less about location and more about skill — regardless of location — the geographic distribution of venture capital should follow suit. If venture capital is more decentralized and democratic, entrepreneurs in emerging entrepreneurial hubs gain new access to capital. Cities like St. Louis or Detroit present massive opportunities for founders who want to partner with large corporations in verticalized industries such as agriculture, automotive and transportation, and insurance.

Cliff Holekamp, a professor with Washington University and a venture capitalist with Cultivation Capital, is focused on supporting and retaining entrepreneurs to build businesses within the Midwest. Raised in California but transplanted to St. Louis, Holekamp has seen the United States transition from a country dependent on its manufacturing states that thrived given their industry dominance and technical prowess to now investing heavily into its technology and financial sectors. Holekamp discusses how these cities have evolved:

"St. Louis, a rustbelt city, was one that was heavily dependent on manufacturing and was famous for its high proportion of Fortune 500 companies headquartered there until the 1980s. In the 1980s those companies started to be acquired by multinationals or went out of business (Purina by Nestle, Anheuser Busch bought by InBev). We were a company town, our students and residents worked at these companies. We got too confident and no one planned for the adverse. That's typical of the Midwest and we've seen it play out in most cities across the United States. There were a lot of old-school manufacturing companies that in their heyday were thriving but as the economy changed and evolved, these cities were not entering into the future and were suffering as a result of change. They were being, as a Silicon Valley investor might put it proudly, 'disrupted.' In Chicago, venture capital was slow to grab a foothold. These large cities were focused on industry, but these industries were not evolving. In 1904, St. Louis was a thriving metropolis and the fourth largest city in America. Since then, the city became complacent and lost its focus on innovation and entrepreneurship. By the end of the 20th century, it just wasn't in the DNA of our people anymore. We were big company people but as those big companies failed, we needed to evolve. In fact, we had to evolve. Around 2012, we began to force this change."

Holekamp reflects on a trend I noticed as I traveled to cities across the United States for *Disruptors*. In small towns such as Aberdeen, South Dakota or Pippa Passes, Kentucky, entrepreneurs with bold ideas are not being provided with the same opportunities as entrepreneurs on the coasts are being given. It is less of a financing problem and more so a knowledge gap on what is available to these founders. The outlier geniuses that do emerge in these towns end up abandoning their communities and building their businesses and hiring teams in the economies of Boston, New York or San Francisco. Holekamp began to focus on building a robust ecosystem that retained its entrepreneurs. He says:

"When we started, we held competitions that gave entrepreneurs $50,000 to start. There was no follow-on capital. So as a result, those companies would be seeded in St. Louis but then they would have to move to California or New York to get that next round of capital. We launched Cultivation Capital to fund companies through the Series-A round so that we can create an ecosystem to allow them to stay in this city. Angel markets were local but follow-on capital was elsewhere."

Entrepreneurship is meant to be a democratic vertical where 'geniuses' can start a company without too much restriction. The problem that exists in 2019 is not only that the opportunities are not equally available to women or people of color, but they're also out of reach to 'geniuses' who are bound by the places they are born. Holekamp is one investor focused on addressing the geographic distribution of wealth and venture capital. Another is Steve Case, the former CEO of America Online who partnered with Revolution's Rise of the Rest fund, which is specifically designed to fund entrepreneurs outside of the coastal cities. Their portfolio spans multiple industries but is able to identify unique opportunities, such as Freightwaves out of Chattanooga, Tennessee, a fast-growing company building telematics software for the freight industry.

Given that he has grown up surrounded by the freight industry, Craig Fuller, the founder of Freightwaves, has the unique insight and determination to solve problems that he has witnessed his entire life.

Holekamp believes that access to talent and a capital network are important to foster and support entrepreneurial genius but places importance on a 'dense ecosystem'. He says:

"We need talent and capital in an environment that is dense enough to create a community — which I define as a group of people with shared experiences. When you create a community, it defines a culture and that culture attracts more people to join the community. The big enemy to entrepreneurial communities is lack of density because if you don't have people physically located near one another and sharing their ideas around common experiences, they'll never bind to one another's challenges and struggles or inspire one another with success and vision. We didn't initially understand the important interplay between talent, capital, and density, but fortunately, these essential three elements all came together in downtown St. Louis at the T-REX incubator around 2012. We ended up with enough critical mass and that created the genesis that has built upon itself and given us the momentum we have today."

Looking to the Future and Avoiding the Hype

From 2007-2019, mobile smartphones opened up opportunities for new venture-scale businesses. With high-quality cameras in everyone's pocket, Instagram and Snapchat were concepted as mobile-first businesses. As GPS technology was embedded into these handheld devices, companies such as Uber, Lyft, and Waze, became integral to our everyday lives. The surge in smartphone usage was followed by a decrease in the cost of the device while the chips in these devices continued to evolve and support more activities. In 2017, consumers saw augmented reality (AR) and virtual reality (VR) startups leverage smartphones to change the way we interact with the world around us. Over the past decade, smartphones have been an entry point for people in developing countries to access financial credit, remain in contact with their friends and families, monitor the health of their businesses, and gain access to important knowledge previously not available to them. In 2018, Apple paid developers who built and monetized apps on the Apple App Store over $38 billion and venture capitalists were behind many of those projects. In China, applications such as WeChat on mobile dominate everyday life through transactions, communication, entertainment, and commerce.

As smartphone penetration compounds, mobile devices and their users continue to produce treasure troves of data. For storage needs, VCs backed cloud infrastructure projects; and for projects that leveraged smartphone data, they backed geniuses solving problems in healthcare, communication, productivity, education, social, and one of the most lucrative of all, mobile gaming. As this data is stored, new applications for artificial intelligence have emerged and venture capitalists are funding opportunities at the intersection of machine learning, computer vision, and smart devices. Through machine learning, robotics have become a hot investment area for venture capitalists who are funding companies that aim to automate mundane tasks from invoice processing to packing boxes. VCs have also been eager to fund the next-generation AI projects and are funding companies surrounding autonomous vehicles to the tune of hundreds of millions of dollars a year.

In the next section, I'll share theses from investors looking at how investment opportunities within specific industries will evolve and present themselves. In comparison, other investors are interested in the next platform shift, similar to the previous transformations incited by the Internet, software, and mobile. And others still, as they wait for this shift, are continuing to invest and search for opportunities around using data for more complex businesses in computational biology or applied robotics. Josh Nussbaum of Compound, for example, shares his take on this next generation of venture capital investing:

"I'm excited about applying data to complex activities like computational biology, where we are now capturing health data, understanding what it all means, matching it to physiological data, and understanding certain diseases to develop drugs. This same frame of thinking can be applied to robotics and teaching them to process complex environments to eliminate the need for humans to do repetitive or mundane processes. I've been fascinated by the rise in voice interfaces. Airpod adoption may be the tip of the iceberg. With airpods, you can see 'always-on voice computing' becoming a reality as Siri uses data and behaviors to become more intelligent. Another area of interest is around decentralized apps on ethereum or blockchain. This idea of the world becoming decentralized is interesting especially with world events, such as Brexit and Donald Trump being elected, that show the divide in communities. These patterns are driving people into niche communities, where people have more in common in digital interest groups than they do in their own countries."

Investors like Nussbaum remain fundamental optimists that technology will continue to evolve, and entrepreneurs will find ways to build disruptive businesses on top of it. Yet, as entrepreneurship becomes more commonplace and more and more individuals attempt their own startups, an obvious question presents itself: is 'genius' being diluted as more 'tourist entrepreneurs' flood the ecosystem looking to make their own mark?

Genius: Diluted

'Genius,' as defined earlier in this book, is a term reserved for a few outliers in society. With over $56 billion poured into venture capital funds in 2018, the discipline of funding only true 'genius' has wavered. VCs have not been as stringent as they once were in the past with who they fund. Similarly, more 'entrepreneurs' are joining the modern day gold rush and attempting to start companies that are merely solutions in search of problems or that lack true customer validation or value. As referenced earlier, these 'tourist entrepreneurs' may experience the lifestyle but rarely commit to the challenge of starting a company. Yet, they still get funded. As more founders join the ecosystem, how has the abundance of capital and entrepreneurial ideas diluted the ecosystem? Are we up against an overcrowded entrepreneurial market where geniuses are hard to spot? Beth Ferreira discusses this phenomenon:

"The number of people who are starting companies each year is insane. These are all talented people, but you also want the most talented people working on the best ideas, not all starting companies. Founders need to be at the right place in their life and with an idea they're passionate about that they're ready to sacrifice everything else to do it and accomplish it. My concern is we celebrate all the wrong things and people are getting funded that shouldn't be funded. We need to be more selective. I think there is a disconnect on what it means to take capital. You have to really believe who you're about to build something really big. If you're not in that place, you 100% should not take capital. Not everyone has that ability to build and throw it out there in the world. You have to find what your iteration tolerance/spectrum is."

The 'Zuckerberg effect' — chasing entrepreneurial dreams in hopes of becoming billionaires — has led to flocks of new founders entering the ecosystem. Separately, employees are leaving established companies (like Fab, mentioned above) to launch their own businesses. While the market will stabilize and weed out the ventures that shouldn't exist, Matthew Hartman of Betaworks recognizes that investors need to be more discerning during this upswing in venture capital. He says:

"I bet Mark Zuckerberg's story pulls people out that would have otherwise been in private equity or investment banking, who were chasing wealth. Yes, I can see the entrepreneurial pool being diluted in 2019. As investors we need to be better about deciphering between the noise and the real. Are you starting a company for its own sake? An idea that you can't shake? If not, you're probably chasing the wrong things and an investor needs to discern if you'll quit at the first challenge."

Entrepreneurship and startups have become pervasive in our culture and with it, there are more people starting companies without the required experience or insights. At a high level, investors like Ellie Wheeler believe it is a good thing that entrepreneurship has become more accessible, but are weary of 'tourist entrepreneurs.' She explains:

"There are those people who are tourists — this is a hot space, I can go do something big — typically they use a lot of lingo, they just don't have that 'genius' factor, and they're coming at it because it's a shiny new object. Those people do not have staying power. Yes, there has been an influx into the tech ecosystem and overall that's a good thing, but we also need to be conscious that there are now going to be more people chasing that dream but they don't have what it takes. It is an unfortunate byproduct of the tech media being only about fundraising announcements. It's a necessary evil on a path to something else, but celebrating fundraising announcements is not a valuable use of time, at all. It's changing the definition of success."

Wheeler however, agrees with Beth Ferreira that VCs will need to be more disciplined through this next generation of investing. As more funds enter the ecosystem, venture capitalists will need to be disciplined with the metrics they follow but still seek out higher returns to justify the massive funds that they have raised. As discussed earlier, the definition of success can be far different for a founder and a venture capitalist because not all businesses should be venture-backed. There are countless examples of founders who never raised outside capital and they owned 100% of their business. In that instance, a $10 million sale of a company is $10 million directly to the founder. If the same founder raised $5 million in capital, a $10 million outcome is not as exciting for the founder or the investors.

As investors take their stakes in companies and search for higher valuation multiples, there is a prevailing 'greater fool theory.' Investors will often overstate the success of companies within their portfolio to find an investor who can now fund the next round of a company, which may or may not even deserve a higher valuation. The greater fool theory is prevalent in a venture ecosystem that is focused on growth, at all costs. This leads to founders raising and spending more capital without a sound business model. These businesses often have negative unit economics or are venture subsidized the entire time. As entrepreneurs and investors, it is important to have a disciplined perspective on the fundamental economics when evaluating a business opportunity. Jonathan Teo, a former partner with General Catalyst, discusses the greater fool theory and how as an investor, he remains disciplined on staying away from the frothiness of high valuations and public fundraising announcements. Teo says:

> "We always make this comment internally that we don't invest with the 'greater fool theory' in mind. We look at companies that have a strong potential to be public, independent companies with solid business models in place. If you look at many consumer packaged goods companies out there today, they're not being built on strong fundamentals but instead have business models that are venture subsidized. These businesses won't scale well because over time, as they stop finding customers organically, they'll spend more venture dollars to acquire more customers. As a result, their margins will be compressed, eventually driving their prices up. Eventually, this all leads to a serious attrition of customers. There are a lot of issues at play in these businesses but because they are in this growth mode where they are building a brand, some investor may jump on board. Companies like these are fueling the 'greater fool theory' and you may get a less sophisticated who wants to jump on that kind of growth. These types of exits and outcomes are never good for anyone — the founder or the VCs."

As Teo suggests, the main result of an influx in capital into a 'hot' company is the excess spending of that same capital. What happens when there is too much money? Entrepreneurs find a way to spend it — often not efficiently

— and you're left with a situation of startups outspending each other in order to try to acquire as many customers as possible. In 2019, consumers are likely familiar with businesses that offer $50 for the first at-home meal kit or $10 to use the new food delivery service. While consumers love these initial benefits, if they do not continue to use the service, the business loses that money they spent to acquire them in the first place.

Teo, like other investors, believes that in some cases, for a short period of time, this model may work to spur growth; but it is important to look for deals not based on public perception or false success metrics. At the time of our conversation, Teo was searching for deals that were not getting done because that specific industry was unpopular. With other investors, he was staying away from 'hot' companies that were raising money only on a growth story, but lacked a solid business model. Capital that feeds growth is typically not just feeding an unsustainable model but also breeding really bad behavior from an entrepreneur. It's facilitating the need for them to spend on marketing and branding instead of answering the tough questions to get intimate with their value proposition and figure out the real problem they're trying to solve. Teo believes in the future, the market will stabilize and weed out these companies. He says:

> "I think this bad behavior will get slowly filtered out. Prices are an assumption of demand. There has been more demand for private equity because products are not making their way to the public markets. Some of the exits you see in the space are purely around the greater fool theory and no one is regulating this. You have entrepreneurs and investors feeding this frenzy for a land grab, but it is not sustainable. We should start seeing far less capital come into companies at insane valuations, because it becomes clear that you may not be able to get downstream financing at a high price. Unsophisticated investors all make the same mistake. They're not looking into the underlying business to understand what drives their sustainable advantage. You see a lot of investors trying to jump on the coattails of growth, and

growth has been all of what Silicon Valley investors have spoken about over the past few years; but growth should be fueled through discipline and core business values. I think the future looks great for technology and entrepreneurship, but we need to return to basics."

Beth Ferreira sees this pendulum starting to swing back to this direction. In the first quarter of 2019, she saw investors demanding more proof points. Whereas 18 months prior, Ferreira reflects, it was easy to raise capital only on a pitch deck. She explains:

"The pendulum has swung, and most logical investors want to see a proof of concept, revenues or a working product. When you look at some of the companies that have traditionally been started out of business schools, they took the time to build a proof point. Warby Parker didn't raise capital at first, they just tested out their theory and when they had the proof of concept, then they started thinking about that. I think there is a disconnect on what it means to take capital. That's why we like to back engineers because they are system thinkers. There are a couple of groups of people I'm advising who see problems and they try to build a product as their first instinct. They build one that doesn't work and keep testing it and finally stumble on something that works.

A decade from now, venture capital will look entirely different than it does today. The industry will continue to go through dramatic shifts in order to better serve entrepreneurs. In 2019, Matthew Hartman of Betaworks was in the process of launching Betaworks Fund II on the back of the success of the first fund. As he looks at the landscape around him, he recognizes the volatility surrounding venture capital: AngelList's impact, the noise of ICOs, venture capital funds growing larger in size, pre-seed funds emerging with access to new capital flows, governments and corporations all entering the ecosystem.

Hartman recognizes that Betaworks too must evolve in order to stay relevant and his solution to this noise is to focus:

> "With everything that is going on around us, how do you do early investing at a scale where you're adding a lot of value? As the competition for breakout deals increases, we need to be focused. Our solution is to focus on areas of interest and find the best companies in that space before anyone else does. For example, we launched Voicecamp and Botcamp. In Botcamp, we accepted eight companies into our office that were exclusively building technology around chatbots. We invited the big players, like Slack and Facebook, that could leverage this technology. We helped them think about product, market, launch strategy and by inviting enterprises, we could actually help them. At the same time, our team is also building companies so that we collectively learn a ton with the founders. We raise money for those companies that we're building so we get a sense of the funding market for those companies. At the end of Botcamp, we end up knowing as much as anybody about that ecosystem. We can share that information with our companies, and we can learn to make better investments."

Across the board, venture capitalists seem to agree that funds — especially new ones — will be forced to have a point of view on why they are differentiated. Beth Ferreira, Matthew Hartman, Rebecca Kaden, and Keith Rabois all touched on this. Some of them do this through the people they hire, some through their industry focus, and some through their expansive theses. The proliferation of ways to finance a company will no doubt force venture capitalists to differentiate their offering. And if the trend of more sources of capital persists, there will be plenty of cases where 'genius' entrepreneurs will no longer need to touch venture capital money, because there will be an abundance of other sources of capital available to them.

CHAPTER 10
LOOKING FORWARD AND CONCLUSION

"In order to be in venture, you have to be a persistent optimist and believe in the inevitable march forward in technology. You have to assume that everything is always going to get better. To assume it won't is limiting, close-minded, and self-defeating."

Andrew Parker, Spark Capital

In Search of Greatness, a documentary released in 2018, examines patterns of athletic genius exhibited by Wayne Gretzky, Jerry Rice, Serena Williams, Pelé, and Tiger Woods. It begins with an account of the "Combines," where aspiring professional athletes compete fiercely across a series of physical tests such as the 40-yard dash or total weight bench-pressed. While designed to quantify athletic ability for scouts to base their recruiting efforts on, these tests rarely indicate future success. Tom Brady, the winningest NFL quarterback, demonstrated little potential based on the Combine tests in 2000. For the 40-yard dash, Brady was clocked at 5 minutes and 28 seconds — the slowest recorded time for any quarterback at the Combine as of 2019. Today, Tom Brady is undeniably an athletic genius. Scouts for the NFL had harsh criticism for this future star, as revealed by Brady in a social media post:

"Poor build, Skinny, Lacks great physical stature and strength, Lacks mobility and ability to avoid the rush, Lacks a really strong arm, Can't drive the ball downfield, Does not throw a really tight spiral, System-type player who can get exposed if forced to ad lib, Gets knocked down easily."

The same goes for hockey legend, Wayne Gretzky. In public interviews, Wayne Gretzky often speculates that he 'would have been ranked the lowest' in many measurements people now see as important. In Search of Greatness argues that athletes may have some biological or physical disposition that sets them apart, but it is the other, unquantifiable factors that allow them to achieve greatness. In that vein, Gretzky alludes to his obsession and creativity with the sport of ice hockey that allowed him to break all scoring records for the NHL. It was Serena Williams' and Michael Jordan's insecurities about being second best, the documentary indicates, that sparked an intense competitive nature, and made the sports of tennis and basketball synonymous with their names.

In writing *Finding Genius*, and through the series of conversations I have had with entrepreneurs and venture capitalists, I have come to understand that entrepreneurial genius cannot be measured or quantified through aptitude tests. It is not something a person is born with. It is not, as popular culture stories would suggest, a spark of genius that appears overnight. Instead, genius manifests itself by learning through unstructured environments, a sense of creativity, and having an unmatched tolerance for risk and failure. Genius is the result of an obsession with a problem and having the competitive drive to find the best solution to that problem. Venture capitalists have proven, through the success of the companies they have backed, that entrepreneurial genius can be found, nurtured, and supported. The open debate remains whether this search for genius is happening efficiently and equitably.

Unstructured Creativity & Learning

Ilya Fushman believes that geniuses emerge from unstructured and uncertain environments. After earning a Ph.D. from Stanford University and a failed startup attempt, Fushman worked for venture capitalist industry titan Pierre Lamond at Khosla Ventures. It was his role as head of business development at Dropbox, however, that earned him his reputation in Silicon Valley: he joined Dropbox when the company was only 50 employees and helped scale the organization to profitability. He then brought that operating experience gained at Dropbox back to venture capital, first as an investor at Index Ventures and as of 2019, as a GP with Kleiner Perkins. Over his venture career, Fushman has backed companies such as Slack, KeepTruckin, UiPath, and Robinhood. All of these companies, as of writing this book, are valued at over a billion dollars and each one is being led by founders lauded as 'geniuses' by those in Silicon Valley and beyond. According to Fushman, there's one characteristic that sets the founders of these companies apart: they are all immigrants.

Prior to Fushman 'making it' in the United States, his family emigrated from the Soviet Union, to Israel, to Germany, and finally to New York in a matter of a few years. When they arrived in New York, his family struggled to create a life for themselves and crammed into a one bedroom apartment where Fushman spent five years sleeping on a futon. As he recalls, it is an understanding of these 'lows' that eventually gave him a willingness to 'lose it all' and to take uncharacteristic risks to succeed. The qualities that set apart founders are only developed by growing and learning in unstructured environments where a person's character and mettle is tested. Reflecting on his investments in UiPath, KeepTruckin, and Slack, Fushman says:

"When Kleiner Perkins was raising this fund, its 17th fund, we did a study and found that out of our last fund, 70% of our founders were immigrants. This was not by design. Between Stewart [Slack], Shoaib [KeepTruckin], Eliot [Plastiq], Daniel or Marius [UiPath], there is a commonality between all of them that drew me to their individual genius. There is a commonality where in order to be a great founder, you need to take the right risk at the right time, but more importantly be willing to take that risk and make that leap, where you know you may lose everything. I believe that a 'nothing to lose' background or mentality, that is shaped over several years, prepares you for that. With my own background, and the situations I have been through, I know that what I'm doing now is so infinitely better than all of that. My background isn't the lowest of lows, but if I lose it all and if I go back to that situation, I'll be fine. I'm willing to set it all on fire to some extent to go the bigger distance. That's the mentality you see in entrepreneurs that are doing really well. There is nothing holding them back and they know that if they fail, they'll be okay. Immigrants exhibit that behavior because they've had to do that. They have started from nothing and know they can go back to that. You need that level of conviction to become a great founder. If you're in the middle, have too much opportunity cost, you may not go all the way in. The risks will hold you back."

The universal theme in every conversation I had with every venture capitalist was that entrepreneurial genius is determined, in part, by the risk tolerance of a founder. Some claim that this is a trait that great entrepreneurs are born with; but the majority, including Fushman, believe it is a trait developed over time. While Fushman sees this in immigrant founders, other VCs search for this characteristic in alternate settings: repeat founders, founders with atypical career paths, or minorities that have historically been marginalized yet still found ways to succeed. I had this same finding when writing *Disruptors*: the successful founders had a willingness to lose it all. They put themselves in unstructured situations to see how they would react and thrive. They tested and strengthened their instincts, their creativity, and their ability to learn about new concepts and areas without instruction. In writing *Finding Genius*, the theme reemerged, as I learned that venture capitalists search for a tolerance for the unstructured and for experience operating in high-risk environments. When looking for genius, VCs search for the 'antifragile' entrepreneur.

When the German national team won the FIFA World Cup in 2012, a study was commissioned to understand what set the players on this team apart. The purpose was to use these findings to train the next generation of athletes. It turns out, according to the research, that the players who went on to make the national team had spent more time learning through unstructured play, rather than structured play dictated by drills, regiments, strict scheduling, or disciplinarian coaches. The unstructured play in small back alleys prepared players for faster reaction times. Shooting on smaller-than-regulation size goals improved accuracy. This is evidence of the 'implicit learning' that happens when individuals are not being taught in obvious ways. With languages or musical instruments, children learn by implicitly observing others and developing an ear for the right pronunciation or tune. While exceptional athletes or musicians have a certain disposition that sets them apart from others, their true genius evolves through unstructured paths or learning, because they willingly seek out new and innovative ways of learning.

In the documentary *In Search of Greatness*, Gretzky says that his performance on the ice was less about his size, speed, or strength — all factors tested by the Combines for athletic genius — but instead his obsession with the sport from an early age that led to a creativity and vision about the sport that had not been held before. Gretzky not only chose to pick up a hockey stick but, from the age of four, he also obsessively watched every hockey game and memorized where the puck would go at all points during the game. In doing so, Gretzky formed his own thesis on the sport. This kind of unstructured, implicit learning allows individuals to find their own path to success, as opposed to conforming to a structure put in place by others before them. Similarly, there is no clear or defined path to entrepreneurial genius; it is in allowing founders to take those risks and to fail that genius begins to develop. Through failure, genius founders can develop the creativity to attack problems that seem impossible to solve. We see this in examples of entrepreneurial geniuses like Elon Musk focusing on commercial transport from the earth to the moon, or building hyperspeed tunnels underground for faster transportation. Venture capitalists seek to fund repeat founders because they know that these individuals are comfortable with non-conformity and a lack of structure. In fact, they thrive when they are not confined to a set of rules, roles or responsibilities.

Genius entrepreneurs are built to withstand risk and ambiguity, are humble enough to recognize their shortcomings, and act as beacons for others to rally around toward a shared vision. They are storytellers who develop a passion for change and possess the persistence to see that change come true. Like the artists, athletes, and inventors mentioned throughout this book, entrepreneurs are wholly committed to their pursuit of genius. The most successful founders are eccentric, focused, and have a disposition far removed from most people.

More than a decade ago, Fred Wilson of Union Square Ventures described the qualities of entrepreneurial genius as a desire to accept risk, an ability to construct a vision and sell it to others, a conviction in one's self, and a magnet for talent. Many of these traits have been reinforced by the dozens of partners behind successful venture funds.

The Role of Venture Capital

Both *Disruptors* and *Finding Genius* share a common belief: that those exotic, hard-to-quantify, genius traits possessed by the iconic entrepreneurs who VCs have backed are birthed out of chaos and unstructured environments. The best venture capitalists find ways to support this entrepreneurial path by forming structure around an entrepreneur's vision, but not blocking it or giving overly-prescriptive input when the answers are not immediately obvious. As told through the anecdotes shared by the VCs in this book, starting a company is an irrational endeavor — one that venture capital thrives on. Alignment is hard to find but the intelligent, pattern-recognizing, and experienced venture capitalists can be the trail-wise sidekicks they are meant to be. Fushman elaborates on this with a key takeaway:

"Founders have to bend their risk curve over time. To start a company, you have to ignore everyone's feedback. If you think of the big companies and best founders, they don't listen to anyone. Drew [Houston] started Dropbox at a time when you couldn't define the market. There were other companies in the space that had been acquired by Microsoft but those weren't big outcomes. You need to ignore the inputs and feedback, but slowly start paying attention to the market and what people around you give feedback on. That's important to me — a founder opening their aperture for learning and listening over time. It's the same about building products. You have to be deeply opinionated about building a product in the beginning but over time as your product user base grows, your users have a better sense of what they need. They will tell you, if you ask them the right way, of how you should build and change and evolve your product. You have to go from being opinionated about a product to taking that as an input to your process and change your trajectory."

Looking Forward

An important lesson shared by Walter Isaacson in *The Innovators* is the concept that innovation and disruption are shaped by 'expanding the ideas handed down from previous generations.' He writes: 'The best innovators were those who understood the trajectory of technological change and took the batons from innovators who preceded them.' Venture capital continues to do the same in its relatively short span of operating as an asset class built to support entrepreneurs. Even as more capital floods into the ecosystem, venture capitalists as of 2019 seem more committed than ever before to finding more equitable ways of allocating this capital. This shift has begun at the LP level and continues to flow to GPs who demonstrate a commitment of funding founders of diverse gender identities, ethnic backgrounds, and geography. Similarly, while some outsiders from the technology ecosystem believe that the opportunity and the scope of venture-scale businesses has hit its peak, insiders believe this is a pessimistic tone for the potential of genius entrepreneurs determined to change the world. In our interview, Andrew Parker of Spark Capital disagreed with the prevailing sentiment that entrepreneurial genius has been diluted and that the future looks bleak. He responds to this claim with an alternative outlook:

"That assumes the universe of exciting or interesting ideas or possibilities is finite and that doesn't sound right or optimistic to me at all. The next really innovative trend or idea is going to come from a totally orthogonal vector that people aren't thinking about today. It's not some zero-sum game where there are only 100 ideas in the world and once you have 1000 entrepreneurs chasing those 100 ideas you don't need the 1001 person. Instead there are unlimited pools of opportunities to come from some combination of future technologies, progress, business model innovation, and international markets, and that future is already here.

SECTION 4
THE FUTURE VENTURE CAPITALISTS ARE BETTING ON

RAYFE GASPAR-ASAOKA
CANAAN PARTNERS

I had the pleasure of meeting Rayfe Gaspar-Asaoka, an investor with Canaan Partners, through our shared interests in the future of mobility and industrial automation. At the time we met, Rayfe had just closed an investment in Apex.AI, a company working with automotive developers to implement complex artificial intelligence (AI) software into vehicles to support autonomous driving. Bold initiatives such as these are often established by teams of Ph.Ds., scientists, and subject matter experts; and the founders of these sophisticated technology companies search for investors who can match them at an intellectual level. As entrepreneurs within this industry will attest to, Rayfe is that type of an investor. In collaborating with Rayfe, I have been consistently inspired by his ability to break down complex topics and technologies to reveal the true value they provide to those without technical experience. Case in point: AI.

The study of AI has a rich history that dates well before it became a topic of conversation in popular media or culture. This field has attracted top researchers, scientists, entrepreneurs, academics, and programmers from all over the world. The widespread potential applicability of AI across all industries and its impact on the global economy are not overstated. When I approached Rayfe about contributing a chapter to *Finding Genius*, he immediately saw the value in sharing the framework he uses to help ask the right questions to determine if an AI company is built for long-term success. As you will learn through this chapter — a primer on AI, as well as a forward-looking perspective on industrial automation — Rayfe is a systems thinker and a technologist who also has an ability to tell a story. That's a rare and valuable combination.

In earlier chapters, I discussed the importance of developing an 'information edge.' Rayfe is able to set himself apart from other investors who cannot evaluate a technical product or application. As Rayfe reveals in this chapter, venture capitalists are 'often investing in AI companies before any commercial maturity. This means that understanding the AI technology at a fundamental level is critical to the investment decision, especially given all of the hype and promise around AI.' This specific market segment requires a deep technical know-how if investors want to succeed by identifying winners early on. Rayfe shares a framework for investing that cuts through the noise to determine what is truly an AI-first company with the potential to create long-term value. These frameworks and questions are not only relevant to AI companies but also provide a relevant foundation from which entrepreneurs and venture capitalists can think about other industries or nascent technologies.

BUILDING AN AI TOOLKIT AND INVESTING THROUGH THE HYPE
Rayfe Gaspar-Asaoka, Canaan Partners

In 2017, Andrew Ng, Stanford professor and one of today's giants within the field of artificial intelligence (AI) famously said "Artificial Intelligence is the new electricity. Just as electricity transformed almost everything 100 years ago, today I actually have a hard time thinking of an industry that I don't think AI will transform in the next several years." On the surface, that seems like a very bold claim. But taking a step back, what is artificial intelligence and why does it have the potential to enable change in every facet of the way we live, work, and interact with the world?

AI is a technology that allows machines to perform tasks at a level comparable to, and in some cases, superior to that of a human. While AI has been dramatized over the decades through futuristic science fiction stories, AI is already here, and in fact, powers a lot of today's world without us even realizing it. Every time we open up our Netflix app, there is an AI algorithm running in the background that personalizes our recommendations based on our past history and preferences. Or whenever we make a command to Siri, Alexa, or Google Assistant, there is an AI algorithm that processes our voice into a machine-readable command and action. And just like a human, the AI technology powering these actions is constantly ingesting data (more shows watched, more commands heard) and continuously improving.

But as an early stage investor in startups, it is important to understand not only the differences between the various types of AI, but how to sift through the current AI hype. The challenge is finding the companies that leverage AI as an essential pillar of their long-term success versus those that are using AI as a marketing buzzword. In this chapter, I'd like to share a couple of the frameworks that I use to help me understand a company's AI technology (their "AI toolkit"), long-term potential for success, and a particular application of AI that I am excited about today.

What's in Your AI Toolkit?

Given the near-infinite combinatorics of tasks humans can perform, the field of study of AI is a broad one that can be broken down into various subspecialties, each with its own set of algorithms and models that are optimized for a particular task. The major fields of AI today are machine learning, deep learning, and reinforcement learning, although up and coming areas such as transfer learning and Generative Adversarial Networks (GANs) are quickly becoming table stakes in today's AI applications. I think of each of the different subfields and algorithms as tools for an engineer to use as part of their AI toolkit. Each tool in the AI toolkit has its own strengths and weaknesses based on the setup of the problem and the data you are given. Below is a short definition of each, with a few examples to help you better understand the use cases of each.

Machine Learning (ML)

Machine learning is one of the foundational domains within AI. Many of the building blocks that were developed in the field of machine learning have served as a framework for other domains as well. In our toolkit analogy, machine learning is the hammer, a versatile, must-have tool that everyone must have.

There are many different types of machine learning models, but they all share the same workflow: 1) ingest data (known as "training data"), 2) make predictions based on that data, and 3) optimize the predictions over time. The recommendation algorithm for Netflix is a real-world example of a machine learning algorithm. Every time you start up the Netflix app, it ingests data (your watch history), makes predictions on that data (shows relevant to your historical preferences), and then optimizes that over time (based on how close your selections match the recommendations).

While there are many ML models (and more coming out of research every day), each problem can be broken down along two axes that help to structure the type of algorithm to use. On the first axis is classification versus regression; this is simply defining whether the answer to the problem should be discrete (classification) or continuous (regression). For instance, if you are trying to build a model to predict the price of Bitcoin in 10 years, the answer is a continuous one, with it ranging from $0 to priceless, and every number in between. This would fall into the camp of regression machine learning algorithms. On the other hand, a model that predicts whether or not an email you receive should be marked as spam or pass through into your inbox is discrete (spam or

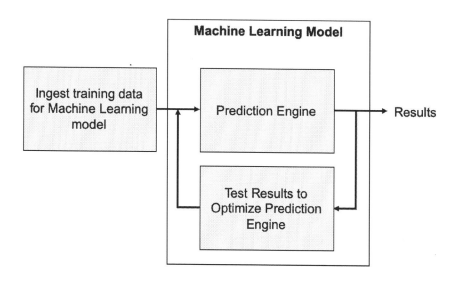

inbox), and best defined as a classification problem. ML algorithms can be built to work with both linear data (linear regression) and non-linear data (logistic regression, neural networks, etc.).

The second axis is supervised learning versus unsupervised learning. Supervised means that you have historical, accurate labeled data, known as "training data," which you can feed the ML model to in order to produce an accurate, initial prediction. Unsupervised simply means that you do not have that labeled, accurate data set to begin with, so the ML algorithm puts a stronger emphasis on the observations of the initial outputs in order to quickly optimize. For example, in the spam filter example above, if the input data used to train the ML model is a set of emails and corresponding classification of spam or not spam, then this would be a supervised learning problem. However, if you only had an initial dataset of emails and did not know whether or not it should be labeled as spam, this would be an unsupervised learning problem, as you are relying on the feedback from the ML algorithm to identify the differences between a regular email and spam email without explicitly labeling one or the other. The benefit of an unsupervised learning algorithm over supervised is that you do not need to individually label the training data set; but the tradeoff is that you often need more data and feedback loops in order to produce a strong prediction from your ML model.

Deep Learning (DL)

If machine learning can be thought of as the hammer in your AI toolkit, deep learning is the set of screwdrivers; they can be incredibly useful in certain situations, but there is a bit more complexity (head type, size of screw) involved in order to use it properly. The recent rise in the use and effectiveness of deep learning algorithms is one of the biggest drivers of today's excitement around AI.

Most of today's deep learning algorithms are based on a neural network, which is a type of non-linear machine learning algorithm. A neural network algorithm is built to mimic the structure of the neurons in our brain. Each node (neuron) is connected to other nodes, and those connections are weighted based on the type of data being processed. In the same way the neurons in our brain associate information together, a deep learning neural network is built to do the same. Each node of the neural network captures certain features of a dataset in order to make a prediction on new, incoming data. Relating this back to the way it works in the human brain: when we meet someone new, that experience is broken up into certain features that we unconsciously store, such as the shape of the person's face, where and when you met them, and the sound and spelling of their name. And with each new meeting, we continue to capture those features in neurons and form connections between people and places based on how related these experiences are. The more neurons (or nodes) available, the more features from that information we can capture, resulting in more accurate predictions.

There are various flavors of neural networks, such as convolutional nets (CNNs) and recurrent nets (RNNs), each with their own specific set of use cases. CNNs are often used to make image predictions; a real-world example of a CNN is the FaceID algorithm on the iPhone. FaceID uses an initial scan of a user's face to build a CNN with each node capturing features that are used to uniquely identify a person. Each time forward, when that user places their face in front of the phone, the algorithm will make a prediction of whether or not that face matches the features stored in the CNN. If there is a strong match, the phone unlocks. In contrast, RNNs are better suited for time-series data. An example of an RNN application is the algorithm powering your Alexa or Google home speaker; as you speak, it captures the speech data over the course of that sentence, and once you are done speaking, it then processes that data together.

What has made DL neural networks so powerful recently is the number of nodes and layers of nodes that can now be computed. However, DL algorithms are not only very compute- and data-intensive, but the complexity of the inter-actions between nodes leads to what's commonly referred to as a "black-box" solution. Just as you unconsciously store features from an experience into neurons, it is not easy to determine what features a neural net extracts from a data-set. You may remember someone because of their name, while I may remember that person because of the features of their face. A DL algorithm is the same;

the complexity of the neural net makes it difficult to understand why the model outputs something, despite it often being highly accurate.

Despite all of that, the prediction power of deep learning algorithms compared to traditional machine learning often outweighs the "black-box" cost. And with the exponential increase in compute capabilities thanks to processors like GPUs and cloud computing, as well as the massive amount of available data today (80-90% of today's data has been created in the last two years), deep learning algorithms are now one of an engineer's preferred tools to use from their AI toolkit.

Reinforcement Learning (RL)

The third, major field of AI that I often see companies use is reinforcement learning. In your AI toolkit, reinforcement learning is the set of wrenches. Just like deep learning, it is a more specialized tool in the AI toolkit that requires upfront preparation to use effectively. Reinforcement learning algorithms are often used when the objective to a problem can be optimized through rewards in a "cause-and-effect" manner. We see this type of behavior in the real world every day. For example, when a dog owner is teaching their dog to sit, they will often do this by giving the dog a treat (a "reward") when the dog performs the behavior, and no treat (a "punishment") when they do not. Over time, the dog will learn to associate sitting on command with a treat.

Reinforcement learning algorithms are similar. Unlike deep learning, which requires an extensive set of upfront training data, reinforcement learning models are best used when there is a goal (e.g. teach the dog to sit), along with the ability to train the model by providing cues along the way (e.g. treats when the dog sits, no treats for they do not). Today, reinforcement learning is widely used, from the control algorithms that optimize the path of a robot within a warehouse, to being used to compete in the most complex video games and puzzles.

This is just a short introduction that scratches the surface of the complexity of the subdomains within AI. But while billions of dollars and decades of effort are spent pushing the limits of one particular specialty within AI in research, it is the ensemble models that combine multiple domains of AI expertise and research together into a single solution that have produced some of the best performing AI today. Just as you would use more than just a hammer to build a house, the best solutions are often constructed by combining multiple tools from an engineer's AI toolkit. For example, the famous 4-1 chess win by Google Deep Mind's AlphaGo against Lee Sedol in 2016 is built on a combination of deep learning methodologies coupled with reinforcement learning.

As an early stage investor in AI startups, I am often investing in companies before any commercial maturity. This means that understanding the AI technology and differentiation at a fundamental level is critical to the investment decision, especially given all of the hype and promise around AI. This leads into the next framework I want to share, which is around investing through the hype.

Investing through the AI hype

There is no shortage of companies using some sort of AI to build a new product or service, ranging from the latest consumer app to the next enterprise software that promises to reinvent the way an enterprise works. The power of machine learning, deep learning, and reinforcement learning is real. The challenge today is cutting through the noise to determine what is truly an AI-first company creating long-term value versus one masquerading itself as an AI company in order to take advantage of the current market hype.

One way that I look at the potential of an AI startup is by using a two-by-two framework that evaluates the company along their technology and business model innovation. On one axis, I look for companies that have differentiated data sets or algorithms. Differentiated datasets can be both proprietary datasets as well as unique access to scalable, labeled data. An example of this is Netflix's dataset of user preferences based on their watch history; or Facebook's photo tagging feature, which allows them to amass a large number of labeled photos, done almost entirely by leveraging their user base.

On the algorithm side, this is often in the form of a new mathematical model out of academia, or a unique combination of existing AI models that has mized to solve a particular problem. Access to this proprietary dataset and/or algorithm allows the company to build a long-term competitive moat around their technology. As you already know from the AI toolkit description above, there is a strong feedback loop between AI algorithms and data. The better the data, the better the algorithm will perform at future predictions. And the better those predictions, the better the output data, which is then fed back into the algorithm. What this means it that a company with even the slightest head start with a better proprietary dataset or algorithm will have an ever-increasing advantage over their competitors. This winner-take-all characteristic of AI is one of the things that makes these companies so powerful.

The second way to evaluate an AI company is by the innovation of their business model. Companies that can build a business model that leverages their differentiated AI in a way that is fundamentally disruptive to the traditional economics of their competitors will build long-term value that cuts through the noise within a sector. For example, Amazon's Kiva robots are used to bring products from one end to the other of their 1 million square foot fulfillment center. This drastically reduces the number of humans needed to do retrieval, and instead allows them to focus on tasks that require more cognitive load, such as picking and packing items into a customer's box. The use of these AI algorithms that enable their robots to autonomously navigate the warehouse disrupts the traditional unit economics of the business. Amazon not only has AI powering their backend logistics, but like Netflix, they have built a recommendation engine on the frontend that personalizes the site for each individual user. The use of AI throughout the business is one of the reasons Amazon has built the largest e-commerce websites in the world but can offer a superior customer experience with a disruptive model of 2-day, 1-day, and even 1-hour shipping.

Companies that excel on both axes will not only have a differentiated business model but will enjoy the dataset/algorithm defensibility in a space where competitors struggle to survive the new world order. As an investor, I use this framework as a starting place to help me ask the right questions to determine if an AI company is built for long-term success. It is often the case that companies excel along one axis but not the other. This results in short-term success, but competitors that come along with better access to unique datasets/algorithms or innovative business models will ultimately win out. The companies that will succeed in this next wave of AI will need to excel along both axes. Not only will these companies change the way an industry views their business, but by the time the competition figures it out and tries to challenge them, it will be too late to break the AI company's defensive moat of better data and algorithms.

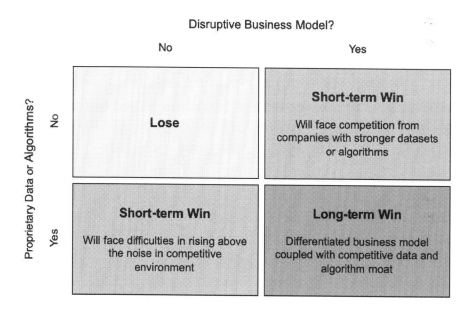

AI + Physical world = Intelligent Robots

Building on the framework for investing in AI startups, one area that I am particularly excited about is at the intersection of AI and the physical world, aka intelligent robots. Today's world is still largely manual and human-labor intensive. Take the largest industries in the world today that leverage physical labor; from construction, to manufacturing, to agriculture, 80% of the tasks are still done by humans, with relatively simple machines to aid in very specific pieces of the remaining 20% of work. Today's robot is often designated to repetitive tasks in very constrained environments. But as companies continue to use their AI toolkit to enhance robots to deal with more complex scenarios, I predict that 80/20 split of human/machine will not only flip, but intelligent robots will unlock new business models. Humans no longer will be limited to simplifying the manufacturing line based on the low-level capabilities of robots but will be free to set up complex environments that are better optimized for rapid production of improved service. Early stage investors are often searching for the next big platform shifts in technology and industry, and I believe this has all of the makings of a big one.

One of the biggest barriers to intelligent robotics penetrating industries such as agriculture or retail has been the high capex with unproven ROI. However, there has been a commoditization of sensor hardware over the last decade, largely driven by the rapid innovation cycles in consumer smartphones and personal electronics. HD cameras, flash memory, and compute processors are pennies compared to what they used to cost. This not only has greatly lowered the barrier for startups to take on the capex required to build robots, but it has enabled new business models such as RaaS (robots-as-a-service) that allow once skeptical industry incumbents to now consider intelligent robots as a viable solution to augment human labor. In addition, this has exponentially increased the amount of sensor training data that a young startup can capture and process for their AI algorithm, which rapidly levels the playing field against the incumbents. Today, startups like Blue River Technology in agriculture and Bossa Nova in retail are leading the charge, but this is just the beginning.

AI is at the heart of these robots' ability to make decisions and take actions in massively unstructured environments. It cannot be understated how different intelligent robots are versus the machines we think of today. Human perception is a highly complex process dependent on our past, current, and future predictions of the world. The physical world is incredibly unstructured. The analogy of a nicely organized Excel table doesn't exist in real life. While humans are innately skilled at perceiving and making decisions with imperfect information, machines are historically not. The reason why robots were only used to automate 20% of the physical world was because the environment needed to be structured enough for a robot to make sense of it. Take the industrial robot arm from ABB or Kuka that is used to build an automobile; it takes months to program that robot to do a single task along the manufacturing line. Because of that, a company needs to produce thousands, even millions of a single line in order to be profitable. But as these robots improve their ability to rapidly adapt to learn and execute new tasks in a complex, unstructured environment, it will open up new ways to build a business with entirely new economics. We have already seen this happen with Amazon's acquisition of Kiva changing the economics of logistics, and this is continuing with companies like Zume in the food space, and Google's Waymo and GM's Cruise in transportation.

When I meet with startups building intelligent robots, I go back to first understanding where the company falls along the two frameworks I shared in this chapter. First, what is in their AI toolkit? What combination of ML, DL, and RL are they using? And second, do they have access to proprietary data/algorithms coupled with a disruptive business model? There are a number of startups that are building intelligent robots applied to traditionally labor-intensive industries that excel along both of these frameworks. From my point of view, intelligent robots are the "how" to Andrew Ng's statement of AI transforming industries. And while we are in the early innings of it all, I predict that today's startups that are leveraging AI to build intelligent robots will be tomorrow's giants.

ANDREW KANGPAN
TWO SIGMA VENTURES

The common conversations surrounding AI are around how the technology will replace humans: a discourse that forebodingly points to a dystopian future. As the authors of the thesis chapters explore, this may not be the case. Through decades of technological advancements and study of the human body, AI has the potential to elevate human performance to heights never before seen. With a better understanding of how our bodies function, down to the organs and genome itself, the most genius entrepreneurs are using technology to eradicate disease, repair organ function, and optimize humans for their best attributes and qualities. This is an interest area that Andrew Kangpan, an investor with Two Sigma Ventures, is focused on. He writes in this chapter that 'as our lives become more quantified, we will have a better understanding of how our decisions impact our lives both positively and negatively. This in turn will allow us to optimize the trajectory of our health in a way that allows us to more knowingly accept the benefits and risks of how we choose to live our lives.' Within those words lie the crux of his thesis: we are interacting with technology in ways that we never have, creating truly novel insights into the human body, and with that, there is immense potential.

This discussion is one that Andrew has considered in his venture capital career spanning FF Ventures and now Two Sigma Ventures, a data-focused fund in New York City. In 2016, nearly three years before publishing this chapter, Andrew wrote in a post on Medium:

"Lately, there's been a lot of excitement regarding new forms of human-computer interfaces. The way users interact with their computing devices are becoming more varied as we shift beyond traditional point and click. Textual conversations, voice commands and VR/AR experiences are new user interfaces that present interesting questions in relation to how their eco-systems will continue to develop and impact markets they penetrate."

These questions became more focused in 2018 as he honed in on how data science and technology intersect with the human body. In a post during that same year, Andrew posed three questions: How is our health trajectory affected by our daily choices? How can we catch disease and deliver treatment earlier? How can we account for individual variability when we treat disease? In this chapter, Andrew begins to answer some of these questions and explores a key point made earlier in this book: investment theses are often the result of years of research and deep introspective thinking informed by the entrepreneurs they meet.

OPTIMIZING HUMAN HEALTH AND WELLNESS: DATA, AI, AND THE FUTURE OF THE QUANTIFIED SELF
Andrew Kangpan, Two Sigma Ventures

In 2007, Gary Wolf and Kevin Kelly began to organize a diverse group of tech-enthusiasts called the "Quantified Self," which informally gave name to the band of individuals using digital technology to measure all aspects of their lives. "Numbers are making their way into the smallest crevices of our lives," Wolf once wrote in reference to the movement; "with an accelerometer and some decent algorithms, you will soon be able to record your sleep patterns with technology that costs less than $100."

The technologies being employed at the time were crude. Members of the "Quantified Self" would hack together readily available computing com-ponents as a makeshift solution to translate aspects of their lives into digital form. Writing for the Financial Times, April Dembosky observed an early prac-titioner of the movement, a "quiet middle-aged man," who hacked together his own tracking solution, "a pulse monitor clipped to his earlobe, a blood pressure cuff on his arm and a heart rate monitor strapped around his chest, all feeding a stream of data to his walkie-talkie computer."

The accuracy and utility of these projects are questionable, but what Wolf and Kelly foresaw was the inevitable ubiquity of wearable computers that would track our lives — long before Fitbit, Apple, and Samsung entered the market with the devices that most consumers know today.

At the time, the individuals who were part of this Quantified Self movement were a relatively small subset of the population who believed that new digital technologies could lead them to a deeper understanding of themselves. "A new culture of personal data was taking shape," Kelly wrote. "We don't have a slogan, but if we did it would probably be 'Self-knowledge through numbers.'"

The movement has since propagated to nearly every corner of the world. San Francisco plays host to a collective of approximately 5,000 people who meet to explore "Consciousness Hacking." The community describes itself as exploring technology to catalyze psychological, emotional, and spiritual flourishing. About 500 people in Stockholm meet to discuss the very same topic. Nearly 1,000 people meet in Brooklyn to discuss "biohacking," which focuses on exploring applications of novel biological technologies such as affordable genetic sequencing. In fact, one search on "Meetup" for the term "Quantified Self" surfaces 90,900+ members and 228 Meetups in over 115 cities and 25 countries.

The concept of knowing oneself for the purpose of self-development is not new. An early known example of this type of behavior was a self-recorded account of the 17th century physician, Santorio Santorio. In one famous experiment Santorio used a self-weighing chair to meticulously weigh himself, including everything he ate and drank, and his waste for 30 years. The crux of these experiments was the idea that you cannot change what you don't understand, and that through numbers one can build an understanding of the self.

The intellectual underpinnings for the Quantified Self stretch far back. Philosophical giants from Michel Foucault to Martin Heidegger have also given heavy consideration to the "care of the self," emphasizing the importance of self-knowledge. While philosophers used discourse to examine their own thoughts and conduct, it could be viewed as an activity of gaining true knowledge that could drive meaningful personal growth. To this end, members of the Quantified Self movement, as Dembosky writes, "are fond of referencing Benjamin Franklin, who kept a list of 13 virtues and put a check mark next to each when he violated it. The accumulated data motivated him to refine his moral compass."

Athletes have long measured time and resistance as a means to quantify fitness. Individuals with chronic conditions have long measured aspects of their behaviors and physiology (among other variables) to manage their body states. In many ways, the most recent boom in quantifying ourselves is an elaboration of an age-old concept.

So what was happening in the late 2000s that gave way to our current landscape?

Cheaper, Faster, Smaller

"Moore's Law" is a commonly used term that describes the doubling of the number of transistors on integrated circuits every two years. The term "law" connotes a physical inevitability, but in reality the reference more accurately describes a common commercial framework that engineers have utilized to drive progression across a variety of technical fields. Moore's Law is likely the most famous technological observation of our modern era. It is so famous that it often takes on a popular meaning to encompass exponential technological change in general.

Exponential change is a simple concept that is impossible to fully understand. A famous mathematical problem known as the "wheat and chessboard problem" emphasizes this reality well, as posed below:

"If a chessboard were to have wheat placed upon each square such that one grain were placed on the first square, two on the second, four on the third, and so on (doubling the number of gains on each subsequent square), how many grains of wheat would be on the chessboard at the finish?"

This problem has gained notoriety over the past hundreds of years, and often appears in stories about the inventor of chess. Sessa, an ancient Indian minister who is said to have invented chess, is said to have requested wheat — in accordance to the wheat and chessboard problem — as a prize for inventing the game. The king, not realizing the hidden implications of the request, willingly agrees, only to have his court tell him that the request has bankrupted the kingdom's supply of grains. Opinions still vary as to whether the king rewards Sessa with a position in his court for his clever request or executes him for making him a fool.

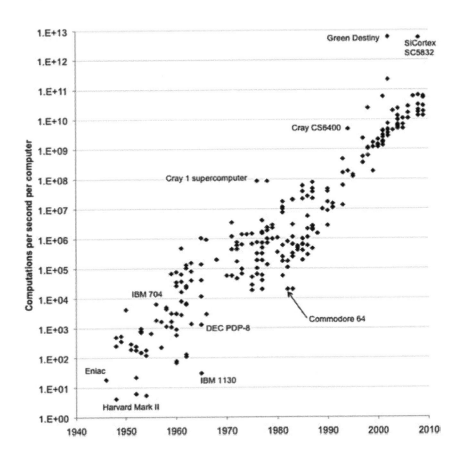

Figure 1 - Exponentially increasing computational capacity over time (computations per second) — Koomey, Berard, Sanchez, and Wong (2011)

The general lesson is that exponential progression accelerates so quickly that its velocity defies intuitive logic. This factor is one of the driving forces behind the advances in the Quantified Self movement.

Examining the progression of personal computers in the 2000s provides a tangible, recent record of technological progression in action. At the beginning of the decade, the price of these PCs was extraordinarily high compared to today's standards. A notable example is the Gateway Performance 1500, which carried the brand new Pentium 4 Processors, sold for a price tag of $4,272 (accounting for inflation.) A few years later in 2003, Apple released their Power Mac G5, which was the first personal computer to utilize new 64-bit processing architecture. The cost at the time for the G5 was $2,587 in inflation-adjusted terms. Near the end of the decade, in 2009, HP released their 2140 Mini-Note, which sold for $554 in inflation-adjusted terms. In the span of a decade, personal computers moved from a price point that only a few families could afford to a price that opened the market to a significant portion of the country. Indeed, in 2000, the consumer PC penetration per capita in North America was approximately 26%, while in 2009 the number reached 51%.

Computers were not just getting cheaper; they were also becoming more powerful. The benefit of being able to place more transistors on a chip is that the computer can conduct more mathematical operations in the same amount of time. Furthermore, as computing power increases, the more capacity it has to execute instructions in parallel, retrieve data from memory, and (more generally) have room for ingenious engineers to make the machine run faster. Every time you turn on a computer, decades of computer science innovation powers the task at hand.

The magnitude of this improvement cannot be understated. From approximately 1975 to 2009, the computational capacity for computers doubled every 1.5 years. Said another way, computers effectively doubled in power 23 times over the past 34 years. To put that in perspective, if you had $2 that went through approximately 23 cycles of doubling, you would have $8,388,608.

Size is another factor at play. An implication of Moore's Law is that while the total potential power of a computing system increases dramatically, the form factor of moderately powerful devices decreases. Engineers have pushed the size of transistors down to 10nm, which is nearing the physical limits of what is possible. Practically, that means that smaller computers can now have the same power, if not more, than the much larger ones did even a decade ago.

The exponential change in computing price, power, and form factor is one of the most extraordinary, ongoing technological achievements in human history. It has fundamentally transformed all aspects of our society: how we socialize with one another, educate each other, and conduct business.

This ongoing innovation is also the underlying force that enabled useful and affordable mobile computers, which become the central player in the Quantified Self story.

The Mobile Shift

In 2005, Steve Jobs recruited a group of Apple engineers to work on a project, code-named "Project Purple 2," that would fundamentally transform the world's relationship with computers. The project's goal was to build a computing device, which employed a multi-touch screen obfuscating the need for a keyboard and mouse and would take the form factor of a mobile phone. It is reported that approximately $150 million was invested into this project over a 30 month period.

Steve Jobs officially announced the project in his keynote address at the January 9, 2007 Macworld Conference. This was more than a new product announcement — it marked a platform shift from a computing paradigm that was primarily based on PCs to one that was (and continues to be) based on mobile smartphones.

Technology investors often refer to "platform shifts" as moments when a new group of technologies (typically a combination of hardware and software) become a new paradigm for the development of computing applications. A variety of driving factors play into these shifts, which are hard to isolate, but the economic implications are significant. An explosion of new business opportunities often arrive alongside a new computing platform, opening the floodgates for early-stage startups and large companies to release innovative products and services. Frequently, early-stage startups are able to profit off of these platform shifts more quickly than large organizations.

Ownership of mobile smartphones has exploded since the iPhone's first release, when virtually no one had a mobile phone. In the span of a decade, four out of every five mobile phone users in the US now own a smartphone. This number is even more striking when you look at people between the ages of 18-29 — approximately 94% own a smartphone.

Mobile phones have effectively become the center of the computing universe, displacing the desktop as the central hub. Put more simply, we use mobile phones for everything. Nearly every indicator of usage supports this claim. For instance, 2016 became the year where the combined traffic for mobile and tablet devices outpaced desktop worldwide.[1] In 2015, the number of "mobile-only" adult Internet users exceeded the number of desktop-only Internet users.[2] In that same year, more Google searches took place on mobile devices than on computers in over 10 countries including the US.[3]

However, it's not only the centrality of mobile devices that is so transformative. As smartphones are always internet-enabled, we are now a society that is pervasively connected to each other. 26% of American adults now report that they go online "almost constantly," and three out of four Americans go online on a daily basis.[4] Pervasive broadband has enabled a plethora of innovative services — such as ride sharing, music streaming, and dating-by-swipes — that have transformed the way consumers interact with businesses and with each other.

The centrality of mobile smartphones and the persistent connection to the Internet laid the foundation for a new class of computers — wearable devices

---

1. https://techcrunch.com/2016/11/01/mobile-internet-use-passes-desktop-for-the-first-time-study-finds/
2. https://www.comscore.com/Insights/Blog/Number-of-Mobile-Only-Internet-Users-Now-Exceeds-Desktop-Only-in-the-U.S
3. https://searchengineland.com/its-official-google-says-more-searches-now-on-mobile-than-on-desktop-220369
4. http://www.pewresearch.org/fact-tank/2018/03/14/about-a-quarter-of-americans-report-going-online-almost-constantly/

— that would create the conditions for the first truly mainstream Quantified Self use case.

The Emergence of Modern Wearable Computers

As consumer demand for smartphones continued to rise, the miniaturization and accessibility of computing components created a new opportunity for companies to commercialize a new class of computing devices. These devices were affordable, wearable computers that were beginning to show signs of a product-market fit. "Can a $99 rubber wristband inspire owners to move more, sleep better, and eat smarter?," wrote Thomas Ricker in a review of the Jawbone Up Fitness Band published on November 6, 2011.[5] Jawbone's band was "very much post-PC," according to Ricker, meaning it utilized the smartphone as a central hub rather than a desktop computer.

While a variety of companies in previous decades had tried to commercialize wearable computers, the early 2010s saw a tidal wave of new products specifically targeting the fitness market. The first two years of the decade saw the introduction of modestly successful devices that primed the market for the bracelet form factor. Notably, in September 2010, Apple released the 6th-generation iPod Nano, which came with a wristband attachment converting it into a wearable wristwatch computer. Jawbone was one of many companies that were part of the race to capitalize on the application of computing technology to fitness.

Fitbit is probably the most well-known company in this market today. Originally called "Healthy Metrics," the company was founded in 2007 with a particular focus on building accessible activity trackers. In the beginning of the decade, the company generated approximately $5 million in revenue. Demonstrating the growth in popular demand for fitness-focused wearables, the company went on to generate $1.9 billion in revenue in 2015, which is the year that it filed for an IPO targeted to raise $358 million in new funding.

The popularity of these new devices translated to one clear message: fitness was the killer app that would drive mass adoption of wearable computers.

5. https://www.theverge.com/2011/11/6/2541783/jawbone-up-review

To a certain extent, the Quantified Self had now become a popular phenomenon with a significant portion of the population interested in tracking at least part of their daily lives.

Yet fitness is not the only application of wearable computing that was being developed for the mass market in the early 2010s. Wearable computers were becoming a new platform for developers to build new applications.

Eric Migicovsky is a notable trailblazer in this early market. After having successfully completed Y Combinator, the most premier startup incubator in the world, Migovsky was unable to raise capital from traditional venture capital funds. On April 11, 2012 Migiovsky's company, Pebble, launched a Kickstarter campaign with an initial target of $100,000. Early participants paid $99 for a Pebble and within two hours of going live the project had met its target. Moreover, the campaign went on to raise $10.26 million in funding from 68,929 people — at the time, the world record for the most money raised via a Kickstarter campaign.

What was so notable about the Pebble was not just that it offered fitness applications in a wearable form factor, but that it also offered a variety of functions that served as an early template for what was to become the modern smartwatch. The Pebble was originally slated to ship with pre-installed apps, including a cycling tracker and a golf rangefinder, in addition to displaying notifications and messages from the connected smartphone. However, the beauty of the device was that it enabled a plethora of applications to be built for it with future generations seeing applications including games (e.g. Pixel Miner) and transportation (e.g. Uber.)

Gadi Amit, the founder of New Deal Design and the person responsible for the design of the Fitbit Activity Tracker, made an apt comment on the future of wearable computers: "You could imagine five years from now each one of us will probably have about 10 of these. Two or three will be customized to some physical or medical needs we have. Two or three will be recreational. Two or three will be data oriented, identity, authentication, and so on."[6]

Indeed, the emergence of wearable computers had just begun.

6. https://vimeo.com/155594490

Moving Beyond Fitness

In 2017, worldwide shipments for wearable computing devices was approximately 121 million across five categories of devices: smartwatches, smart clothing, ear-worn devices, wristbands, and sports watches.[7] This number is set to grow dramatically over the coming years. In 2019, the number of total devices shipped is expected to increase approximately 27% over 2018 to approximately 190 million devices. By 2022, the total is expected to reach approximately 373 million devices. Accompanying this expected growth in device shipments is an expanding set of use cases.

Healthcare is one market that has industry commentators excited. Health providers are seeking technological solutions to help better manage their patient populations and subsequently the overall cost of delivering healthcare. There are more clinical trials incorporating digital health solutions than ever before. This will only increase as the FDA rolls out programs, such as the digital health software certification pilot program, that make it easier for digital health solutions to be approved. Insurance companies, recognizing the potential value of wearables in managing health, are starting to offset or fully reimburse the cost of these devices. As of 2017, less than 5% of large health systems had deployed full-scale digital health pilot programs. Thanks to many positive tailwinds, this number is expected to increase to 40% by the end of 2020.[8]

These medical wearable devices will look significantly different than the bracelet form factor most fitness bands have adopted. Sensor-embedded textiles have become a market that many believe will be a significant part of the health management solution. For example, Owlet is a company that has created a smart sock for babies, which allows parents to have a constant and accurate read of a baby's heart rate and oxygen level with the help of a pulse oximetry (pulsox) device positioned within the sock.

Likewise, Nanowear is a trailblazer in this market building medical-grade smart textiles focused on healthcare applications across a broad array of

7. https://www.gartner.com/en/newsroom/press-releases/2018-11-29-gartner-says-worldwide-wearable-device-sales-to-grow-
8. https://www.gartner.com/smarterwithgartner/wearables-hold-the-key-to-connected-health-monitoring/

medical conditions and chronic disease states. The company's technology provides healthcare providers with continuous diagnostic data through a wearable that is effectively worn by the patient as a piece of clothing. The brilliance of these new, emerging solutions is that they move away from simple, descriptive quantifications of our behavior to prescriptive information that can diagnose targeted issues.

Beyond just measuring data exhaust from the individual, companies are also finding ways to measure aspects of the immediately surrounding environment. Deloitte Wearables is a company in Canada building a sensor that can be attached to a miner's helmet. The product is able to detect all types of environmental risk factors including hazardous gasses, radiation, temperature, and humidity. The company is using this data to provide alerts for emergency situations and allow for more effective communication. Rather than trying to surface descriptive statistics related to the individual, the company is focused on surfacing data related to an individual's surroundings and placing that information in context.

Wearables, however, are just one part of our ongoing Quantified Self story. An explosion in data and newly accessible computational techniques are creating a vast array of opportunities for entrepreneurs to build the next breakthrough company. The rapid growth in biological data, such as genomic information, is an ongoing trend creating the foundation for an entirely new generation of companies.

The Smallest Crevices of Our Lives: The -Omics Revolution

Genomic information is now accessible to the mass market. At the beginning of the millennium, an entire human genome cost $100 million to sequence. That cost has plummeted to approximately $1,000 representing an improvement that has accelerated faster than the pace of Moore's Law. Looking at the cost per genome, one will notice that in approximately 2008 the cost began a precipitous decline at a pace significantly faster than the years 2001 to 2007. This is attributed to the transition of Sanger-based chemistries and capillary-based instruments ("first generation" sequencing platforms) to next-generation sequencing (NGS) platforms.

The implication of this price decline is evidenced by studying the increasing accessibility of popular genetic testing services such as 23andMe. In 2007, the price of a full testing service was $999 and by 2016 the price for the product decreased to $125. On Black Friday, Target sold the autosomal-only service kit for $59 and Amazon sold the full service (ancestry plus health data) for $99. This trend has led to an astounding acceleration in the number of people who have access to personal genetic data. Around one in 25 American adults now have access to this information, with more than 12 million people having tested themselves through a consumer genetics company.[9]

Growth in the total sequenced base of individuals in the US has created a plethora of opportunities for entrepreneurs to offer services based on this data. More broadly, the growth in this information has provided a degree of granularity into our own identity that has up until now been unavailable to the average person. This progression will not just stop at genomic information. Companies across the globe are beginning to offer services that provide more granular information beyond the genome, such as our epigenome (modifications on the genetic material of a cell) and proteomics (proteins that are produced or modified in the body).

However, it is not just the explosion of this new data that is creating new opportunities. Novel ways to make sense of that information, namely modern applications of AI, are creating a new class of companies that will take our understanding of human health and wellness to a new level.

Accessible AI

The explosion of digital information in the past decade has coincided with a resurgence and democratization of one of the most promising technological fields of this generation: artificial intelligence (AI). AI is a broad encompassing umbrella that refers to a collection of analytical technologies that enable

9. https://www.technologyreview.com/s/610233/2017-was-the-year-consumer-dna-testing-blew-up/

systems to interpret data, learn from that information, and achieve specific goals and tasks through adaptation.

Artificial intelligence is not new. The modern field of research stretches back to the mid-20th century when computing giants such as John McCarthy, Marvin Minsky, and Herbert Simon produced programs that were solving real-world problems such as checkers, word problems in algebra, and proving logical theorems. Its progression has been filled with many boom periods and so called 'winters,' a prolonged period of reduced funding and interest, following hype cycles similar to many emerging technologies. In a modern context, AI has captured the public's imagination by surpassing humans in various domains such as Deep Blue's defeat of Garry Kasparov at Chess in 1997, IBM's Watson's defeat of Ken Jennings at Jeopardy in 2011, and AlphaGo's defeat of Ke Jie at Go in 2017.

What is new about the field of AI is the ability for a broadening swath of the population to access the technology. Developers no longer need to know advanced mathematics to implement artificial intelligence into their products. Readily available software libraries, such as TensorFlow, make it easier for developers to utilize deep learning models. Since its release in November 2015, TensorFlow has become the dominant software library developers use to apply advanced data analysis to their programs. While the exact number of users is hard to pinpoint, there are a variety of indicators illustrating its popularity, such as the more than 118,000 stars it has received on GitHub and the usage of the software in companies such as Airbnb, eBay, Intel, and Snapchat.

The accessibility of these tools has opened the floodgates for early stage companies to bring new products and services to market. Banks now utilize modern software to help them better detect fraud and confirm the authenticity of transactions. Physicians use software that helps them detect abnormalities in images such as mammograms. Hospitals are beginning to utilize software to protect their connected medical devices from external cybersecurity threats.

All of these challenges are being addressed be a proliferation of AI-enabled software, much of which has emerged in the past 5-7 years thanks to advances in this field. The application of this technology in the context of optimizing human health and performance is beginning to take off. This is creating an investing boom, with investors hoping to find generation-defining companies that will fundamentally transform how we care for ourselves.

Investing in the Future of the Quantified Self

Our lives are now bathed in data, and with increasingly accessible tools to make sense of that information we can begin to address even more useful questions about ourselves and the lives we lead. However, for investors, general trends only serve as a weather vane, not a signpost. Having confidence in where the world is going doesn't answer the billion dollar question of which companies will capitalize on that change.

Finding and supporting the opportunities that have the greatest chance to find outsized success is the key role of the venture capital investor. Determining the characteristics that define what a 'good bet' is will drive consistent, and hopefully optimal, decisions when it comes to investing in early-stage technology companies. When thinking about the Quantified Self, several characteristics come to mind:

Availability of novel datasets — the company has access to data that is novel, and that others do not have access to

Application of novel analytical technologies — the company is leveraging an approach to analyzing vast quantities of information in a way that was not possible before and is nontrivial to replicate

Why now? — the company is capitalizing on fundamental shifts in society, technology, and the economy that create the macro conditions for success

From fun facts to behavior change — the company is generating insights that not only provide interesting information, but also have the ability to enact meaningful behavior change

Pervasive penetration — the company's technology has the potential to touch the lives of a broad swath of the population, not just a small niche of power users

Smart data management — the company is able to navigate the complexities of managing user data, which includes regulatory considerations, societal attitudes towards data privacy, and security provisions to protect information from being stolen

Moats — the company has the ability to protect the value they deliver from competitors either through inherent features of their product, aspects of their organizational structure, or other factors

These characteristics are by no means exhaustive, but they illustrate the types of considerations that early-stage investors explore when identifying areas ripe for investment and assessing companies raising capital. Taking these factors into account, a couple of areas come to mind as territories that may yield the next generation-defining company: making care personal and taking control of our health trajectory.

Making Care Personal

We have more data about our health than ever before — from our genome, to our behavior, to our health record. For example, approximately 84% of all non-Federal, acute-care hospitals have adopted a basic electronic health record, which has increased from 9.4% just over 10 years ago. While much of this information is still hard to access and analyze, entrepreneurs are quickly finding ways to liberate its use for a variety of novel applications. This data will create a more holistic picture than ever before of each individual's health, and will in turn serve as fuel that drives a more personalized healthcare system. From clinical decision making to more intimate primary care experiences, entrepreneurs are creating products and services that will fundamentally transform the way we think about care.

Spring Health is a company that embodies this fundamental shift to personalized care. The company is an online mental health clinic that uses clinically-validated techniques to offer personalized wellness recommendations, such as treatment options and exercise regimens. Users complete a dynamic questionnaire that adapts to each respondent based on their responses. The company then takes this dataset and utilizes their matching algorithm, which has been fine-tuned through the analysis of aggregated clinical trials and medical records, to identify personalized care plans.

This is a fundamental shift in how people access mental health treatment. Nearly one in five Americans struggle with mental illness, yet despite its pervasive reach, the experience of treatment for most patients is antiquated and inefficient. Not only is the company fixing a significant challenge, they are doing so at a time when mental health and wellness is top of mind for our society. By leveraging data that has just come online, and analyzing it in a novel way through the application of modern machine learning, the company has been able to create a platform that has the potential to greatly impact the way our society cares for our collective mental well-being.

Taking Control of Our Health Trajectory

We intuitively understand that our health is impacted by a variety of factors. Our daily choices, such as diet and exercise, can dramatically impact the trajectory of our health. Furthermore, all of us are impacted by decisions in different ways based on our genetic code, environmental factors, and more. The impact of these decisions takes years to manifest, and have traditionally been almost impossible to isolate.

Omada Health is a company empowering millions of users in this way. The company has developed a digital care program that takes a fundamentally novel approach to disease prevention and maintenance. Omada is building what CEO Sean Duffy calls a "21st century provider," one that is supercharged by digital information and persistent care. The company uses connected devices to surface medical biometrics for each of their users in real time, providing a real-time picture of actions they can take to optimize for better health outcomes.

Additionally, they provide users access to online coaches who can intervene when issues arise. While Omada started with diabetes, they are quickly moving into additional indications such as hypertension and high cholesterol.

Omada is transforming the way in which we care for ourselves. By taking actions earlier on in the progression of a disease, the company is helping millions of patients take more control of their health outcomes. Digital information and telemedicine provide the company with the ability to deliver care at a scale that was impossible a few years ago. As we are all growing more accustomed to wearing devices that surface information about our lives, the company is leveraging that behavior to transform how we view and treat disease.

Gary Wolf once described the Quantified Self movement as a "macroscope" applied to the individual human. He was describing the growing ability to quantify the individual as the summation of all their "countless moments, behaviors, and locations."[10] Over time, this macroscope has become both more broad and more sharp in focus, as we now have a more holistic and granular understanding of the human condition than ever before.

In turn, entrepreneurs are now equipped with the resources and tools they need to build innovative products and services that will radically change our understanding of human health and performance. These new products and services will serve as the foundation for a new class of generation-defining companies that will transform how we live our lives.

---

10. https://www.webcitation.org/66TEHdz4d?url=http://aether.com/quantifiedself

BRIAN YORMAK
STORY VENTURES

Rayfe Gaspar-Asaoka and Andrew Kangpan shared their perspectives on artificial intelligence and its impact on industrial automation and human-to-computer interaction. As revealed through their experience, the applications of AI are so far-reaching that it will eventually touch every aspect of our lives. One such application — for the future of mobility and transportation — has absorbed the largest volume of venture dollars. The study of autonomous driving dates back to the early 1920s and automobiles are 'smarter' today than they have ever been. Modern vehicles come with automatic parking, emergency braking, detection of hazards on the road, and can even keep a car within its lane. While these are all intelligent functions that have been developed through millions of dollars of funding and partnerships with the automobile industry, the players within this ecosystem are eagerly chasing one end goal: Level 5 autonomy or complete driverless cars.

Brian Yormak of Story Ventures began his career in the center of mobility at Fontinalis Partners, a well-regarded venture fund focused on technologies that relate to the automotive industry. For this role, as part of a fellowship with Venture for America, Brian relocated to Detroit, the heart of the American automotive industry, where he developed a unique perspective on mobility startups and the data systems important for complete automation, especially as it relates to the future of transportation. These experiences led Brian to found Story Ventures, a venture fund based in New York, with his brother Jacob. Together, they are focused on investing in sensory systems, data infrastructure, and intelligent software: all building blocks for an autonomous future.

While Brian has a thorough understanding of how cities, states, and governments can grow 'smarter' by leveraging the data created within their ecosystems, in this thesis chapter, Brian focuses exclusively on the future of mobility. Just as automation will impact the jobs of those in factories, autonomous driving will impact over 3 million truck drivers. At the same time, it will provide unique access for those who are hearing or visually impaired and have trouble with transportation. Brian discusses the factors necessary to make driverless cars a reality, and shares what he believes are good investment opportunities as the industry continues to mature.

Earlier in the book, I discussed how the cost of starting a business has gone down dramatically. In the automotive industry, technology has improved, and the cost of sensors has declined, creating more opportunities for entrepreneurs who want to build applications for the driverless future. While many focus on the negative aspects of automation, Brian is wise to point out that the $80 billion invested between 2014-2017 into a future of autonomous vehicles is likely to have a positive impact: over 1.2 million deaths annually are caused by automobile accidents, 93% of which are caused by human error. In this chapter, Brian shares the perspectives of investors on both sides of the table: those who believe that Level 5 autonomy is within reach and those who believe that we are still decades away from this becoming a reality. These differing perspectives help establish a foundation from which entrepreneurs and investors can find unique opportunities.

NEXT GENERATION TRANSPORTATION AND MOBILITY
Brian Yormak, Story Ventures

In Greek mythology, Hephaestus was the blacksmith for the gods. He crafted the armor of Achilles and the arrows of Cupid. However, even as a god, Hephaestus recognized that being the sole source of labor created production limitations. To keep up with the gods' demand for crafted steel, he built automatons: self-operating machines that followed a predetermined sequence of operations. Together, they built tools worthy of Olympus.

The story of Hephaestus and his golden automatons served as one of the earliest inspirations for the concept of intelligent physical machines, and their potential to complement — or even replace — human labor. Today, the expected impact of automating labor via intelligent machines is commonly disputed. Some foresee machines replacing workers en masse. They worry for the fates of blue collar laborers (e.g. truck drivers, assembly line workers, cashiers), and envision accountants, lawyers, and investors joining them soon thereafter. These concerns are supported through analyses by leading academics and economists — a 2017 McKinsey report suggests that anywhere from 39 million to 73 million US jobs are at risk of being replaced by the year 2030.

Proponents of automation are eager to dismiss these concerns as unnecessarily pessimistic. In their view, our robot future will ultimately benefit society by enabling people to focus on work that is safer and more rewarding. In 1970, approximately 11 out of 1,000 workers were killed on the job in the US. Nearly 40 years later, following the passage of the Occupational Safety and Health Act (OSHA) and subsequent regulations, the worker fatality rate had dropped to 3.6 workers per 100, a 67% decrease.

Our society has debated the pros and cons of automation before. During the Industrial Revolution, the steam engine, conveyor belt, and power loom brought about mass-scale mechanization. A generation later, the world moved towards special-purpose machinery, factories, and mass production. Each of the industrial revolution and subsequent periods resulted in material improvements in the standard of living — from 1810-1850, real wages doubled, and over the course of the 19th century, the economy grew by 6x (the growth rate had been almost entirely flat during the previous 100 years). Moreover, the impact of industrialization wasn't merely economic: mortality rates plummeted, efficient transportation systems bloomed, and high-speed communications systems connected towns and families across the country. Still, 19th century America wasn't spared from short-term labor displacement. Unemployment levels reached as high as 8%, and working conditions left much to be desired.

The transition from an agrarian to an industrial society tore at the fabric of American society. Familiar modes of work were destroyed, families uprooted themselves, small town ties disintegrated, and the religious and mystic were gradually supplanted by the secular and scientific. It's difficult to comprehend the suffering and pain this transformation inflicted on generations of Americans.

From the long lens of history, it is also difficult (and perhaps foolish) to quantify the impact of the industrial revolution. Of course, with a much shorter lens, this sort of analysis is even harder. What is clear though is that the technology developments of the 1800s transformed the world, and today, we're at the precipice of another unavoidable revolution: the automation revolution.

The inventions of our age will meaningfully expand the scope of automation in every aspect of life. Once again, society will need to reshape the workforce and adjust to new global economic realities. Opportunity is everywhere. Many will step in and forge a new path, taking advantage of the mass restructuring of the industrial and cultural landscape. Many more will be at risk. There are approximately 3.5 million truck drivers and 8.5 million Americans (~3% of the population) employed across the trucking industry. If certain prognosticators are correct, the majority of these jobs will disappear. And that's only a single industry — unlike previous industrial transformations, ours might be broad and undiscriminating in its impact.

In order to better grasp the potential impact of automation we must first understand whether predictions about the exponential improvements in machine automation are accurate. The logic for a compounding rate of machine prowess revolves around three concepts: the ability for machines to (i) sense their environment through better receptors, (ii) store, process, and communicate sensory information, and (iii) leverage ever-improving software to derive insights from organized data. Companies investing in autonomous vehicles (AVs), for example, are making a bet that the technology needed to enable autonomy across each layer of the data stack is sufficiently mature.

At the first layer of the stack, the manufactured sensors needed to make AVs possible can be likened to human senses: the ability to see, to hear, to touch, to taste, and to smell. Just as humans with bad vision struggle to under-stand the letters on an eye test, an AV with bad sensors cannot understand its environment well enough to make an informed decision.

One reason AV companies believe now is the right time is that hardware sensors have fallen in price by more than half over the past 30 years. Better yet, these sensors are now able to capture information with such high fidelity that vehicles can recognize the curve of the road, the speed of the car next to it, the speed limit of a road, and a person crossing the street. There are a few sensors in particular, such as cameras, sonars, LiDAR's, and radars, that form the foundation of an AV:

Camera: The vehicle has a number of cameras that capture context (e.g. what a sign says) and color. This data provides visual information that the other sensors cannot capture.

Sound navigation and ranging (Sonar): A sonar system emits pulses of sound and listens for echoes to approximate the distance of surrounding objects.

Light detection and ranging (LiDAR): A LiDAR sensor, which typically sits on top of the vehicle, sends a beam of light out and creates a colorless, context-less, three-dimensional replica of its environment, based on the speed with which the light returns to the sensor.

Radio detection and ranging (Radar): A radar sends out radio frequencies to build maps of the environment, based on the time it takes for the radio signal to return. This system differs from LiDAR in that radio waves have less absorption and can therefore travel longer distances and identify items that LiDAR systems cannot recognize (e.g. LiDAR systems struggle to see through dust.)

The combination of data coming from cameras, sonar, LiDAR, and radar sensors enables a vehicle to create a three-dimensional rendering of the world, similar to what we see with the human eye — a clear indication that data capture systems are approaching the necessary quality (and cost) to replace human tasks.

The second layer of the stack dictates what happens when data is captured by autonomous machines. The challenges here are immense. Guido Vetter, the Head of Analytics at Daimler Motors, stated that "flexibility and scalability are what you need for AI and advanced analytics, and our whole operations are not set up for that." If we take Daimler as an example, historically the company stored all data on premise (servers located on facility grounds.) However, given the amount of data generated by these AV sensors, the physical space and cost constraints of storing it on premise have become untenable. Daimler, along with many other companies, has begun to shift data storage to "the cloud," a shift that should not be underestimated in significance. Whereas the company previously relied on in-house expertise to store information, it now mainly utilizes third-party providers such as Amazon Web Services (AWS) to store and process the logarithmically expanding amount of data required to enable autonomy in vehicles.

The third layer of the stack is where companies such as Daimler leverage machine intelligence to derive insights from the data, a primary driver of autonomy. These companies use algorithms to run extremely complex probabilistic regressions on massive amounts of data — artificial intelligence (AI) — to turn plentiful, rich, labeled data into the autonomous functioning of machines. In order to better understand how these algorithms work, consider an analogy: four tennis balls are located on a white wall in the shape of a square. The balls alone are just that — physical objects. The square, of course, is not actually 'there:' our minds organize a pattern and abstract a shape. The mind allows us to form conclusions from the non-physical. Similarly, an autonomous vehicle's ability to abstract conclusions is a result of applying algorithmic analysis to raw perceptual data. Recent advancements in the quality of these algorithms play an integral part in the process with which AVs navigate their environments.

Thus, it is not surprising that demand for workers with AI talent has more than doubled — from 2015—2018 job postings for "machine learning engineer" grew 344%, and three of the top four paying jobs include computer vision engineer, machine learning engineer, and data scientist. This spike should only further accelerate innovation and the speed of commercializable automation.

Technology optimists believe that with the emergence of this data stack — sensors, data infrastructure, and AI — autonomous vehicles, along with a number of other robotic systems, are poised to meaningfully change our world. These same individuals also point to the 1.2 million deaths annually due to automobile accidents, 93% of which are caused by human error. It should come as no surprise then that from August 2014 to June 2017, an estimated $80 billion was invested into AVs by the auto industry and venture capitalists. As of 2019, there are already three startups that have raised north of $1 billion from investors — Cruise, Nuro, and Aurora — with many more that have raised well over $100 million. Similarly, many large manufacturers such as Ford, GM, and Toyota have invested well over $1 billion into internal programs focused specifically on autonomy. New rideshare companies such as Uber, Baidu, and Lyft are following suit. Gabe Cunningham, an investor at the mobility-focused venture capital fund, Fontinalis Partners, explained the interest in the autonomous vehicle sector: "this is a transformative shift in how society moves, touching trillions of dollars in the global economy. To realize that vision though, there is an expansive amount of research and development capital that will be needed to reach the necessary milestones. Ultimately, the big question is not if AVs will become a reality, but what companies have the resolve and technical capabilities to bring these vehicles to market at scale over the next decade and beyond." Gabe's sentiment is one that is generally shared across the industry: autonomy is an impending reality but the winner(s) will have to invest an incredible amount of capital to deliver on the market opportunity.

The long-term implications of this transition are massive. Those immediately affected include 3.5 million truck drivers, and 1 million taxi / rideshare drivers. There will also be significant secondary effects. One fifth of organ donations come from vehicular accidents. One third of all civil trials have to do with motor vehicles. Highway motel occupancy will decrease drastically. The auto insurance and claims market will contract. Police forces will lose revenue generated from ticketing drivers. All said and done, millions of jobs will be indirectly affected, likely with a net negative impact, at least in the near term. These changes warrant concern but they shouldn't completely obscure excitement. In transitioning to autonomy, millions of lives will be saved from auto accidents. Senior citizens, children, and the disabled will be able to use transportation solutions currently inaccessible to them. Vehicles will communicate and synchronize decisions that should improve road congestion — today Americans spend more than 6.9 billion hours a year sitting in traffic — and decrease CO_2 emissions and fuel consumption. Finally, decreased transportation costs will open up access to more places for more people in a way that will produce benefits not currently imagined.

While the potential impact of autonomous vehicles should not be understated, AVs are just one example of how the data stack will transform a cluster of industries. Julian Counihan, for example, is betting on this transformation. As a partner at Schematic Ventures, where he focuses on supply chain and manufacturing, Julian has invested in companies such as Plus One Robotics, Symbio, Root, and Azevtec. When discussing these opportunities, he focuses "on technology within industrial sectors where the automation problem is less challenging." He says:

> "The industrial environment can be controlled to eliminate difficult variables, and infrastructure can be modified to simplify operational complexity. Still the same concepts apply regardless of business type. Industrial application systems will fuse sensor data to understand the environment and leverage machine learning to arrive at optimal decisions. Having been a part of a few robot companies, I find the difficulty of full automation can be understated. Unless the problem itself can be changed, the added cost to address the final one or two edge cases can push a solution past the point of commercial viability.

The key to a robot company's success is as much finding the right problem as building the right technology."

Not surprisingly, Julian shares a similar sentiment to Gabe and even expands upon the scope of what may be defined as automatable; but he also acknowledges that entrepreneurs must be very careful to figure out the right time and capital structure to achieve their goals.

iRobot, manufacturer of the Roomba autonomous vacuum, is one of the first companies to create a consumer-grade autonomous robot. To date, the company has sold north of 15 million Roombas. Folks that have interacted with the product likely recognize the value of autonomous cleaning, but also understand the limitations: the robot misses certain areas, dies before re-docking for charging, and displaces items that it bumps. However, these limitations will likely lessen in the near future. Colin Angle, iRobot's CEO, predicts a "big leap" where the Roomba "remembers what's going on in the home." Such a leap will be made possible by improvements the data stack. The Roomba i7+, launched in 2019, has a myriad of sensors, a camera, and an on-board computer processing unit, all of which allow the vacuum to see a room and memorize the layout. The Roomba will soon be able to clean every part of a room — even if the layout of the room changes — and map out a path back to the docking station. It's not a reach to think that the Roomba might soon also be able to apply different cleaning techniques to certain floor surfaces and report incidents such as a spilled glass of wine in order to minimize long-term damage.

Jacob Yormak, my partner, and managing partner at Story Ventures, agrees an immense opportunity exists around automation. At the same time, he dismisses the notion that AVs and other autonomous machines are anywhere near ready to replace the most complicated forms of human intelligence. For now, AVs fall into the bucket of artificial narrow intelligence (ANI), whereby they are able to complete a single, narrow task. This is compared to artificial general intelligence (AGI), whereby a machine would be able to complete multiple, generalizable, complex tasks (think: The Terminator). As Jacob says:

"The current state of artificial intelligence is still very limited — we are just scratching the surface of ANI. Though the media may suggest otherwise, we are far away from machines replicating the most complex forms of human intelligence. Think about babies: they are born with complex sensors that are almost always on, incredible internal communication systems, and algorithms that have been honed over thousands of years. Improvements across the data stack have enabled machines to complete real-world tasks in narrow verticals such as selecting when to turn on a road, or how to lift a package on a conveyor belt, but the algorithms used to make these decisions quickly break down with even minor deviations from the originally intended purpose."

This recognition that machines do not have general intelligence highlights a key insight — in the near term, automation will be limited to highly repetitive tasks with predictable variations.

These hesitations cited by Gabe, Julian, and Jacob provide a necessary reminder that robotic systems are not yet ready to take over the world. At the same time, the billions of dollars being poured into companies working on these systems clearly demonstrate the immense economic opportunity in commercializing autonomous systems. There are millions of repetitive, logic-based jobs carried out by humans today: cashiers (3.4 million), food preparation and serving workers (2.7 million), customer service representatives (2.1 million), and freight movers / laborers (2.0 million). These represent just a small sampling of jobs that will be susceptible to automation. Given the economic advantages, this transition to automation seems inevitable — as do the adverse impacts to millions of American lives.

Going forward, we can resist this change, though history suggests that it is difficult to deter the momentum of technology. Conversely, we can embrace the efficiencies of this new wave and construct solutions to aid those at risk. To the latter, we are already seeing some progress. Lambda School, a trade school focused on coding, is one of the many institutions emerging with real signs of success to help individuals transition into jobs that will be in demand for the foreseeable future. This is part of a larger trend as venture capital funding for education technologies reached an all-time high in 2018 of $1.45 billion. Andrew Yang, a 2020 presidential candidate, is running on the platform of universal basic income in which every US citizen over the age of 18 would receive $1,000/month. Famed innovators including Bill Gates and Stephen Hawking have proposed a robot tax in which companies that leverage automation would have to pay higher taxes to compensate the US people for the labor displacement. Each of these solutions, if wielded properly, have merit and can partially remedy the challenges ahead. Yet, there is no silver bullet. A portion of the population will, once again, struggle to navigate the changing landscape.

I believe that those investing in and building the future of automation are confident that the end result will be an improved material and non-material standard of living. However, it is important that as the world moves forward, we determine best practices to support those caught in the riptide of our impending revolution.

ADRIEL BERCOW
FLYBRIDGE CAPITAL PARTNERS

The merits of universal basic income (UBI) — or a monetary stipend provided to all citizens of a country — is a hotly contested topic in the US in 2019. Candidates like Andrew Yang and Elizabeth Warren are establishing their platforms in preparation for the 2020 presidential election and have explicitly voiced support for this type of government program. This debate has become more relevant over the past two decades as automation has significantly impacted the livelihoods of truck drivers, factory workers, typists, farmers, miners, and other laborers whose jobs have been replaced or reduced by machines and automation. The differentiation between 'unskilled' versus 'skilled' labor is becoming less clear as the effects of automation are now far-reaching across all industries and geographies. In the developed world, even individuals with higher education or specialized skill sets are at risk of being out of a job as more startups seek to automate all kinds of work at a fraction of the cost. As this debate rages on, the central question is: What will happen to humans in a future where automation will replace most menial tasks? Rayfe Gaspar-Asaoka from Canaan Partners provided a perspective on artificial intelligence that shows that this reality is not far away. In this chapter, Adriel Bercow, an investor with Flybridge Capital, explores the factors driving this discussion in a thesis focused on the 'future of work.' He writes, a 'combination of evolving demographics, a widening income and skill gap, and an education system that was not built for today's digital economy have created an investment opportunity.'

Throughout this book, I have hinted at the ethical dilemmas some investors face as they invest in businesses that are replacing the jobs of humans. Some investors believe that more jobs will be created as a result of the persistent progress made through technology, while others argue that investments need to be made to build this infrastructure for a future economy. Adriel addresses many of these points, asking questions such as: How will workers receive professional development, ongoing training, and worker classification and credentials? What is the software infrastructure needed to support the enterprises shifting to a contingent workforce? What other industries are ripe for the gig economy? His perspective will further explore what is driving the future of work and the investment categories that will look to answer these questions in the decades to come.

Adriel approaches this topic with a sense of responsibility and optimism. While some may look at this topic with a grave outlook, Adriel adopts the perspective of a venture capitalist who genuinely believes that the world can be made better through technology. He provides a convincing case that venture capitalists are in search of the founders who are building the answers to problems that automation presents.

THE FUTURE OF WORK
Adriel Bercow, Flybridge Capital

"Work" in the 21st Century

"What do you do for a living?"

While this opener has been the dominant conversation starter for North Americans for decades, it has also been a cultural norm that is viewed as contentious and divergent from the values in Europe and other regions. In their new book, The Bonjour Effect: The Secret Codes of French Conversation Revealed, authors Julie Barlow and Jean-Benoît Nadeau warn the reader not to initiate a conversation about work with a French person due to their beliefs in viewing each person from an egalitarian framework no matter what their job is. They also become indignant at being "put into a box," not wanting to be judged for their work. However, for many of us in today's labor force, our chosen employment has become the defining representation of who we are as individuals.

Jessica Pryce-Jones identifies in her book Happiness at Work that the average American spends 90,000 hours at work over their lifetime. Tack on the more than 100 hours commuting every year (US Census Bureau) and for most Americans over one-third of their life and half their waking hours during any given working day are consumed by their job. Consequently, it has become more commonplace for individuals to define themselves by their occupation. As writer Annie Dillard once said, "How we spend our days is, of course, how we spend our lives."

We have reached an inflection point in society where work no longer has the same structural constraints it once had; the question of what one does is more tied to how one spends their day rather than their title or job. Today, the "lawyer-in-training" may also be participating in the gig economy driving an Uber as they strive to pay off their student debt. The "photographer" traveling the world is now an influencer with hundreds of thousands of followers making a six-digit income through brand sponsorships. Where the term "entrepreneur" used to imply struggling to find a job, now it signifies a business builder providing dozens of others employment. "Working in finance" today might refer to developing algorithms that are increasingly replacing the once-lucrative trading jobs on Wall Street.

Although it is impossible to predict the future, we can ask questions that will help define the future of work. As globalization sets in and technology progresses and becomes democratized, enterprises and individuals are continuously reimagining what is entailed in a given job, who does them, where, when, why, and how they will get completed. This ultimately determines the very definition of "work." Opportunities are effectively being created in new sectors due to the exponential evolution of technologies, an anachronistic education system, cultural shifts amongst the workforce, and growing income and access inequality. This chapter will further explore what is driving the future of work and the investment categories that will look to answer these questions for the coming decades.

The Driving Factors

To better understand what the future of work holds we need to explore the different "driving factors" that are shaping today's global economy and its workforce. These are catalysts for change. Many are well-researched macro trends across the private, public, and non-profit sectors. When combined, their interconnectedness becomes apparent and may shed light on future possibilities.

Advancements in technology

Advancements in technologies including artificial intelligence, automation, the blockchain, and the democratization of access to mobile phones and the Internet are transforming the nature of work for enterprises and the labor force. Simultaneously, they have trillions of dollars' worth of impact on the economy. Over the last 45 years, we have seen the transistor count follow Moore's Law, increasing from less than 5,000 to more than 10 billion. We have progressed from the World Wide Web to major technology milestones such as Google search, Amazon Web Services, IBM's Watson, Facebook's DeepFace, Amazon's Alexa voice technology, the blockchain, and Deepmind's AlphaGo. There are now over four billion Internet users with access to nearly 600,000 Wi-Fi networks (WiGLE). Not only are individuals frequently online, but they are accessing it through handheld devices, evidenced by the nearly three billion owners of smartphones, according to a report by market researcher Newzoo.

What does this all mean? The workplace is increasingly becoming digitalized in order for employees and enterprises to connect, communicate, collaborate, and compete. Enter artificial intelligence, machine learning, the blockchain, and automation and the outcome is that new and innovative methods are being developed to accomplish those four C's. However, with advancement comes change, which can have a negative impact on those on the receiving end. There has been extensive conversation around the effects that automation and digitalization will have on the larger workforce — many of which are quite alarming. While these issues are important to be raised as credible concerns, it is equally critical to understand that these challenges will act as catalysts for opportunity (to be discussed later in the chapter.)

Automation

One of the more highly debated topics is the disruption or repositioning of work. According to a McKinsey Global Institute (MGI) study, up to one-third of work activities could be displaced by automation as soon as 2030. This would result in the need for 75 million to 375 million workers — which accounts for 3%-14% of the global workforce — to switch their occupations. Bain's Macro Trends Group has shared a similarly daunting outlook, which they call "The Great Transformation." An analysis they put together claims that automation could reposition labor two to three times more rapidly than past transformations in agriculture, manufacturing, and construction — ultimately displacing 20%-25% of the labor force over the next couple of decades. While MGI found that less than 5% of jobs have activities that can be fully automated with existing technologies, at least one-third of constituent activities could be automated in about 60% of occupations.

Consequently, all workers will need to adapt as the technologies they work alongside are evolving to become increasingly capable replacements. We have already seen this transition for decades as machines have superseded physical labor resulting in productivity gains in industries such as manufacturing and construction. Technology has also altered or replaced routine service occupations including secretaries, switchboard operators, travel agents, and file clerks. Robots and computers can now recognize, translate, and respond to human speech, drive automobiles, identify a universe of images, and diagnose and support medical operations.

In the coming era, many aspects of cognitive occupations that once required years of education and training such as law, medicine, and finance, will be augmented or replaced by computers. Advances in artificial intelligence will mean that technology will outperform humans in areas in which data is a key function of that job or industry. It is entirely possible that in the next few years a non-trivial percentage of the core skill sets of most occupations will be skills that are not crucial to today's workforce.

On a global scale, MGI calculated that automation could affect 50% of the world economy and nearly $14.6 trillion in wages. In order to adapt, members of the workforce must attain a higher degree, specialized education, or refocus on activities that require soft skills such as creativity, emotional and social adeptness, and other cognitive capabilities that are inherently too human to automate.

Student loan debt and the broken education system

In Brookings Metropolitan Policy Program's analysis covering 90%of the workforce in industries since 2000, it was found that two-thirds of today's new jobs require either high- or medium-level digital skills. In order to meet the demands of the digitalized labor market, the Georgetown Center on Education and The Workforce believe 65% of jobs will require education beyond high school by 2020. The "catch 22" of higher educational attainment or advanced degrees is the high financial commitment involved.

Over the last decade, the student loan debt totals in the US have skyrocketed to nearly $1.5 trillion (as of the end of 2018.) According to a report by the Federal Reserve Bank of New York, that accounts for one in five adult Americans or 45 million individuals carrying student loan debt. This report states that the total student loan debt is on average $37,000, a $20,000 increase from 13 years ago. This is a powerful driving factor for the future of work. Unlike previous generations, it is no longer financially viable to take the first accessible nine-to-five job out of college.

How did we get to the point of a student loan crisis? The amalgamation of exponentially increasing tuitions (more than quadrupled in the last few decades), lower wages, globalization repositioning jobs internationally, and the need for additional education to succeed in the rapidly changing labor market have all exacerbated this issue. Yet the depth of the problem lies within the actual structure of our education system creating unprecedented income inequality and a drastically shrinking middle class.

One of the key aspects that led to the United States becoming the leading global economy is education. In the early twentieth century, the US responded to technology advancements like electricity, air travel, the telephone, and the automobile by expanding public high school education and establishing the state university systems. In Claudia Goldin's "America's Graduation from High School: The Evolution and Spread of Secondary Schooling in the Twentieth Century," she reports that through the first four decades of the 1900s high school attendance rose from 18% to 73% and completion went from a mere 9% to 51%. This greatly impacted US labor share (economic output that accrues to workers in the form of compensation) over the next couple of decades as workers averaged 65% of the national income. The labor share effectively helps explain the extent of the wage gap between growth in labor productivity and growth in real hourly compensation. Yet, after years of relative stability, the labor share fell to unprecedented lows and is now 10% less than what it once was. This is particularly important for workers because it both describes the degree to which they are compensated for their work and is a direct comparison of the output they helped produce with the compensation they received.

Although there has been strong economic growth over the last five decades, according to the Brookings Institution, wage growth has been stagnant, averaging just 0.2% annually since 1973. This has accentuated income inequality and constricted the middle class. Those at the top of the income distribution have seen an increase in wages, while those at the bottom have had a substantial drop in real wages. That gap in compensation is largely being attributed to a steady rise in corporate/owner share of the national income. In most cases, employment and wage growth are concentrated in jobs that require high social and analytical skills. For common low- and middle-income jobs, such as cashiers and truck drivers who are at high risk of elimination due to automation, individuals will be forced to receive better or additional education and training or to find new fields of work.

Unfortunately, the performance of the public education system is measured by college enrollment, not career identification and placement in high-paying, sustainable jobs. Schools have focused primarily on developing knowledge within more traditional subjects rather than fostering collaboration, problem solving, critical thinking, and cognitive skills. The challenge is that today's technological breakthroughs have exponentially surpassed the necessary innovations within the education system in order to adjust to the modern labor market. In many industries that have been digitalized, employees need to have specific applicable job experience. This leads to increased competition and demand for the top academic programs and a stronger need for advanced degrees.

Interestingly, there is an extreme dissonance between employers and the higher education system. According to a study by Gallup and the Lumina Foundation, 96% of college administrators believe their graduates are workforce ready, whereas only one-third of business leaders agree. Due to the lack of collaboration between employers and educators, we are left with an antiquated education and skills training system. With success not being tied to employment outcomes, both workers and employers are forced to adapt rapidly. This drives the future of learning, hiring, and ultimately, work.

Millennial workforce

An interesting paradigm shift being observed in today's economy is the changeover from the employer to the employee determining how and where work is occurring. A major reason behind this is the rise of Millennials in the workforce. Already emerging as leaders in industries such as technology, by 2025 they will make up 75% of the global workforce.

Millennials are a driving factor for the future of work because they have unique demands and expectations compared to previous generations. In order for employers to attract and retain high-performing talent, they are compelled to adapt. As we shift from industrial globalization to knowledge globalization, digitalization is decoupling people, information, and systems. This enables the worker to obtain employment that more accurately aligns with their needs and values. In order for employers to achieve success at a global level, they can no longer compete by simply procuring any available talent. They are moving to a model centered around acquiring superior (defined by experience and/or skill) talent.

This shift in the labor pool empowers Millennials to dictate workplaces and corporate culture. As consumers, they are socially and environmentally responsible and expect the same from their employers. In addition to caring for the environment, they choose to acquire experiences over material objects and are attracted to communities with shared interests and values. Millennials spend more on wellness than any other generation and that is reflected in demands they have of their workplace. While they have a strong work ethic beyond traditional hours at an office, they also desire environments that support work-life integration.

Due to growing up digitally connected, Millennials have an expectation of instant feedback and are willing to seek new opportunities if their job does not allow them to learn and grow both personally and professionally. This leads to a desire for flexibility in the workplace in order to acquire the life experiences and skills Millennials believe are associated with growth. As such, many Millennials would rather make less money at a job they love than remain in one that does not align with their needs and values. Unfortunately for employers, today's unprecedented access to employment through online job boards, marketplaces, and digital platforms leads to a transient workforce if they are unable to meet the demands of their employees.

Without strong ties to any particular organization, Millennials have gained a reputation for "job-hopping." A Gallup report found that only 29% of Millennials are engaged in their jobs. With 60% open to different job opportunities, a high turnover ensues, costing the US over $30 billion dollars annually. The challenge for organizations is to understand that Millennials are consumers of the workplace and employers will need to identify how to attract, acquire, and retain their employees.

The Investment Categories

As Carl Sagan once famously said, "You have to know the past to understand the present." Historians, policymakers, academics, and the like seek to make sense of today's world through studying and reflecting on the past. Not only do we examine and learn from history in order to apply it at a macro or societal level, but as individuals, we reflect upon how we shape the future from the past.

Perhaps the past and future are more alike than we realize. The idiomatic expression 'hindsight is 20/20' means that it is easy to be knowledgeable about an event only after it has occurred. Every past event or idea has a cause or multiple causes that may be retrospectively obvious yet were not so from the outset. While we may not be able to predict the future, we can examine the present as well as the past to understand what will shape the future.

Making sense of how previous economy transformations have altered the way we work demonstrates how our current society might evolve to meet the challenges of the future of work. By examining the human motivations that drive today's digital economy, we now see how we are encountering a paradigm shift around work. As the interactions between human and machine become more intertwined, our motivations have started to move from extrinsic to intrinsic. Where we were once motivated by extrinsic values such as income, prestige, and external validation, they are now being supplanted by intrinsic desires such as autonomy, creatively applying one's skills, a bias towards community, and the urge to develop one's knowledge and ability. This shift of how we are motivated continues to demonstrate itself in how humans participate in both the open development of technology and how work is being performed

Being cognizant of the driving factors in today's digital globalized labor economy enables us to identify the investment categories that will create financial and societal value for investors, employees, industries, and communities.

The Gig Economy

No longer is working nine-to-five for a single employer with a structured payroll the predominant way today's workforce makes a living. The rise of independent workers has created what is called the gig economy or the on-demand economy. According to MGI, there are over 160 million people in Europe and the US — or 20%-30% of the working-age population — who participate in the gig economy. Many other reports have projected that over half of us will be engaged in the gig economy by 2020. While these freelance workers span across demographics, they tend to be divided into two segments: those who make their primary income from independent work and those who do independent work to supplement their income.

This model is continuing to become mainstream due to driving factors such as the Millennial workforce, advancements in technology, and income and education inequality. Simply put, the gig economy is the culmination of mobile and Internet access becoming democratized, a highly connected Millennial generation seeking flexibility and autonomy, and the need for additional revenue streams in order to cover education, student debt, and increased costs of living. As a result, independent work is quickly evolving as digital platforms create online marketplaces that facilitate on-demand connections between workers or service providers and customers.

Whether it is the ability to hail a ride through Uber or Lyft, access software developers to build a website through Upwork, get at-home meal delivery through DoorDash, or even have your dog walked using Wag, the rise of digital platforms is providing millions of individuals independent work while generating billions of dollars in revenue by facilitating services. Both entrepreneurs and investors continue to find it an attractive market as still, only 15% of freelancers are using these marketplaces to find work (MGI). With 61 million Generation Z'ers expected to be joining the American workforce in the next few years, many more will opt to join the gig economy. In fact, 46% of the generation's workers are already freelancing according to Upwork. Other factors such as traditional workers pursuing their desire to become independent, an increase in demand from businesses and consumers for independent services, and the population of unemployed and inactive workers freelancing for employment are expected to fuel growth in the gig economy.

While the rise of the gig economy could have many economic and financial benefits, there are still various challenges and opportunities that can be addressed by entrepreneurs and their venture capital counterparts. According to the US Bureau of Labor Statistics, 10.6 million people whose primary source of income is independent contractor work do not currently have access to health insurance. Because policymakers are not keeping up to speed with this shift in work, freelancers are ineligible for existing financial products and government programs. Therefore, startups like Trupo are being built to protect independent workers. Sara Horowitz, the founder and former director of the New York-based Freelancers Union, launched Trupo to provide a short-term disability insurance product that will cover up to half of an independent worker's typical income in the event of a serious injury or illness. As Horowitz declares, "We're not waiting... government can't or won't do it. We're building the safety net ourselves."

However, it's not only health insurance that needs to be addressed in the gig economy. Other companies like Catch and Joust are extending beyond portable benefits and are building financial products to counteract wage and income variability. Catch's curated and simplified benefits services offer health insurance, retirement savings plans, and tax withholding directly to freelancers, contractors, or anyone uncovered. As Catch co-founder and COO Kristen Tyrrell states, "In order to stay competitive as a society, we need to address inequality and volatility. We think Catch is the first step to offering alternatives to the mandate that benefits can only come from an employer or the government." Additionally, Joust has built a digital bank platform specifically for the needs of the independent professional and freelancer providing a range of centralized services including tax payment tools, income and invoice smoothing, and the ability to incorporate a business in minutes.

Since the use of gig work platforms has also grown by more than 30% in emerging economies, new freelancers now span beyond the traditional strongholds of IT, mobility, delivery, and data processing to all industries (BCG Henderson Institute). We are seeing a rise of independent work in virtually every industry including finance, healthcare, agriculture, construction, business-to-business (B2B), retail sales, and education. For employers, freelance workers are often less expensive because they don't require the added 25-50% overhead of a 401(k), healthcare, and other benefits while allowing for a nimbler workforce. While the first wave of the on-demand platforms has led to investment opportunities focused on worker wellbeing, the gig economy penetrating additional industries and regions raises new and exciting questions.

How will workers receive professional development, ongoing training, and worker classification and credentials? What is the software infrastructure needed to support the enterprises shifting to a contingent workforce? What other industries are ripe for the gig economy? What countries? How do we improve and sustain freelancer productivity through collaboration, communication, and connection?

As we look to the future of the gig economy and questions such as these begin to emerge, venture capitalists will be in search of the founders who are building the answers.

The Creator Economy

Picture this: you are seven years old; you film yourself opening new toys and explaining all the features while playing with them. You upload them to YouTube and a few years later you are earning $22 million dollars a year from pre-roll advertising and sponsored posts. Sounds like a fantasy, right? Well, for Ryan of Ryan ToysReview, it's a reality. When Forbes released their list of the highest paid YouTube stars of 2018, the seven-year-old sat at the top with his channel, which has 17.3 million followers. How is this possible?

We have entered a new era of our economy called the creator economy. Again, looking at history to understand the present, we can determine that in the first half of the twentieth century we were in the producer economy categorized by industrial manufacturing driving the economy. As we optimized for productivity through the assembly line and other innovations, we began to shift towards the consumer economy. Production costs fell, technology began to permeate across the public, delivery of media went from newspapers and the radio to television and the Internet. The question was no longer how do we raise production and improve efficiency, but rather how do we reach consumers in order to increase sales? Where businesses' successes were once characterized by mass production, these new consumer-oriented businesses forever shifted the ways companies operated. To grow sales and profits, organizations prioritized advertising, offered installment credit, and created regional and national chains to reach more consumers.

Enter the creator economy: an individual is now able to monetize their skills, passions, and interests through their creations by leveraging today's technology and global reach. Unlike previous times, today's economy is defined by individual interactions, engagement, and data. Why is this the future of work? As long as an individual or community is able to maximize interactions while reducing friction for a user or consumer, prospering no longer needs to be tied to a traditional occupation within an organization. Take Ryan for example. He is able to leverage the YouTube platform to acquire hundreds of millions of views on his videos generating data and thus, a remarkable income.

YouTube is just one of the many companies enabling today's creators. Companies like Shopify, Wix, Mailchimp, and Facebook/Instagram are providing the software infrastructure that allows a creator to set up an e-commerce store, build a website, engage consumers through email, and acquire new consumers through marketing. Platforms like eBay, Etsy, Indiegogo, and Patreon permit individuals to reach a mass audience in order to sell their creations or collections as well as have their consumers and fans support them financially.

While we are still in the very early stages of the creator economy, we are seeing opportunities spring up across a diverse set of categories. Individuals who have learned how to optimize for interactions and engagement are now able to make an income in areas such as playing video games (Twitch), hospitality experiences (Airbnb), teaching resources (Teachers Pay Teachers), skill sharing (Masterclass), and more. Splice, an audio sample marketplace and music production collaboration tool with 2.5 million users has now paid out $15 million to artists since 2013. As the CEO and co-founder states, their platform lets "people behind the scenes get an opportunity to step into the light with an amazing revenue opportunity, but also an opportunity to be seen for their creative contributions."

With the progress of technology, more individuals will be able to gain access to powerful tools and platforms that will empower the digital-savvy workforce to participate in the creator economy. There are still many industries, shared interests, skills, and arts that will drive interactions and engagement across the world, giving birth to a new model for making a living.

The Automation Economy

"In the new technology, machines and automated processes will do the routine and mechanical work. Human resources will be released and available for new activities beyond those that are required for mere subsistence. The great need is to discover the nature of this new kind of work, to plan it, and to do it."

Although it is believable to think this quote is from today, in fact, it was written by Howard R. Bowen, the Chairman of the National Commission on Technology, Automation, and Economic Progress, a group that was established by President Lyndon B. Johnson in 1964. The Council was enacted in order to identify aspects of technological change and recommend legislative and administrative steps to be taken by the government. While it was a period of growth for national income, wages, urban populations, and access to education, it was also a time of conscious social change. One of the conclusions of their assessment was the fact that "technology destroys jobs, but not work." The narrative that large-scale automation will lead to mass unemployment and economic uncertainty has become a common thread of nearly every major technology shift. However, automation is not a new occurrence and historical evidence suggests that the long-term effects on employment have actually been positive. Advancements in technology have allowed workers to do their jobs better and faster, which in turn, has increased output, incomes, and raised living standards.

Whether we realize it or not the automation economy is already here. Impressive developments have been made in artificial intelligence and the technology that powers automation. This is driven by exponential increases in computing power and by the immediate availability of a massive quantity of data, providing improved and novel automated capabilities. From discovering new drugs to algorithms that are able to predict our personal interests, to the development of self-driving cars and drones, to virtual assistants and software that can translate languages or invest our finances, we have seen the potential of new technology.

To date, the digitally connected consumers are the ones who have primarily benefited from automation. This technology has improved the efficiency, convenience, and arguably quality of lives through new products and services. Everything from hailing a taxi, booking a flight, and buying, receiving, and returning a product, to accessing nearly unlimited entertainment and ordering groceries and meals is being powered with elements of automation.

However, with a projected $8 trillion to be invested in automation over the next decade, businesses will also be rewarded for entering the automation economy (Bain & Co). Leveraging automation, companies are disrupting large sectors of the economy such as transportation, logistics, human resources, healthcare, finance, real estate, manufacturing, and agriculture. Depending on the industry and type of problem they are solving, automation investment opportunities tend to fall in two buckets: an application that makes work more efficient, productive, and accurate, and an end-to-end autonomous solution that replaces humans entirely.

For many entrepreneurs applying artificial intelligence and other technologies to the application layer of their business, they are finding ways to optimize and automate workflows and create a competitive advantage. Founders who combine a unique insight or domain expertise in their target industry with strong technical capabilities will ultimately have the recipe to drive massive degrees of improvement against incumbents. For example, Convoy is leveraging automation to tackle the highly fragmented $260 billion trucking industry in the US, which according to McKinsey & Company is 20% of the $1.2 trillion global total. CEO Dan Lewis and his co-founder Grant Goodale came from Amazon, where they gained domain expertise working on a massive logistical task. Through this, they recognized the proliferation of mobile phones amongst truck drivers and the power the devices could have in addressing the 40% of miles driven without a load. As a result, Convoy's apps use automation to match trucks and shipments. They enable drivers to bid automatically for loads, submit their bills, and get paid, and shippers to post a job, get real-time quotes, and track their shipments. Although their revenues are still dwarfed by the incumbents, in less than five years they have already raced to a valuation over $1 billion while raising $265 million from venture capitalists.

With autonomous vehicles in the not too distant future, the several million truck driving jobs are expected to be highly impacted but, according to Lewis, it's unlikely they will become obsolete. "It's not just about driving," says Lewis. "You need a driver's knowledge about a guardhouse or signing documents. The driver's role will definitely change, but he'll be around a very long time."

Companies like Waymo — the autonomous-vehicle developer that spun out of Google — has taken a different strategy within the automation economy by building the infrastructure needed to remove the human altogether. As their Chief Technology Officer Dmitri Dolgov stated, "We're not building a car, we're really building a driver." By partnering with car manufacturers and ride-hailing companies like Lyft, they are able to scale their technology at a more rapid pace than competitors such as Tesla and Uber (which is building its own self-driving technology.) This method of building self-driving software that other companies can utilize is helping make autonomous cars a reality.

While automation in some domains (such as driving) has the potential to displace a large number of jobs, the technology is arguably still a ways off from reaching its potential. As entrepreneurs, investors, software developers, and engineers continue to invest capital and resources to its development, there is a growing demand for companies that help build the automation tools of the future. As a result, the robotic process automation (RPA) sector — tech that tasks intelligent agents with performing repetitive, often tedious tasks usually undertaken by humans — has been drastically growing. UiPath, which raised its most recent round of venture capital at a valuation of $7 billion, develops automated software workflows meant to facilitate the highly repeatable activities in a common workflow of legacy systems. For example, they are able to integrate modern tooling in areas like accounting where they can automate a process such as scanning a check and recording the payer and amount into an Excel spreadsheet, enabling the human worker to increase their bandwidth and productivity. Their capabilities to assist customers in entering the digital economy have paid off for the founders, employees, and investors alike as they went from $1 million to $100 million in annual recurring revenue (ARR) in less than two years and are on track to do $450 million in ARR in 2019. With big insurance companies, financial services, and other workflow-intensive organizations looking to digitization to stave off growing competition, other RPA startups have also found rapid success. Automation Anywhere, which has raised $550 million that values the company at $2.6 billion, has machine learning-powered systems to automate tasks that normally take hundreds of thousands of employees. In March 2018, it launched its IQ Bot solution that learns by observing human behavior and has already accumulated more than 65,000 users. CEO and Co-Founder Mihir Shukla is confident they will "help bring AI to millions." He believes that "like the introduction of the PC, we see a world where every office employee will work alongside digital workers, amplifying human contributions. Today, employees must know how to use a PC, and very soon employees will have to know how to build a bot." This process of humans teaching machines is a critical part of the investment to deploy automation. Ironically, we are entering a period where humans are working with the machines that may just ultimately replace them.

One of the more exciting areas of the automation economy is collaborative automation. While there are many short-term gains to be had from the other methods of automation, companies and humans will see the most significant improvement in performance when machines and humans work together. Through understanding one another's collaborative intelligence, humans and AI will be able to enhance each other's complementary strengths. Where humans have soft skills that cannot be replicated by technology (e.g. collaboration, abstract thinking, leadership, creativity, and social skills) machines are able to analyze and react to quantities of data at speeds that are impossible for humans. H. James Wilson and Paul R. Daugherty of Accenture believe the key to collaboration at the human-machine interface involves three necessary roles from both the human and the machine. The latter is responsible for "interacting" with humans to give workers more bandwidth, "amplifying" our cognitive skills, and "embodying" human abilities to broaden workers' physical strengths. On the other hand, humans need to "train" machines to accomplish tasks, "explain" the outcomes and objectives of those activities, and "sustain" the responsible and ethical use and application of machines.

Montreal-based Age of Minds is built based on the thesis that ethics in AI is one of humanity's biggest challenges this century; one of the answers is to have AI augment humans, rather than replace them. CEO and Co-Founder Dorian Kieken believes "that a full circle of learning: AIs learn from humans who learn from AIs who learn from humans, can lead to vast and continuous improvements for both." He insists that, "human and AI collaboration is crucial because not only can we achieve more but it's our best insurance against AI/human misalignment and so, a good investment in the future of our species."

Waves of automation have reshaped what work is done and how work is done throughout history. Automation in agricultural led to automation in the industrial and manufacturing sectors and today we are seeing it in the service sector. For many workers in the industries that are being automated, it is certainly a concerning time full of unknowns. But for the entrepreneurs who are embracing change and the investors who believe in and support them, the automation economy is one of the most exciting epochs in the history of technology.

Workforce Development

The combination of evolving demographics, a widening income and skill gap, and an education system that was not built for today's digital economy has created an investment opportunity in what is called workforce development. This refers to the human capital services that empower individuals to find work and then succeed in their profession. To recognize where the opportunities lie, one must understand the journey of a worker in the labor force from education or apprenticeship to exiting the workforce with financial stability. There are three areas in particular that are emerging in order to solve the challenges this generation's workforce is facing: career identification, corporate learning and development, and upskilling and retraining.

As previously discussed, today's education system has not been able to keep up with the rapidly evolving digital economy and graduates are forced to discover the appropriate employment for themselves while navigating a challenging job market. Balancing student debt, an uneven fit between their interests, qualifications, and knowledge, and what different prospective employers really want from their employees has culminated in unprecedented employee "job hopping." A CareerBuilder survey shared that employers expect 45% of their newly hired college graduates will remain with the company for under two years, and the study showed that by age 35, about 25% of young employees would have already worked five jobs.

So how do we solve this? There are hundreds of job boards such as Indeed and Hired that are enabling workers to find and apply for employment, some with the simplicity of three buttons on a mobile app. However, not everyone knows what opportunities are out there, much less the ones that align with their interests and values. To empower individuals to identify the right career path there has been a rise in education technology companies known as bootcamps like General Assembly and Codecademy that are teaching job seekers everything from product management to coding. These programs are not meant to necessarily replace the traditional education path but instead are a form of vocational schooling to aid people in navigating today's employment landscape. Some of these programs are focused on helping place workers in specific industries that have a supply gap, while others are exploring unique business models designed for today's economy.

Where the current paradigm asks students to make a large upfront investment in their future earnings, under the emerging model of the income share agreement (ISA), a third party will make that investment and only see a return when the student lands a financially profitable job. One of the better-known proponents of the model is Lambda School, founded in 2017. The program provides risk-free education in fields where there are worker shortages like nursing, programming, and cybersecurity. Under the ISA, students are required to pay 17% of their income for two years after graduation, if they find a job that pays $55,000 a year or higher. Lambda caps the ISA payment at $30,000, so a highly-paid student isn't penalized for success. If they do not find a well-paying job within five years, they owe nothing.

In today's labor market, employment is no longer limited to credentials or prestige but instead favors skills. Lambda recognized this and built their program based on the skills that are desired by employers. Designing their curriculum for employment means they are aligned with the outcomes of their students. As Austen Allred, co-founder and chief executive of Lambda School shares, "(Lambda School's) model meets students where they are. We work to minimize the barriers to entry that exist in other education and training models. That means no down-payments, no credit checks, available entirely online, and a clear cap on repayment. We only get paid when our students do." Although only a couple of years old, they raised a $30 million Series B in January 2019 that already valued them at $150 million. Investors such as Geoff Lewis, the founder of Bedrock and protégé of billionaire Peter Thiel, Google Ventures, Y Combinator, and actor-turned-venture capitalist Ashton Kutcher all recognize the incredible opportunity this model has to be applied globally. As of April 2019, the company has confirmed this by launching its first cohort in Africa.

It is not only startups that are building in the workforce development sector. Employers are also expanding their human capital efforts to a rapidly growing segment called corporate learning and development. Arguably the most valuable asset of a company is its people and in an extremely competitive job market, it has become increasingly vital to acquire, engage, and retain one's employees. The reason engagement, in particular, is so important is because it is a representation of a worker's deeper emotional and behavioral connection to a job and company. Gallup found that high turnover of Millennials costs the US economy $30.5 billion each year.

Part of the reason behind this turnover is that only four in ten Millennials are satisfied with their chances of being promoted in their company. If 60% claim that opportunities to learn and grow are "extremely important" to them, according to Gallup, then it is evident that they don't believe organizations are investing enough in their employees.

This need for workforce development is a key factor in why the corporate training market has grown to over $200 billion worldwide (Bersin by Deloitte). With the digitalization of the workplace and shifting consumer behavior, a new paradigm has emerged in how workers learn, train, and progress. While corporate training is not a new concept, technology has evolved the delivery from e-learning through online universities and course catalogs to continuous learning through video and MOOC (massive open online courses) providers to today's digital learning through the personalized and timely-centric micro-learning and learning experience platforms. As the workplace evolves and new workers (both demographically and geographically) enter the labor force, new opportunities will continue to arise within the corporate training industry.

Another issue is the need to address those who are seeking career mobility or no longer employed due to job displacement. In the third key area of workforce development, re-skilling and upskilling will become crucial due to its close tie to the loss of jobs expected from automation. As work continues to be digitized, individuals will need to outpace competition from both humans and technology. To close that information gap, companies will need to understand what the skills associated with sustainable employment are and in what industries there are high demands for workers. Although it is hard to predict, looking at sectors such as technology, professional and technical services, hospitality, healthcare, and education, they will all continue to have hiring surges as they grow. Some companies in industries that are already facing automation, such as automobile and telecommunications, are anticipating the necessary human-centric jobs by investing in services to improve the skills of their workforce.

Startups like Upskill are working to enhance the operational capabilities of these workers in functions such as field service, material handling, and manufacturing by leveraging next-generation technology like augmented reality. Their Skylight smartglasses product is so highly effective that GE technicians who wore them saw a 34% increase in productivity after just their first use. Paul Boris, VP of Manufacturing Industries at GE, was so impressed, he claimed:

"In just three to five years, I can't imagine a person on the plant floor that doesn't have a wearable device to help them do the job." While automation will likely have an impact on what jobs are done in many industries, we also have an opportunity to use the new technologies being developed to our advantage and provide workers the tools to succeed.

Future of Work

Whether we explore the future of work through the lens of the enterprise or the worker, there is no denying that we are entering both exciting and unprecedented times. When historians look back at what the next few decades bring, the companies that are founded today will set the foundation for the relationship between humans and machines. Access to information and technology is increasingly becoming democratized, putting the power of change into more hands than ever before. We have the unique opportunity to shape how industries, institutions, communities, and humans will metamorphose, operate, and build value for generations to come. Responsibility will be in the hands of the entrepreneurs and their venture capital counterparts to steer us into a future economy that is guided by ethical use of technology, unbiased employment opportunity, and the tools for individuals to prosper.

The unknown can be daunting and filled with uncertainty. However, as we learned to navigate through the industrial revolution, technical revolution, and most recently the digital revolution, we will soon prosper through the next technological revolution. As Professor Klaus Schwab, Founder and Executive Chairman of the World Economic Forum, says in his book The Fourth Industrial Revolution, "The more we think about how to harness the technology revolution, the more we will examine ourselves and the underlying social models that these technologies embody and enable, and the more we will have an opportunity to shape the revolution in a manner that improves the state of the world."

How humans will produce, share, and distribute value will appear different than in the past but will be driven by the factors of today. We might not know what the future will hold but it is the understanding of how we got here and where we are headed that will influence our framework in defining the next revolution. It is up to both society and its entrepreneurs and investors to utilize the most advanced technology in our history to build the future of work.

**WENDY XIAO SCHADECK
NORTHZONE**

In 2008, the foundation for blockchain technology was established in a whitepaper by a person, or a group of people, anonymously using the name Satoshi Nakamoto. Over the decade that followed, the technology protocol became the foundation on which entrepreneurs began to build a new generation of applications. The protocol, simply stated, decentralizes decision making and authority over digital transactions. In the first generation of the Internet, most of the large technology companies, governments, and financial institutions managed our data and transactions through a centralized authority. With blockchain, decision making shifts to the masses; through complex verification processes, blockchain technology is said to be unhackable and monetary transactions or changes in ownership of property or contractual rights can never be tainted by dishonest practices. This brings an element of trust to an Internet that has been subject to data breaches — in itself a promising premise worth betting on. In fact, many experts have been quick to proclaim blockchain as the 'new Internet.'

In the earliest stages, the technology evolved through the hard work of developers and entrepreneurs. They devised applications and use cases where blockchain would be most suitable. Cryptocurrencies, made commonplace through Bitcoin, were built using blockchain technology, and promised a future of global financial inclusion and access. But this currency had little use in the real world. Governments were slow to accept it and the regulatory bodies failed to control speculation and swings in value. Similarly, many blockchain-based applications were built with grand plans but worked less efficiently than existing solutions. This is common for a new protocol when it is first introduced and over time, these protocols become the standard.

This is what venture capitalists are betting on. Between 2008-2014, a few million dollars were invested by venture capitalists in blockchain startups and applications. In 2018, however, investments ballooned closer to $4 billion in that year alone. In 2019, organizations including Facebook, MasterCard, Goldman Sachs, and IBM began innovating using blockchain technology, making applications built on this protocol mainstream.

The merits of blockchain technology and the use cases are still being contested in public forums, but this technology should not be overlooked, for reasons that Wendy Xiao Schadeck, an investor with Northzone, will share in this thesis on Web Infrastructures 3.0. I had the privilege of meeting Wendy when I first became interested in better understanding blockchain. When new technologies emerge, there are always venture capitalists who develop a surface-level understanding and can speak in broad strokes, but Wendy is not that; rather, she is a representation of a quality I spoke about often throughout this book — an individual who goes deep within a sector to better understand the nuances and landscape prior to making decisions. In order to become proficient on the technology, I signed up for a blockchain class hosted at Columbia Business School, for which Wendy had created the curriculum. She specializes in blockchain investments with Northzone and has become prominent within the venture ecosystem for her understanding of this important technology. While blockchain is still in its early days and the use cases and future of it are being publicly debated in real time, Wendy provides a deep foundational knowledge of why this technology is important and how it can radically change the Internet as we know it.

WEB 3.0 INFRASTRUCTURES: BLOCKCHAIN
Wendy Xiao Schadeck, Northzone

The Evolution of the Web

"The Web as I envisaged it, we have not seen it yet. The future is still so much bigger than the past."

Tim Berners-Lee, Inventor of the World Wide Web

Since the beginnings of the Internet, people have been replicating real-world behaviors more efficiently in the digital realm — this is the initial driver of web adoption. For example, email was a more efficient way to send a message, and many of the early web pages were essentially more accessible digital newspapers. As more people began interacting in more ways online, we began to discover new internet-enabled use cases that could only and uniquely exist in the digital realm. Describing Snapchat streaks or Tiktok trends to someone in 1998 would simply not compute as it would require language portraying concepts that didn't exist back then. There is a layering effect between behavior change and technology that drives the evolution of the web, and the constant expansion of the Internet is a function of trust and technology working in tandem to define the new rules of engagement in this digital realm.

Starting with the first iteration of the web, the adoption of Internet protocols such as TCP/IP provided a trusted basis for transmitting information, which powered the web's formation. However, these protocols didn't define much else. Web 1.0, or the "read-only web" according to Tim Berners-Lee, was an anonymous place, where you could trust that information will get from point A to B, but there was very little trust in the information itself. The only business transactions were one-to-many, a few large trusted content producers selling static information to everyone else. AOL's homepage c. 1995 gave you various links to online resources such as "Today's News," "Sports," and "Finance," like pages of a newspaper. Like most of the Web 1.0, it had limited rules of engagement and offered users only two options — search and consume. As more publishers came online and eventually earned the trust of its consumers, information became more and more commoditized as it became more widely available. Web 1.0 didn't create huge Internet companies because there was only so much you could do to monetize commoditized information; but it did give us the information age.

Starting in Web 2.0, the "read-write web," companies built tech platforms to create trustworthy environments online, forming new markets where many-to-many business transactions could take place. These companies defined the Internet rules of engagement even further, but largely within their own controlled ecosystems. This allowed participants to interact in more ways online because they trusted the platforms to dictate and enforce the rules. As a result, these Web 2.0 intermediaries took a large cut of the value and defended their positions using network effects and data monopolies. This was the era that spawned the large technology companies of today. Facebook began by successfully building a trustworthy environment for chatting with your college buddies by tying online profiles to real-world identities in the form of a .edu email address. This allowed the company to outcompete Myspace and other more pseudonymous social platforms, where the trust was lacking, and ultimately allowed Facebook to leverage their user data moat to build a huge advertising business. Similarly, Uber created a trusted ecosystem for ride hailing by enforcing its own rules of engagement between rider and driver, and as a result, it keeps a large percentage out of every transaction. Although we are now in an era where there is growing distrust towards these tech giants of the Web 2.0 era, these companies gave us unique and huge digital economies and greatly expanded our vocabulary of behaviors online.

We are now at the beginning of Web 3.0, and technology standards are being developed to establish the trusted basis for transmitting value as well as information, creating automatic dependencies between the two — money tied to data. This is important because we aren't reliant on a company to establish the rules of engagement online; they are written directly into the fabric of the web. Millions of devices globally can contribute to an infinitely elastic supply of compute power while earning a financial reward directly — without any company taking a cut. Fully digital economies can exist, where digital assets can be unique and valued without reliance on a central provider. Financial systems can be truly inclusive, and payments transferred directly and cheaply, at the marginal cost of doing the digital accounting. Securities can be transparently linked to their underlying assets, and risk traced directly and transparently as to encourage wider adoption. The digital commons can be governed collectively, where creators can profit directly from their work. The full implications of Web 3.0 are still not fully clear as we are still early (it would have been hard to foresee Snapchat streaks from 1998, as per the earlier example), but the initial clues are promising.

Protocols Powered by Tokens

> "Blockchains are a new invention that allows meritorious participants in an open network to govern without a ruler and without money. As society gives you money for giving society what it wants, blockchains give you coins for giving the network what it wants. Blockchains combine the openness of democracy and the Internet with the merit of markets. To a blockchain, merit can mean security, computation, prediction, attention, bandwidth, power, storage, distribution, content..."

> Naval Ravikant, AngelList

Tokens account for units of value built on top of a protocol. Tokens are the powerful incentivizing force which allow protocols to coordinate trusted economic activity on the web. They help bootstrap network effects by first providing financial liquidity for future network value. This then attracts early adopters to contribute specific work, data, and capital for the network (in exchange for tokens.) Lastly, as the supply side becomes more robust, the demand-side participants can buy and sometimes pay via token for the network's services. Bitcoin is the most basic example of a token — Bitcoin is the native token for the Bitcoin blockchain, which is a protocol for financial transactions. Bitcoins derive their value based on the future expected value of the protocol, priced on the market. Miners do work for the Bitcoin blockchain by recording transactions on an immutable ledger; for this work, they are rewarded in Bitcoins. Way before the Bitcoin blockchain became useful for real-world adoption, the supply-side of miners became very robust due to this ability to capture and get liquidity for future protocol value. Projects are experimenting with a variety of other token models, which derive their value from different aspects of protocols — for example, Work tokens, Currency tokens, Non-Fungible tokens, Security tokens, Discount tokens, Stablecoins, DAO tokens, etc. The economics behind these are fundamentally different, and it is perhaps simpler to think of them as potential business models on top of protocols. There can also be more than one token per protocol, and they can also be layered on top of one another as basic economic building blocks for a new digitally-native value chain.

Protocols vs. Institutions

"One of the areas of blockchain innovation I am most excited about is building open, permissionless, and decentralized technology infrastructure. The three areas that seem most obvious to me for decentralized infrastructure are compute (code execution), storage (storing files, etc.), and bandwidth (network infrastructure)."

Fred Wilson, USV

If you reduce the role of an institution or a protocol down to the very core, the aim is to get a bunch of people and machines to work together towards a common goal; usually that's the production of some sort of good or service. It then stands to reason that whichever entity can do this cheaper will have an advantage over the other and grow, while the other shrinks (adapted version of Coase's Theorem for those fluent in economic theory.) Well-designed tokens allow crypto protocols to coordinate people and machines more cheaply than institutions by cutting out middlemen, simplifying contracts, and reducing political friction.

We haven't yet seen the line drawn between where companies end and protocols begin, but bolstered by tokens, protocols have a lot of room to grow and can be expected to take significant share from current companies. One hypothesis is that the future of the web could be composed of a few wide-ly-used crypto protocols responsible for much of the transactional, low-value tasks in addition to thousands of highly specialized institutions focusing on user experiences. For example, institutions win when the market depends on physical goods — real estate, e-commerce, services, etc. — as the touch points with meatspace usually cannot be perfectly governed by a digital proto-col. Institutions also win when control/design and subjectivity are required, in products such as gaming experiences, wallets, and arbitration. On the flip side, protocols win when the market is self-contained and digitized, as the economic logic within games. They also win when consistency and censorship resistance are important, allowing developers to build on them without having to worry about the rules being changed arbitrarily. Lastly, protocols win when coordi-nating a very large number of workers across discrete, measurable markets, such as a market for global compute power.

Where Adoption Starts

"Crypto-powered governance markets will solve the tragedy of the commons and drive future abundance at the same level of scale as the stock market and the corporation. In a pervasively connected world, it will be more global and democratized than what we've seen before."

Mike Maples, Floodgate

How exactly does the value erosion happen from Web 2.0 to Web 3.0? And where will the wedges be created in the existing web businesses, dominated by giants? One potential answer to this is wherever there are digital market failures in our society today.

In economic terms, a market failure is any time the free market fails to allo-cate resources efficiently, usually requiring government intervention. There are a few types of market failures, but let's focus specifically on the tragedy of the commons. The commons refers to a pool of scarce resources, shared by all, but not governed by any, so it's often exploited and depleted. The only solutions proposed by economic theory are privatization — letting an enterprise govern it, or nationalization — letting governments govern it. Well-known examples of tragedy of the commons include global warming, depletion of our natural resources, and a lack of funding for public schools.

This was until economist Elinor Ostrom proposed a solution which won her the Nobel Prize in 2009. She observed that many communities have successfully governed the commons by adhering to a set of rules. These rules are largely encoded into the fabric of trust built within the small communities she studied; she never thought them to be socially scalable to our large, modern societies... until crypto protocols came along.

For the first time, the rules for governing a common resource can be encoded and enforced digitally, within crypto protocols, without the need for an enterprise or a government. If we can account for the resource and enforce rules around its consumption digitally, Ostrom's findings can extend beyond the small communities where this already works in practice.

Crypto protocols will have a harder time managing the physical commons because rules like access rights are harder to enforce in the physical space without some sort of central party intervention (e.g. clean air, oceans, schools, roads, etc.) However, applied to the digital commons where all the value can now be traced and tracked for the first time, real-world adoption begins to look more near term. However, the idea of a valuable digital commons is still somewhat new to us because digital scarcity is new. What makes this really big is that any scarce resource can be thought of as the commons and managed by crypto protocols if producers and consumers are willing to produce into and consume from the "collective pot." The problem with this line of thinking has always been the corrupted incentives of the central party required to manage the allocations back to society.

Again, crypto protocols solve this problem — far better in fact than even the most uncorrupt central authority, because protocols can deliver services at monopoly efficiency while maintaining perfectly competitive prices. This means that any time a protocol or an enterprise is competing to deliver a service, a protocol can deliver it more cheaply by making it a commodity. The usefulness of this economic model extends thus beyond the commons and into other types of market failures such as monopolies or oligopolies. It is perhaps a useful framework for thinking about how to economically break up the Web 2.0 giants discussed earlier.

Time will tell the extent of adoption and how many of our resources we'll be able to manage as commons. However, aligning our incentives with the collective using crypto protocols is powerful because it is how our society works today, but not how our businesses work. Our incentive structures fail in the face of increasing human connectivity because they fail to capture the growing impact of our actions on our networks and vice versa. In the future, our decisions' impact on others will perhaps be greater than on ourselves, so continuing to operate in single player mode in a multiplayer world is not only wrong but dangerous.

Technology vs. Human Protocols

"One of the challenges of this sector which I think is not getting enough attention is this: what is the cost to society of not trusting?"

Dan Ariely, Economist

In this industry, we tend to overemphasize the role of technology and underplay the other forces driving the growth of the digital economy. The crypto world promotes "trustless" as an ideal, which is not surprising given that the Bitcoin whitepaper deems the elimination of the need to trust (specifically in a third party) as a core value proposition of Bitcoin. It would be foolish to pretend it's possible to completely remove trust from the equation and propose instead that blockchain technologies should be used to enable more trust between counterparties. While cryptonetworks are technology protocols, trust is a human protocol. The former is more scalable across a large, anonymous population, but the latter is more powerful as it is far more adaptive and multi-dimensional. The two need each other to scale.

Trust is essential for growing the economy. In the absence of trust, even with technology, many value-creating transactions wouldn't happen. A simple example is this: I am selling a t-shirt online to you. However, you don't trust that I will send it to you after you send me payment, and I don't trust you enough to send you the shirt before you pay; therefore, this transaction never takes place and the market for t-shirts was not established. Then comes along an e-commerce platform to facilitate this trust by holding funds in escrow until verification of receipt and promising to take recourse on both seller and buyer if either misbehaves. So, we make the transaction, but the platform takes a cut for establishing the market. However, all participants have to trust the platform will do the right thing, and they suck significant value out of the ecosystem. Now, cryptonetworks come along and allow us to program the verification of receipt and escrow into the smart contract such that we can transact without the need for trust in a third party. The elegant technological solution can help establish many new markets and even allow certain economies to leapfrog financial systems where there hasn't been a credible third party to establish societal trust.

The idea is that participants in blockchain networks so fully trust the technology that they implicitly trust the entire network. This could be thought of as an evolution of trust in the most ideal case. However, in reality, especially at this stage of the technology's development, we cannot expect the code to fully account for all edge cases, and this is what's worrying. Abiding too strictly to the trustless ideal allows network participants to offload personal (or community) responsibility for unethical behavior because it is supposedly "programmed into the code." This type of "code is law" thinking puts us in a position where everyone is expected to be cold-hearted and uber rational, and exploitation is the norm. As such, the trust and ethics governing the edge cases dissolve altogether. Countless incentives play such a major role in governing our behavior today, and we can't possibly account for them all by top-down design. There are always unforeseen edge cases, and they can't always be predicted and must be resolved over experimentation and trust.

However, what's optimistic is that the virtuous (or trusted) participant always has a competitive advantage in the market; they are likely to attract more transactions because dealing with lack of trust can be costly and complex.

A few virtuous actors can anchor a market because others will try to mimic them in order to also win business. There have been tons of studies done on reputation games in economic literature — the gist is if we enable a transparent reputation system over time, all players have an incentive to behave, virtuous or not.

Technology's impact on society is so greatly influenced by how we choose to adopt it, and some of the decisions we make right now are fundamental to how and how much crypto will change society in the future. As this technology prepares for the mass market, it will be key to build more trust into these networks: trust that we all will act with integrity where lines are blurry, and code is broken. This will actually speed up adoption.

What Web 3.0 Means for Entrepreneurship

Decentralization is a core value of the early crypto ecosystem, and fundamentally that means resetting the web's rules of engagement such that competition increases naturally and that economies of scale don't form because of unfair advantages. That lays the groundwork for cheaper tech infrastructure, upon which other entrepreneurs can easily build. For example, several projects are looking to build cheaper global payment rails, including Facebook's project Libra. A few others are looking to commoditize file storage, cloud computing, and networking. Most importantly, Web 3.0 companies are looking to commoditize data, which breaks down the biggest moats of Web 2.0. This should dramatically lower the cost of starting an Internet company in the next phase of the web, even more than the existing platforms (AWS/Shopify/Google/Facebook) already have.

"Web 2.0 developers treat data as "the new oil" — a scarce resource to be acquired and exploited. Web 3.0 developers now see that hoarding user data is a liability, and that giving users control reduces the cost, complexity and risk of managing that data while also enabling more powerful online experiences. It also directly challenges the Web 2.0 business model of "user as product" forcing the dominant incumbents to either forgo current revenue and market power or allow Web 3.0 developers free reign to pioneer new business models based on giving users access to and agency over their data."

Brad Burnham, Union Square Ventures and Placeholder Capital

Another big feature of this era of the web is composability — the ability for developers to combine pieces of innovation like building blocks to create something that is very complex with relative ease. Since these pieces are all permissionless, there are no central dependencies nor central points of value extraction. The decentralized finance (DeFi) movement, which includes lending protocols, prediction markets, decentralized exchanges, and a whole host of other tools, is a great example of this. Using different DeFi protocols as building blocks, entrepreneurs can create, test, and launch complex financial derivatives in weeks as opposed to years.

"A traditional business is generally best positioned setting up shop in a location with existing residents, utilities, law, security, and a vibrant market economy. Similarly, developers benefit from building on top of shared resources such as an existing user base, data, security, and running code.... Composability is important because it allows developers to do more with less, which in turn, can lead to more rapid and compounding innovation."

Jesse Walden, a16z

The organizations that win in this paradigm are probably also different too, as protocols are in their essence collaborative, and their incentive mechanisms are decentralized. This means a different approach to leadership is required to manage a different type of organization. The incentives structure between a company and a protocol are vastly different; the community around a protocol is perhaps as important as the technology itself. Whereas entrepreneurs scaling equity organizations need to be able to scale pyramidally, ruling by dictatorship, protocol entrepreneurs need to lead by inspiration, influence, and incentive design, often taking themselves out of the story line in the long run (e.g. Satoshi Nakamoto.)

Ultimately Web 3.0 infrastructures create a whole new basis of competition for startups, where competitive advantage is still undefined. It allows startups to attack the tech giants right where it hurts by commoditizing their moats and leavening the playing field. When developers can easily pick and choose the cheapest infrastructure stack, plugged into specific user data they don't have to create or own, they can build more powerful custom user experiences and business models.

"Information technology evolves in multi-decade cycles of expansion, consolidation and decentralization. Periods of expansion follow the introduction of a new open platform that reduces the production costs of technology as it becomes a shared standard. As production costs fall, new firms come to market leveraging the standard to compete with established incumbents, pushing down prices and margins, and decentralizing existing market powers. The price drop attracts new users, increasing the overall size of the market and creating new opportunities for mass consumer applications."

Joel Monegro, Placeholder Capital

NITYA RAJENDRAN
TRIBECA VENTURE PARTNERS

The 2008 financial crisis wreaked havoc across the global economy and transformed the financial services industry so that it was ripe for disruption. Following the crisis, new laws and regulations emerged, forcing incumbents to look inward; at the same time, it also created immense opportunity for upstarts to enter the industry. After the financial crisis, millennials developed a deep-seated distrust for large financial institutions, a sentiment that was exacerbated by their overwhelming student debt. On the technology side, machine learning and artificial intelligence powered algorithms for more efficient financial plat-forms. Since 2008, the $1.8 trillion financial services industry has gone through monumental shifts and even over a decade later, continues to be upended by upstarts across insurance, personal and business loans, financial advisory, investments, and other financial sectors that power the global economy.

Intricate, complex, and difficult to navigate, financial services is an industry in which an aspiring founder requires deep insider insight to gain a competitive edge. Nitya Rajendran, an investor at Tribeca Venture Partners, develops her investment perspective for a fund that has previously invested in companies such as CommonBond, AppNexus, and ShopKeep. A former investment banker who worked on mergers and acquisitions at Lazard, Nitya understands the business fundamentals and metrics that drive businesses forward and make them more valuable over time. In her assessment, many innovative fintech startups have emerged in the last decade and while incumbents have faced their fair share of challenges over the past decade, some have evolved to keep pace with the digital revolution and have rebranded themselves either through partner-ships or high marketing spend. As Nitya reveals, 'there is a massive opportunity for financial institutions to invest in or partner with startups so that they can reinforce each other, help each other thrive, and help provide more financial tools and access to more customers in innovative ways.'

THE FUTURE OF FINANCIAL TECHNOLOGY
Nitya Rajendran, Tribeca Venture Partners

SECTION I: INTRO TO FINTECH

Disruption is a word we hear a lot these days. Netflix is disrupting Hollywood and video content consumption. Airbnb is disrupting travel and hospitality. Amazon is disrupting retail, grocery, cloud storage, and maybe even pharmaceuticals. While not as immediately obvious, finance is another industry that impacts everyone and is undergoing massive disruption. In fact, venture capitalists invested $12.3 billion into US fintech startups in 2018 alone to further fuel this disruption.[1]

What's causing this recent surge of disruption? The short answer: an increasing amount and variety of data coupled with cheaper and more accessible technology. More data enables companies to better understand consumers and market conditions to optimally price their products. Lower technology costs enable companies to extract more insights from their data and empower more of the population to engage with technology and incorporate it into their daily lives.

Brian Hirsch, a partner at Tribeca Venture Partners whose investments include CommonBond, ShopKeep, and AppNexus, believes that the vast amount of consumer data that companies own has created a shift in the relationships between companies and their consumers. Before globalization and mass markets, banking was localized and largely based on trust and personal relationships. As globalization set in and companies started to reach immense scale, they lost this intimacy because it became impossible to know and track all the nuanced preferences and behaviors of customers across the country and

1. https://www.cbinsights.com/research/report/fintech-trends-q1-2019/

globe. However, in recent years, as data flows more freely and technology is more accessible, businesses have the ability to deeply understand their customers again and reclaim that customer intimacy.

Due to these shifts in the last decade, the financial industry has witnessed an emergence of startups. The fintech startups that will succeed and survive various economic conditions are those that build themselves up as data-centric from the beginning, build more efficient and accessible technology, and appeal to a new generation of financial consumers through transparency and purpose. However, these traits alone will not be enough — the fintech startups that thrive long term will be those that partner with financial institutions in some capacity to give them scale, data, and financial ammunition. Though not impossible, fintech startups that try to go it alone the entire way will be much more susceptible to falter.

Opportunity after the 2008 Financial Crisis

The Atlantic's "The Never-Ending Foreclosure" profiled the Santillan family, who has felt long-term repercussions of the 2008 financial crisis. They refinanced their home in 2003 and 2004 and took on an adjustable rate mortgage, exposing them to the risk of fluctuating interest rates. During the recession, both parents saw their paychecks decrease while their monthly mortgage payment increased to $3,000 from $1,200. As a result, they began to fall behind on payments and by 2009, they were told they would have to pay nearly $450,000 to keep their house. They lost their home to foreclosure that year. The Santillan family also lost out on economic opportunity as they focused on surviving and trying to find places to live, with the family of six often living in hotel rooms or their car. At the end of 2014, the family was able to rent a single-family home. Their oldest son could not afford college after graduating high school in 2009 and finally enrolled in film school in 2017. Although they are on the path to economic recovery, the Santillan family lost nearly a decade of economic opportunity, an incredibly difficult obstacle to overcome.

People everywhere felt the recession's catastrophic impacts in their daily lives, whether with suddenly unemployed family members, houses going under, or less discretionary spending. These scars run deep, leading to distrust and disdain of legacy financial institutions for many, but particularly for millennials who were in their formative years during this period.

The 2008 financial crisis had disastrous consequences and is still fresh in many people's minds, if not still a dark presence in their lives. In the first two and a half years after the recession, 55% of those in the labor force found themselves unemployed or with a pay cut or reduced hours.[2] By February 2010, 8.8 million jobs had been lost since the pre-recession peak.[3] In the year following the crisis, the United States' stock and home values dipped by trillions of dollars, equating to each US household losing on average approximately $66,200 in stock wealth, $30,300 in real estate value, and nearly $5,800 in income.[4]

Following the 2008 recession, the financial industry underwent two major changes: increased regulations and a growing focus on the end consumers' experience.[5] The crisis wiped out many financial institutions and the survivors were increasingly subject to stricter regulations and stress tests. As a result, these surviving institutions turned inward as they were no longer focused on growth but on survival. As The Economist wrote in "A Decade After the Crisis, How Are the World's Banks Doing?," "sluggish revenues, combined with the competing demands of supervisors and shareholders, have forced banks to screw down their costs and to think much harder about how best to use scarce resources." For example, The Economist notes that after Citi spent 20 years dramatically expanding its offerings, it withdrew from many of them post-crisis and re-focused on its primary corporate and investment offerings. Banks also focused on ensuring they were financially sound and could comply with new regulations. Prior to the recession, banks used to conduct their own internal stress tests which would analyze a few thousand data points. Now, banks analyze millions of data points.

2. https://www.pewsocialtrends.org/2010/06/30/how-the-great-recession-has-changed-life-in-america/

3. https://www.bls.gov/opub/mlr/2011/article/employment-loss-and-the-2007-09-recession-an-overview.htm

4. https://www.pewtrusts.org/en/research-and-analysis/reports/2010/04/28/the-impact-of-the-september-2008-economic-collapse

5. https://www.economist.com/special-report/2017/05/04/a-decade-after-the-crisis-how-are-the-worlds-banks-doing

This environment created an opening in which new fintech startups could emerge and scale. When speaking with Brendan Dickinson, a partner at Canaan which has invested in companies such as Lending Club, Ebates, and Instacart, he said, "over the past decade, a lot of incumbents pulled back from the market. It created a great opportunity for lots of new brands to get off the ground where it might have been harder years before."

For consumers, the financial crisis led to a massive loss of trust in financial institutions, leading them to be more interested in companies whose core missions more closely resonate with them. The issue of distrust rings especially true for millennials, who have already been through two recessions in their lifetimes. Because of this issue, millennials are open to trying new and different solutions. Fintech startups have recognized this underserved, unsatisfied market and are working to fill the gap. Startups are employing a myriad of strategies to win over millennials and eventually gain their trust, but a few methods are common: sophisticated technology coupled with an intuitive, easy-to-use interface; social networks serving as trusted sources that amplify word of mouth; and a clear social mission. Matt Harris, a partner at Bain Capital Ventures, has invested in fintech for a long time through Bain's investments, such as Acorns, OpenFin, and SigFig. He told me he has found that people have "a surprising level of willingness to trust new brands that show themselves to be technologically sophisticated and elegant even if they're unknown brands. People are getting their cues from the app's design and from referrals. The way trust is manufactured is a little different for a growing segment in the population, primarily youth and the digitally native." A millennial data scientist echoes Harris' sentiment, saying "I don't really care how well known a brand is. If it has the features I need and everyone seems to like it, it will probably be a good option." However, sometimes the desire for and willingness to try something different can be detrimental to consumers if startups have not followed the proper regulations and do not deserve their customers' trust (I discuss regulations more in depth later in the chapter.)

A primary undercurrent propelling the finance industry forward is the "socialization of finance," which the Goldman Sachs report The Future of

Finance Part III: The Socialization of Finance defines as "the impact of technology and changing behavior on the financial services markets." The report explains that "the financial services industry is becoming increasingly social and democratic as it continues to move online and becomes more automated, at once empowering consumers, disrupting existing banking and credit systems, and creating new markets."

Technology coupled with changing consumer behavior is enabling efficiencies in the financial industry, creating an opportunity for fintech startups to build innovative products that reach more people. A wider swath of the market is gaining access to financial tools: people who have subprime credit scores, people whose bank accounts typically would not meet the minimum threshold to be managed by professional wealth managers, and people burdened with high student loans, as examples. In addition, increased amounts of data extend access of financial products to more people. For example, credit card companies can now price products, such as credit card rates, to people with no credit history using alternative data sources that are now available. Brian Hirsch sees the socialization of finance as one of the most important themes in fintech today as he believes that there are "lower income people around the world that don't have access to the same services that the middle class and wealthy do." Startups that provide money management solutions or access to capital at reasonable rates offer an immense opportunity to provide financial tools and ultimately more financial freedom and power to more people.

The Goldman Sachs report suggests that social networks have acted as a catalyst for the socialization of finance as people are actively sharing their financial experiences on social networks, helping fintech startups gain users through significantly lower customer acquisition costs. Additionally, fintech startups are able to scale rapidly and reach many people using social network constructs. For example, Venmo differentiated itself in the world of payments through the social network they built for users. Venmo allows users to pay or request money from contacts and include a note similar to a check's memo line. Venmo's primary value proposition is the instantaneous transfer of money, a more efficient solution than writing and cashing checks. Another difference from checks is that users can make these payments public to their network so friends can see who is interacting with whom and what activities they are engaging in based on their payment history. Venmo created a sense of virality through its social platform where friends can see their contacts' social activity through the previously boring lens of payments. One of the co-founders, Andrew Kortina, told Fast Company that he and co-founder Iqram Magdon-Ismail wanted to "build a version of [a payments service] that feels more like the apps we're used to using with our friends, like Twitter and Facebook. It became this record of all the things that we were doing — the people we were hanging out with, the places we were going — and it started to look a lot like a news feed. Many think payments are a private thing, but if you think about it, the things you spend money on with friends are: going to restaurants, concerts, ski trips, birthdays. These are the things you would actually talk about the next day over the water cooler at work, so it's natural people want to share."[6]

The memo line has become a fun, interactive space. Users can write straightforward notes such as "Utilities" but many users write more creative notes, employing emojis or jokes. In the Fast Company piece, Austin Carr suggests that "the social aspect of Venmo makes the services feel more authentic and personal — terms rarely used to describe the payments space." Or as The Atlantic notes in "Why the Venmo Newsfeed Is the Best Social Network Nobody's Talking About," "Due to its incredibly intimate look at how your friends spend their money, the Venmo newsfeed has become one of the most interesting, informative social networks out there. But don't say that too loud, or you'll feel like a creep."

Sharing financial experiences has become a natural part of consumers' financial journeys and purchases. The Future of Finance Part III report notes that in a 2015 survey Goldman Sachs conducted, 84% said that reviews of financial tools played a role in their decision-making process. NerdWallet, another post-recession startup, aims to fill the gap of providing transparent evaluations of financial products. According to Inc.'s piece "NerdWallet Weathers Its

6. https://www.fastcompany.com/3019849/venmos-social-increasingly-hilarious-payments-community

Growing pains," NerdWallet's mission is to be a "curated 'Yelp for finances,'" with an "approach [that] certainly fits a post-financial crisis world facing demands, particularly from Millennials, for financial transparency." NerdWallet CEO and Co-Founder Tim Chen founded the company out of his own frustration to try to find unbiased reviews of financial products when trying to help his family members find new credit cards and evaluate mutual funds. NerdWallet seems to have resonated with users as its content and tools received more than 140 million visits in 2018.[7]

In addition to post-recession factors, perception of the financial industry has also proven to be essential in boosting its startup ecosystem and attracting talent. The financial industry was not always an attractive market to entrepreneurs, but Matt Harris believes that the 2009 founding of Square changed the game. Harris explains, "Jack Dorsey started Twitter and amazingly, what he decided to do next was a payments company, Square. I think for a whole generation of entrepreneurs and venture capitalists, that made fintech something the cool kids do." Square's genesis came from one of Dorsey's friends, James McKelvey, who was unable to accept credit cards at his faucet studio. Dorsey and McKelvey came up with Square as a way to help merchants seamlessly accept credit cards through a mobile credit card processor and eliminate the middlemen. Square went public in November 2015, six years after its founding, and as of publishing has a $33 billion market capitalization. Seeing an already successful entrepreneur build a huge fintech startup inspired many others to start their own.

This confluence of post-recession factors has led to a surge of fintech startups in numerous subsectors of the financial industry. Given the breadth of the industry, I will focus on only a few (blockchain is covered in another chapter): student loans, wealth management, and insurance.

The Emergence of Fintech Startups

By looking at post-recession startups such as CommonBond and Ellevest (discussed later in this chapter), it is clear that the new class of fintech startups

7. https://www.nerdwallet.com/blog/corporate-news/nerdwallets-record-breaking-year/

tend to share four characteristics: 1) a technology-first approach; 2) big data as a strategic imperative to better understand customers and run more efficiently; 3) hybrid model combining online automation and the ability to access to humans; and 4) a clear mission that resonates with consumers.

1) A Technology-First Approach

Millennials are accustomed to interacting online or on mobile, so companies are meeting customers where they are and striving to create positive online experiences. Shivani Siroya, the CEO and founder of startup Tala, which underwrites loans to consumers not covered by credit bureaus in emerging markets, said she built the Tala app to "meet our customers where they already are. We're not asking them to meet us in person or through the phone. All the interactions are through digital mechanisms, in-app chat, etc." As cell phones become the primary way people interact with the web, many startups begin as mobile apps before launching websites. Startups are focusing on design and ease of use, making everything seamless and intuitive for new users. David Klein, CEO and co-founder of student loan refinancing company Common-Bond, believes taking a technology-first approach has been incredibly important because, "as technology has continued to improve, it allows you to do things online that you weren't able to do before or enables you to do things much more quickly than you were able to do before. You can make your products stronger. You can make your customer experience faster and more personalized. Your ability to innovate in general is exponentially higher. And it's constant." Employing a technology-first approach enables companies to move many processes online and make them more streamlined, which are beneficial to both companies and their customers.

2) Big Data as a Strategic Imperative

This second characteristic is enabled by startups' strong focus on technology. Fintech startups are employing the latest big data, artificial intelligence, and machine learning technologies to better understand their consumers, predict behavior, and optimize their businesses. Increasing amounts of data to run algorithms on and faster, more accessible technology are pushing artificial intelligence and machine learning forward. The amount of data is growing exponentially and is coming from a wide variety of sources, providing companies the opportunity to analyze customers more fully. For example, robo-advisory startup Betterment tries to understand its customers by taking into account data such as their retirement plans, zip codes, expected growth rate of expenses, social security benefits, spouse's income, and assets at and outside of Betterment. This data allows Betterment to provide personalized solutions tailored to its users.

Another example is Tala, which uses alternative data sets to determine consumers' credit worthiness. Siroya recounted to me that when she worked at the UN and traveled to different countries, she realized "banks in these countries didn't understand how to assess the risk of customers who did not have credit history. They didn't understand their daily lives and it was costly to underwrite them. I could prove they were creditworthy through daily life data and create more customized products for this segment." She built Tala so that it uses behavioral and device data to assess customers' credit worthiness, such as device type and ID, how users engage with the Tala app, and if they read Tala's Terms and Conditions. Opening up the types of data Tala can use to evaluate its consumers creates opportunities to build customized loan products for a massively underserved segment of the population. Siroya was also adamant about using transparent, fair data practices, writing on their website, "Tala is committed to fair lending practices that do not discriminate based on gender, race, ethnicity, religion, national origin, or sexual orientation. As such, we shall seek to follow guidelines that ensure that we do not build any features based on these data points and consider and mitigate if possible the implicit algorithmic bias that might arise with regards to these categories." When employing many data streams and feeding them into machine learning models, potential biases can arise; however, Tala has taken steps to mitigate and eliminate any traces of discrimination in their credit worthiness machine learning models both through the data they ingest and their algorithms.

The more data companies can collect, the more refined their algorithms become. Kenneth Lin, CEO and founder of startup Credit Karma, which offers free credit scores and related services, has said that "data is a powerful driver making innovation go forward, especially in financial services. If I know a lot about you, I can tailor the message and experience [and] help [you] get to a better place."[8] In VentureBeat's piece "Credit Karma: Believe the Hype for 'Artificial Narrow Intelligence,'" Credit Karma's CTO Ryan Graciano said the company uses "data in production, for ad hoc analysis, for data science and modeling, and for online prediction, across all of our products and plat-form." To understand a sense of magnitude, Graciano said that their data set is increasing at the rate of over 1TB per day and his team builds one thousand new models every month to analyze 120 billion observations. If companies such as Credit Karma and Betterment did not have data for their individual users, their solutions would be one-size-fits-all. Ingesting customers' data empowers them to provide custom solutions, while cheaper, faster computing power democratizes access to custom solutions, typically reserved for those willing to pay steep prices.

Incumbents have been working on artificial intelligence as well. JP Morgan, for example, has been forthcoming about its focus on this technology. In the bank's 2017 Annual Report, they wrote:

"Artificial intelligence, big data and machine learning are helping us reduce risk and fraud, upgrade service, improve underwriting and enhance marketing across the firm. And this is just the beginning.... We also need to be more forward looking in many other areas. Doing so will create a better and stronger system — not doing so will actually create additional risk. Following are a few examples: Almost all risk and control functions (think Anti-Money Laundering, Know Your Customer (KYC) and Compliance) could be better performed if we worked with the regulators to streamline what we do and use advanced techniques, like artificial intelligence and machine learning, to improve

8. https://www.cbinsights.com/research/credit-karma-ceo-personal-finance-future-fintech/

the outcomes. The same is true for fraud prevention and customer service."

JP Morgan has $11.4 billion in their technology budget and has been putting it to use for initiatives such as its 2016 launch of COIN (Contract Intelligence), a machine learning solution that sifts through loan agreements in seconds compared to the 360,000 hours lawyers and loan officers were spending annually. This frees up significant time for lawyers and loan officers to focus on more important tasks. Similarly, many startups are leveraging operational efficiencies by automating more, a feature that has enabled startups to keep their teams streamlined. Startups are also able to keep costs low (because they maintain minimal brick and mortar presence) and employ fewer people (because less human interaction is required), leading to efficiencies that enable startups to pass on some of the savings to consumers.

3) Hybrid Model

As prevalent as automation has become, being able to speak with a human can be comforting to consumers. Money is personal and people need to have full confidence that their money is safe. Thus, fintech startups are often creating an online-first approach with the ability to reach human representatives. Brian Hirsch extols the values of a hybrid process that can be automated or manual as he believes it is smart to "have the ability to flip a switch and return any part of automation into a manual process to get consumers to convert. The more informed a transaction needs to be, the more you need to have that type of system in place" — such as for large purchases like mortgages where consumers might need more hand holding. This focus on the customer experience pays dividends in customer conversion as well as customer satisfaction and loyalty.

4) Transparent and Mission-Oriented

Fintech startups are marketing themselves as transparent and morally aligned with consumers. A well-stated mission in addition to clear, transparent major selling points. Hirsch believes that millennials want to see mpanies they support "have heart and care as an organization because every financial institution does that."

Millennials are demanding these multi-faceted changes in the financial industry from enhanced technology to more personalized solutions. According to The Future of Finance Part III, millennials want more transparency, streamlined and automated processes, and 24/7 access. According to their 2015 survey, 33% of millennials do not think they will need a bank by 2020 and 50% are hoping fintech startups challenge and surpass banks. Millennials crave a change in the financial ecosystem. That being said, many others do still trust the incumbent financial institutions, indicating that these institutions will continue to exist for many more years to come.

Disruption and Innovation in the Financial Services Industry

Disruption looks different in the financial services industry compared to other industries where the top 10 companies are more susceptible to being displaced. For example, in the last two decades, Amazon has upended the retail industry to become one of the top players in the space; however, this type of complete upheaval is much harder to achieve in the financial industry. Large financial institutions, such as Goldman Sachs and JP Morgan, are able to hold onto their reins more tightly due to regulations, deeply entrenched customer trust, brand awareness, and their immense scale. It is also much easier for consumers to switch who they buy goods from than change their bank or insurance policy, which tend to fall into the "set it and forget it" category. Due to these factors, it takes much longer and is much harder to have a full flip of market leaders in the financial industry. However, this market is still highly attractive to entrepreneurs and venture capitalists because it is a massive market with plenty of room for new fintech startups to grow. Every major publicly traded bank in America has a market capitalization of billions of dollars. If a fintech startup even captures 1% of the market, it can still become a billion-dollar company. As of Q1 2019, there are 41 VC-backed fintech unicorns (companies valued at over $1 billion) globally that have a combined value of $154 billion.[9] It is not a winner-takes-all market.

Incumbent financial institutions have often viewed the new class of fintech startups as forces of disruption rather than forces of innovation they could benefit from. Last century's innovations primarily advanced financial institutions' offerings.[10] In contrast, these new fintech startups are aiming to seize market share from incumbents. PwC's Global Fintech Report 2017, Redrawing the Lines: FinTech's Growing Influence on Financial Services, found that 88% of legacy financial institutions are worried about losing market share to startups.

In the last few years, financial institutions have been realizing that innovation is vital and that they need to embrace it to remain competitive. Banks are debating whether it makes more sense to build or to buy innovative products from an efficiency and cost standpoint. Employing the former strategy, Charles Schwab launched Schwab Intelligent Portfolios in 2015 to compete with robo-advisory startups such as Betterment, Ellevest, and Wealthfront. Goldman Sachs launched Marcus, a consumer-friendly brand which offers personal loans and savings products that allow consumers to open an account with no minimum deposit. In 2017, over 30 banks, including Bank of America, Citi, Capital One, JP Morgan, and Morgan Stanley, unveiled Zelle, a person-to-person money transfer solution to compete with Venmo and PayPal. These solutions have been incredibly successful as they have all reportedly processed or managed tens of billions of dollars. They have succeeded because they were able to simultaneously create a friendly brand separate from their core brand and leverage their massive resources to market their solutions and scale. Part of their success can also be attributed to the strength of their products. Marcus offers higher interest rates on their savings account compared to many of their competitors and Zelle does not require users to download a separate mobile app and provide their bank account information, offering users a sense of security.

9. https://www.cbinsights.com/research/report/fintech-trends-q1-2019/
10. https://www.forbes.com/sites/ciocentral/2018/07/10/how-fintech-initiatives-are-driving-financial-services-innovation/#11ce28b154fa

Investing in or acquiring fintech startups is also a viable strategy. In the last six years, CB Insights reported in "Where Top US Banks are Betting on Fintech" that the top 10 US banks by total assets have invested almost $4.1 billion across 81 disclosed rounds of funding into startups. One such investment is PayPal's 2018 strategic investment in Tala. Regarding the investment, Siroya says: "PayPal has had a lot of learnings in this category and can help us accelerate our creation of new products. We're seeing real opportunities to partner with financial institutions. So now it's just a matter of how we think about our road map and theirs." Strategic investments such as PayPal's are a win-win for both financial incumbents and startups. Financial institutions need innovation and data-driven technologies, which startups can offer. Fintech startups need capital, data sets, and customer acquisition channels, which incumbents can offer. These relationships will prove particularly crucial to startups in poor economic conditions as incumbents have the ability to cushion their startups with capital if they are hit badly. Startups can also use incumbents' data from previous downturns to prepare themselves. Without this capital cushion and data, startups are much more likely to struggle and not survive an economic downturn.

Financial institutions are beginning to recognize these synergies and view fintech startups as possible partners. 82% of incumbent financial institutions expect to increase their number of fintech partnerships in the next five years, according to PwC's Global Fintech Report 2017. In 2017, 45% of financial institutions were partnering with fintech startups globally compared to 32% in 2016. As a result, some fintech startups that were once solely direct-to-consumer are now creating business-to-business arms to integrate with these partners. However, integration is often not easy due to legacy technology deeply embedded in banks' infrastructure. As a result, PwC reports that financial institutions are working to update their legacy systems with more of an emphasis on data analytics and mobile, or they are building new solutions while also maintaining their older solutions on legacy systems.

Brian Hirsch recommends that fintech startups retain an advisor who comes from an incumbent financial institution to help startups navigate relationships with large financial institutions. A potential concern is whether the Chinese wall can be properly observed if a bank invests in a competitive startup. When putting together the deal, information rights is a key aspect that all the involved parties should discuss; but ultimately, it depends on trust. As financial institutions are making more investments and acquisitions in the space, it remains to be seen if banks are more likely to roll up startups with their other offerings or create a "financial supermarket" with an assortment of financial products they have acquired.

Challenges Facing the Financial Industry Today

There are two major challenges the financial industry as a whole is grappling with: the regulatory climate and data security.

Fintech startups have a leg up on traditional financial institutions because startups can build themselves from the ground up already compliant with current regulations and stay nimble so they can adapt to new regulations as they arise. Incumbents, on the other hand, are weighed down by layers of bureaucracy accumulated over time. Startups can also build systems with the most up-to-date security, a task that is significantly easier than patching a legacy system. Matt Harris points out that it is more time consuming and expensive to work within the boundaries of compliance and that it requires a higher standard for a minimum viable product, but believes it is essential that fintech startups adhere to regulations from the outset; otherwise they risk getting shut down. Brendan Dickinson says Canaan will only invest in startups that fully understand and operate within regulations:

"We have a fundamental thesis at Canaan that fintech is not a 'move fast and break things' industry so you need to understand, respect, and work within the rules set up by regulators. Like other heavily regulated industries, if you break the rules, you'll go to jail and get shut down. We're less likely to fund people who don't have a point of view on how they're going to work with regulators or what the regulatory regime is in their market."

David Klein believes that building compliance into company culture is key. He says:

"From day one, we have considered ourselves to be a financial institution more than anything else. Most fintech companies actually want to think of themselves as a tech company first and a finance company next — maybe because of valuation or because it sounds cooler. But the truth of the matter is, if you think you're a tech company more than you are a finance company, you're likely not going to have the culture of discipline you need to build a sustainable set of controls that's required for a company that operates in a highly regulated space. It's really important to ensure that you are perfectly compliant and have all the controls in place because at the end of the day you are a financial institution that has a lot of responsibility to consumers and accountability to regulators."

Regulations serve as a limiting force for how fast fintech startups can grow compared to startups in other industries, but regulations are essential for consumer protection. Klein believes that there is an opportunity for the industry to build an intermediate regulatory framework that would allow fintech startups to be innovative and achieve scale with less friction: "The way you would do it is make regulatory compliance and capital requirements proportional to the risk your company places on the broader system. So, if you're an early innovator in finance, you have to meet a minimum set of requirements, but beyond that, the requirements are commensurate with the risk you are taking on as a business, and the risk you are putting on the system." In a similar vein, Brian Hirsch believes that financial regulations should be predicated on how large startups are and how long they have been operating. He believes there should be an intermediate step of partial regulations for fintech startups, such as "if the startup is 95% compliant on all these standards, it's good. Then, every year or so as the startup hits certain thresholds in size, it needs to meet more standards. There needs to be some sort of construct that allows for a certain number of non-critical mistakes."

Incumbents have an advantage in scale and power as they can use lobbyists to help them pass regulatory bills in their favor. For example, the New York Times reported in 2013 that bank lobbyists heavily influenced legislation that would roll back part of the Dodd-Frank Wall Street Reform and Consumer Protection Act, with some sections of the final bill reflecting lobbyists' suggestions verbatim.[11]

A major set of regulations impacting fintech companies is the European Union's General Data Protection Regulation (GDPR), which came into effect in May 2018. GDPR requires companies to put controls in place for consumer privacy and regulates how companies collect and use consumer data with the goal of putting power back into consumers' hands. The new regulations impact not only companies that are based in Europe but also any company that has the data of European residents. As a result, many companies, including financial institutions worldwide, are implementing company-wide GDPR policies instead of having different policies for their consumers in Europe and for their consumers in the rest of the world. Fines for not complying with GDPR are potentially massive: either 4% of annual revenue or up to €20 million, whichever is higher.

In addition to regulatory compliance, security must also be a top priority. Security breaches tarnish brands and consumers are becoming increasingly aware of data breaches. They want financial institutions, who are responsible for important consumer data (e.g. social security numbers), to be trusted partners. The Equifax breach in 2017 affected over 147 million people, prompting numerous articles about how consumers can protect themselves. Therein lies the problem: the onus is not supposed to be on the customer. It is up to companies to protect their customers' data. Otherwise, they risk losing their reputations, customer loyalty and trust, and ultimately market share. Securing data is only going to become more difficult once quantum computing becomes viable because the speed at which hacks can occur will accelerate dramatically.

11. https://dealbook.nytimes.com/2013/05/23/banks-lobbyists-help-in-drafting-financial-bills/

As Hirsch puts it, "when we get to the age of quantum computing, all bets are off. There will be a transition period where bad people will get control of the technology faster than all financial systems are able to implement what needs to be implemented" to protect consumers' data and their systems from being breached.

On the flip side, Hirsch believes that "privacy is important but I think many consumers are willing to give up some level of privacy for a better deal. I just think there has to be transparency." For example, he believes a fintech startup could present consumers with two choices: if consumers allow the startup to access and use their data, they are presented with a certain price; otherwise, without the data they could be presented with a slightly higher price. This scenario provides full transparency to consumers and empowers them to make the ultimate decision about if and how their data is going to be used. Siroya echoes the importance of transparency around data, explaining that Tala is "incredibly transparent about what data we ask consumers permission for. Customers have to explicitly go in and give us permission — we're not just taking that information without them knowing."

Hirsch believes that empowering consumers to have full control over their data is the future. He believes "every consumer should have a data file that they're in full control over and they are able to decide what in that file gets shared." Jiko is one startup attempting to build on this vision. Jiko is aiming to create an individual, decentralized bank with users getting their own technological infrastructure that can serve as their individual "Jiko" banks where their data is stored. By eliminating the model of a centralized database (which is prone to hackers), it provides more security and gives users complete ownership of their data and control over who can access it.

The Future

Fintech startups that emerged out of the recession have yet to go through a downturn, so it remains to be seen how they will weather bleaker market conditions. Matt Harris points out that fintech startups will see a slowdown in their growth because "corporations will make decisions more slowly, budgets will be tighter, consumers will buy fewer things, and transaction volume will slow down. The other impact is that people lose their affection for things like trading, investing, and risk when it's pricey." Canaan partner Brendan Dickinson believes the lending industry will be affected the most but that in fintech more broadly, "there will be a shakeout when there's a downturn. Some people will be shown to have no clothes on." Startups that survive the next downturn will further solidify their trust with consumers as they will show their resilience and ability to endure multiple economic conditions. David Klein believes that a downturn will actually give CommonBond the ability to scale further as the company can prove the strength of their credit and underwriting to the capital markets and as a result, can get increased access to low cost capital over time.

Startups are preparing for an economic downturn in a variety of ways. In my discussion with Sallie Krawcheck, CEO and co-founder of Ellevest, she said Ellevest has "built a lot of downturns into our projections, which is a hard thing to do." The company has chosen to be more conservative in projecting clients' future investment gains. She explains: "That means when we give Ellevest's clients a projection for 20 years from now, it tends to be lower than the projections some of our competitors give them but we want to give them a higher chance of achieving their goals. So we lose sales upfront but we believe that we gain credibility through a down market."

Dickinson's advice to entrepreneurs in the space is to not discount financial incumbents. There are many reasons they might be slower to innovate, such as legacy technology stacks or endless layers of bureaucracy. However, they do have two major advantages: immense amounts of capital and scale. Startups that have strong relationships with financial incumbents prior to adverse economic conditions will be in a better position as they will also gain access to these advantages. No matter how strong startups have been or how loyal their customers are prior to a recession, having an incumbent's support will prove greatly beneficial in a downturn and could make the difference between life and death for them.

Many incumbent financial institutions will still exist 30 years from now. Some fintech startups will become huge financial companies. The incumbents and startups that continue to grow will be those that embed a technology-first and strong data analytics approach in their businesses, stay attuned to and respond to customer needs in a transparent way, and remain secure and compliant within the shifting regulatory framework. There is a massive opportunity for financial institutions to invest in or partner with startups so they can reinforce each other, help each other thrive, and provide more financial tools and access to more customers in innovative ways. The financial institutions and startups that can best navigate these trends and symbiotic relationships will end up succeeding — it all depends on execution.

SECTION II: MAJOR PLAYERS IN FINTECH

Student Lending

A surge in post-recession regulations coupled with rapidly improving technology has led to disruption in the lending market. The recession and regulations that followed caused some legacy financial institutions to withdraw from certain areas of lending such as student lending.[12] Concurrently, direct-to-consumer online and mobile distribution channels as well as data analytics strategies have enabled new lending startups to emerge and seize market share from incumbents.

The burden of student loans is known to most, impacting millions of people. One such person is George, a resident at Mount Sinai Hospital in New York. After his parents spent their life savings to send him and his older sister to private high school, he had to take out $120,000 in student loans across his four years of undergraduate studies. Soon after graduating, he enrolled in an in-state medical school because it offered a solid scholarship package as long as he was willing to work at their hospital for a year. However, he still had to take out student loans. He graduated from medical school in 2018 and estimates that he currently has over $200,000 in student loans.

He is far from alone. In the United States, there are 43 million federal student loan borrowers with an outstanding total debt of $1.4 trillion as of Spring 2019. Of the 2017 college seniors who graduated with student loans, they had

12. Goldman Sachs' The Future of Finance Part I: The Rise of the New Shadow Bank

on average $28,650 in debt and research indicates that it takes people over 10 years to pay off their student loans.[13][14] This crisis is a multi-generational issue as 37.5% of those with outstanding student debt are under 30 years old and 62.5% are above 30.[15] The student loan crisis is only getting worse. A 2018 Brookings Institution report, "The Looming Student Loan Default Crisis is Worse Than We Thought" shows that default rates are rising; they project that nearly 40% of those with student loans may default by 2023. Default rates become more dire when looking at specific cross-sections of the population. For example, 47% of attendees at for-profit colleges end up defaulting compared to 13% of attendees at public two-year programs. The report also found that black BA graduates are five times more likely to default (21%) compared to white BA graduates (4%).

A confluence of factors has contributed to the ballooning US student loan crisis. The Brookings Institution attributes the increase in student loans to more people attending college and lower earnings from people who dropped out of college or who attended a for-profit institution. In addition, college tuition continues to rise with an average tuition of nearly $35,000 at a four-year, private, non-profit college, making attending college a huge financial feat.

To fully comprehend the student loan crisis, it is essential to understand the current student loan environment. There are two primary types of student loans: federal loans and private loans provided by financial institutions. The government does not employ a real underwriting model, instead offering Federal Stafford student loans with the same rate to all borrowers. Students often use private loans to fill the gap between what their federal loans cover and the amount they owe to their colleges — an approach George used. When he and his parents were comparing private loan options, he was inundated by daily letters from banks. Ultimately, they decided to choose the bank that gave them the lowest fixed rate because even though the variable rates were often lower, they did not want to be susceptible to rate volatility.

13. https://www.nerdwallet.com/blog/loans/student-loans/student-loan-debt/
14. https://www.forbes.com/sites/tomlindsay/2018/05/24/new-report-the-u-s-student-loan-debt-crisis-is-even-worse-than-we-thought/#488514b7e438
15. https://www.nbc-2.com/story/39538437/student-loans-are-hurting-millennials-net-worth

Many financial institutions used to offer student loan products, but the Federal Family Education Loan (FFEL) program, which enabled financial institutions to originate federal student loans, was disbanded in 2010. In addition, the Dodd-Frank-borne Consumer Financial Protection Bureau (CFPB) turned its attention to student loans to ensure fair student lending practices and handle complaints from student loan borrowers. For example, in 2017, the CFPB fined Citi $6.5 million for misleading student loan borrowers and charging incorrect fees from 2006 to 2015. As a result of mounting compliance costs and FFEL's dissolution, larger banks such as JP Morgan and Citi terminated student loan originations.

Given the startling student loan statistics and the vast number of people who are burdened with enormous student debt, an innovative student loan refinancing market has emerged to alleviate some of the burden. Some major startups have emerged in this space such as SoFi, CommonBond, and Earnest and their core product is refinancing student loans with lower rates. They have all added new products since then: CommonBond now also offers student loan originations, SoFi offers personal loans and mortgages, and Earnest offers personal loans.

The recession provided the perfect backdrop to launch a student loan refinancing company, so much so that CommonBond's CEO and Co-Founder, David Klein, refers to the financial crisis as his "fourth co-founder." That's because people no longer had as much trust in banks and the resulting monetary policy kept interest rates low to encourage economic activity. Klein said: "post financial crisis, the amount of trust that the public had in banks plummeted. There was an openness among consumers that wasn't there before and probably would not have been if it had not been for the financial crisis." Another reason this was an opportune time is that digital natives were beginning to make financial decisions, specifically regarding student loans and the potential need to refinance them. Because of these factors, Klein believes that it was never overly difficult to convince consumers to trust CommonBond. In fact, he believes "there's more of an inherent trust in online-first companies among millennials" and he is starting to see it in older generations as well.

Simultaneously, technology has enabled startups to streamline processes through automation and to run robust data analytics and machine learning models. Klein believes that automation is key to having a positive customer experience. For example, CommonBond has automated most aspects of the refinancing application process, relieving customers of the monotonous burden of filling out hours of paperwork. CommonBond's credit models also bring efficiencies as they can quickly approve or reject candidates and fund loans in a matter of days. A strong data analytics approach has been integral to the startup's success as they are analyzing more than just borrowers' credit scores; they are also examining borrowers' employment histories, industries of employment, and future cash flows, among other variables to create a fuller understanding of potential borrowers. Through the middle of 2019, Common-Bond has done over $3 billion in originations.

As lenders' models receive more data from customers, it creates a virtuous data cycle, improving their models' accuracy, optimizing their loan portfolio, lowering their unit economics, and reducing interest rates for borrowers. As a result, lending startups have a lot to gain from strong network effects. Fortunately for them, digital natives are more likely to advocate on their behalf by sharing their financial experiences on social media and referring friends, spreading startups' reach and feeding their algorithms with more data as they acquire more users.

Due to their better economics, new lenders are also able to offer lower rates and reach those whom traditional lenders have failed to serve. For the 43 million Americans with student loans, refinancing could help them save up to hundreds of dollars on a monthly basis and thousands of dollars in the long run. These student refinancing startups have a strong mission at their core, making them appealing to consumers who increasingly care about supporting companies whose values they believe in. Further leaning into their social mission, CommonBond contributes to its non-profit partner, Pencils of Promise, to fund the education of students in Ghana. The company also hosts an annual trip to Ghana where CommonBond employees and customers can see the impact their donations have made. CommonBond is sending the message that it cares not only about its own customers but also about the world.

In an effort to be transparent, Brian Hirsch believes startups should formulate a mission statement in their early days about why the startup exists and its values. Not only does it make the mission clear to consumers, but it also helps attract and recruit the appropriate talent. He believes that "consumers are smart and they'll read through who's authentic and who's not. I think authentic startups that are trying to do good will have a place in this world and will have a chance for success."

Market education is essential in the student loan refinancing space as many people are not aware of refinancing as an option, or if they are, do not know where to begin. For example, George knows he could refinance his student loans, but he does not know how to do it or where to start. While he has been lucky to have his parents' guide him through the process of taking out student loans, refinancing is new to them, so he would have to navigate this journey on his own and know that there is a real value in refinancing his loans.

From a broader industry perspective, Klein has witnessed a shift in the last few years of incumbent financial institutions wanting to increasingly partner with, invest in, or acquire fintech startups. Lending startups are unique in that they have pre-existing relationships with banks through their warehouse lines and through selling banks securitized loans. In March 2018, CommonBond announced a $50 million Series D round of financing led by Fifth Third. The bank is leveraging CommonBond's success with millennials and CommonBond is leveraging Fifth Third's scale, providing a win-win for everyone.

Out of all the areas of fintech, venture investors believe that the next economic downturn will hit lending the hardest. Matt Harris believes that "you can run however many models you want. Every crisis is different and so you simply can't predict what's going to go pear-shaped, in what timeframe, and to what degree. The 2008 financial crisis defied every model we had." He believes that lending startups can run their businesses more conservatively to cushion themselves for the next financial downturn whenever it hits. However, he also believes that can be tough to do because "all of the other incentives encourage them to do the opposite of that and grow quickly." He also recommends that they "carry higher reserves and go lend to higher, better quality customers;" however, these efforts also entail slower growth and customer acquisition because they force companies to be more selective about their customers. Harris concedes that running businesses conservatively can be tough especially when venture investors are expecting higher valuations, but believes it is best for companies in the long run.

Wealth Management

A prime example of the socialization of finance is the recent movement to bring wealth management services to a broader spectrum of individuals. After the financial crisis, a combination of improved technology, big data, and consumer distrust led to the formation of many robo-advisory startups, which offer automated wealth management services to the next generation of investors.[16] Offering services to underserved markets expands this already massive industry. The Robo Report™: First Quarter 2019 reports $229 billion in assets under management (AUM) across 17 prominent robo-advisors.

Historically, wealth management has only been for extremely wealthy individuals. Wealth management firms typically charge a management fee, which is a percentage of assets held with the advisor. As a result, most firms were not marketing to those outside the upper echelon of wealth holders because the costs of marketing to and serving lower net worth customers exceeded their potential fees. However, everyone needs management of their current assets, not just high net worth individuals. This is especially true as wealth disparities among high-wealth, middle-income, and low-wealth families have widened. Washington DC-based think tank Urban Institute states in its report "Less Than Equal: Racial Disparities in Wealth Accumulation" that between 1983 and 2010, high-wealth families saw their wealth increase by 120% and middle-income families by 13%. However, those in the bottom 20% of wealth holders actually saw their wealth decrease as their debts began to surpass their assets. Wealth disparities are also marked across racial groups. The Institute found

16. Goldman Sachs' *The Future of Finance Part III: The Socialization of Finance*

that the racial wealth gap is three times larger than the racial income gap; the income gap has not changed significantly over time but there has been a dearth of opportunity for Hispanic and black families to build wealth. The financial crisis only made matters worse with Hispanic families losing on average over 40% of their wealth and black families losing 31%, compared to white families that lost 11% on average. Women also do not have the same opportunities for wealth accumulation as they make on average 78 cents on the dollar, a gap that only widens as women become more senior. The lack of opportunities for wealth accumulation is especially concerning because wealth accumulation is essential for income bracket mobility. These stark discrepancies affecting large segments of the population have led to vocal support to make financial support and wealth management guidance more accessible. Michael Barr, former US Assistant Treasury Secretary for Financial Institutions under the Obama Administration and a University of Michigan Law School professor, said:

"After the financial crisis, the problem of income and expense volatility has increased, savings cushions are narrower and many families who were financially secure before are now living paycheck to paycheck.... There is an urgent need for advisors to know about the problems that so many Americans are facing today and many moderate income families would benefit from having a trusted advisor who could help them with very basic financial planning, budgeting and savings techniques. Investment advisors can do a lot to help moderate income families develop the financial wherewithal they need to have greater financial stability."[17]

While traditional financial advisors are unlikely to open their doors to the disenfranchised, some centers have arisen to serve this large, underserved population. In 2008, New York City's Mayor Michael Bloomberg founded the Financial Empowerment Center (FEC) where people can receive free financial

17 https://www.thinkadvisor.com/2015/06/09/former-obama-official-advisors-need-to-serve-lower/?slreturn=20190713220437

counseling. Providing this service is game-changing as New York found that half of its residents had never received financial counseling. Bloomberg Philanthropies is working with local governments to open more FECs across the US. Across its centers, the FEC has helped 34,000 people by reducing their cumulative debt by almost $40 million and building their cumulative savings by nearly $5 million.

While the FEC provides a fantastic option to people in select cities, robo-advisory startups have emerged to empower everyone through accessible, digital options. Betterment, Ellevest, and Wealthfront are robo-advisory start-ups founded in the last decade with this exact mission: to provide automated financial advice and wealth management to everyone. Account minimums range from $0 to $500 on these platforms, encouraging everyone to engage in wealth accumulation.

Sallie Krawcheck, the CEO and co-founder of Ellevest, decided to focus on a specific underserved segment of the market: women. Discussing the genesis of Ellevest, she described to me an epiphany she had: "I had this blinding insight that the retirement savings crisis is a women's crisis. The way to solve it was not just through helping women earn more money at work and not just through the traditional means, which people have tried. But there was something that I had a unique insight into even though I didn't realize it: the gender investing gap."

Solving the gender investing gap has become Krawcheck's mission. Through Ellevest, she hopes to broaden the reach of financial tools to women, who have historically been underserved by wealth management firms and as a result, have not spent enough time and money on investing and managing their wealth.

Robo-advisory startups are employing big data strategies to understand their customers' investing needs and desires and to optimize their clients' portfolios. They can train their algorithms to take various factors into account. For example, Wealthfront asks questions about income, reasons for investing money, and investing philosophy. Ellevest asks similar questions and in addition, takes into account women's specific financial experiences, such as different salary arcs and longer lifespans. Ellevest uses its algorithms to go beyond a wealth management platform that only has female-friendly marketing; instead, its technology enables it to truly better serve women and broaden the access of sophisticated financial tools to women.

While this onboarding process provides robo-advisors a solid understanding of their customers, it also offers customers a streamlined experience that takes fewer than five minutes. Robo-advisory startups are able to automate every element of the process: onboarding, generating investing strategies, and re-allocating portfolios. Providing a frictionless onboarding process is essential because it is likely the first time many of their potential customers have used a wealth management platform. Jon Stein, the CEO and founder of Betterment, says that one of his constant initiatives is to "help reduce the barriers to entry for customers by experimenting with more seamless customer onboarding." Meeting millennials where they are — online or on mobile — also adds less friction to the process. Additionally, automation significantly lowers the amount of required human capital and eliminates the need for costly consumer-facing brick and mortar locations.

Millennials' distrust of incumbent financial institutions has been a key force in helping robo-advisors grow. According to the Goldman Sachs report The Future of Finance Part III: The Socialization of Finance, millennials have lived through two recessions and consequently, often do not believe in active investing or trust wealth managers the way their parents did. Passive investing has skyrocketed in popularity in the last decade: in 2018, 42% of all US stock funds are passive mutual and exchange-traded funds compared to 24% in 2010 and 12% in 2000.[18] In a similar vein, Goldman Sachs reports that the wealth management industry has evolved from a time when personal advisors were sought after to one where consumers prefer an automated platform because they are hesitant to trust humans, who they believe are more prone to error.

Distrust has led millennials to rely more on their own networks and peer reviews for financial advice. Brian Hirsch recommends that startups leverage

18. https://www.forbes.com/sites/michaelcannivet/2018/06/27/the-passive-investing-boom-poses-a-new-risk-artificial-popularity/#70e109503e93

the power of social media and word of mouth referrals, especially from "early customers who become your major brand advocates. It lowers your customer acquisition costs." In fact, unlike other startups, investing platforms are not permitted to request testimonials due to regulations. As a result, social network and word of mouth referrals have to be "very organic where women are talking to other women about what we're doing and telling them to go check us out," according to Krawcheck. Ellevest's customer acquisition efforts have also been bolstered significantly by Krawcheck's own personal brand. Before launching Ellevest, she spent years building her social following and cultivating trust from a group she describes as a "tribe of women and men who were interested in the financial process." Jon Stein echoes that "most of our customers have come to us through word of mouth. Over 50% of our customers say they heard about us through a friend." Further contributing to a positive customer experience are the transparent and often lower fee structures these robo-advisors offer. Lower operating and marketing costs enable these startups to maintain strong unit economics while still having lower account minimums that allow them to reach more diverse and younger investors that incumbent wealth management firms have typically neglected.[19]

These startups also aim to communicate a sense of authenticity to differentiate themselves from the incumbents. Stein conveys Betterment's authenticity as a customer-centric robo-advisory through their product design and workplace culture:

"From day one we wanted to be customer-aligned. It's important to build around the customer and always put the customer first. We realized there was a way to rethink products around customers. Other financial tools have been designed by financial services experts for financial services experts. We wanted to create a solution for regular people. Everyone here at Betterment spends time on the phone and via email with customers."

---

19. Goldman Sachs' The Future of Finance Part III: The Socialization of Finance

To convey Ellevest's values, its slogan is unabashedly female-empowering: "Invest Like a Woman." Krawcheck recalls that when Ellevest first launched, some people said her team would have to dumb down their content and "what was not surprising but still disappointing is that not a single person said 'this is for women; it must be better, it must be more sophisticated.'" Not heeding their advice, Ellevest speaks to its customers in an intelligent and empowering manner. For example, in March 2018 after the Marjory Stoneman Douglas school shooting, some of Ellevest's clients asked if their money was invested in gun manufacturers' stocks. In line with being transparent and value-driven, Ellevest conducted research and published an open letter that there was likely minimal exposure to gun manufacturers and retailers. Ellevest proved they were listening to their customers by responding in an honest way, solidifying customer trust.

The Goldman Sachs report suggests that robo-advisors are typically marketing to a specific millennial demographic — HENRY's (High Earning Not Rich Yet). These consumers have a growing amount of assets, but are still too small for traditional wealth management firms. Attracting them as customers now is part of a long-term strategy because they have the potential to become more lucrative customers in the future. While robo-advisors' intentions are not fully certain, they are still democratizing access to financial tools that would have otherwise been unavailable to large swaths of the population, not just HENRYs.

Robo-advisors are becoming subject to heightened scrutiny from the Securities and Exchange Commission (SEC). In 2017, the SEC released guidance on robo-advisors, advising that they are subject to the same regulatory framework as traditional wealth advisors. Given robo-advisors' increasing market share in a massive industry, it is integral that they follow SEC regulations to protect their clients' wealth and maintain their trust.

The Incumbents

Since 2015, many firms such as Charles Schwab and Vanguard have been launching their own robo-advisory services and have seen great success.

Schwab Intelligent Portfolios and Vanguard's robo-advisory offering launched in 2015 and had over $38 billion and $130 billion in AUM, respectively, by the end of the first quarter of 2019 according to The Robo Report™: First Quarter 2019. Schwab Intelligent Portfolios and Vanguard have far surpassed startups, which have a wide AUM range between $100 million and $17 billion per startup. Incumbents have a built-in network of clients who might want to try out a robo-advisory service, reducing their customer acquisition costs. BlackRock also got into the game with its 2015 acquisition of online wealth management platform FutureAdvisor.

Betterment is in a unique position as it has a direct-to-consumer product and a business-to-business product, Betterment for Advisors. Stein believes that "because of our Betterment for Advisors platform, many incumbents think of us as a partner. We work closely with three institutions that a lot of people would think of as competitors." Krawcheck says that a number of investment platforms have reached out to her to use Ellevest's branding or content but Ellevest has rejected these offers. Interestingly, Morningstar, an investment research company, led Ellevest's first round of funding so they can share information and work through problems together. Both startups have found ways to work with or partner with financial incumbents in a way that felt authentic to who their startups are, providing them with additional scale and resources, strategies that no doubt will prove helpful in the race to seize market share and contribute to longevity and market durability.

While incumbents' movement into the space provides validation, it also threatens startup robo-advisors. However, in the last year, a notable shift has been occurring within robo-advisory startups. They are now adding the human touch to their services so they can cater to those with more assets and upsell HENRYs as they move up the economic ladder. For example, Betterment and Ellevest now provide solutions offering one-on-one access to one of their certified financial planners. Money is personal, so offering people more options ranging from fully automated to a hybrid of humans and automation provides more comfort to people trusting these firms with their assets.

Krawcheck believes that over time, there will be fewer and fewer people and more technology in wealth management companies. She believes, "moving from financial advisors to a digital offering is challenging. People really hate to give up clients. It's better to start with digital and add people."

It is still too early to say if robo-advisory services can provide strong returns; however, it's an easy way for people to start investing instead of doing nothing at all.

Insurtech

In the last few years, the insurance industry has begun to undergo long-needed innovation and as a result, has become a popular area of investment for venture capital firms. Investors poured $3.2 billion into insurtech startups in 2018 alone.[20] The key drivers of insurtech innovation are more data sources and an increasing focus on creating a positive customer experience to drive customer loyalty. Both insurtech startups and established insurance companies are attempting to reach millennials, who are starting to make their first insurance purchases. Brendan Dickinson points out that "millennials are less engaged with insurance out of anybody who's previously been in that age range. All of the carriers are standing at the edge of this oasis in the desert but they see it slowly shrinking because nobody likes them so they're all really concerned." As a result, insurtech startups are targeting this market and hoping to gain millennials' trust through increased transparency and positive customer experiences.

The insurance industry is long overdue for modernization; for example, it is still mostly built on legacy systems from the 1960s and 1970s. In addition, buying insurance is a universal experience — a universally negative experience. Steve Lekas, CEO and co-founder of Branch, a home and auto insurance company, says that what ultimately caused him to found an insurtech startup after a career in insurance was the "recognition that my customers hated me and their belief that I was intrinsically evil." These factors have created an immense opportunity for insurtech startups to emerge.

20. https://www.cbinsights.com/research/report/fintech-trends-q1-2019/

New Data Strategies

In the insurance industry, data is essential; it helps insurance companies understand customer behavior, predict trends, underwrite, and optimize pricing. As a result, insurtech companies are employing an array of new data sources and optimizing their algorithms to offer improved pricing. Spencer Lazar, responsible for Special Projects at insurtech startup Lemonade and a former partner at General Catalyst that invested in insurtech startups such as Lemonade and Shift Technologies, described to me that what drew him to insurtech "was the explosion of new data sources used for underwriting and claims processing; opportunity to disintermediate legacy agent-based customer acquisition models; and new distribution opportunities stemming from the proliferation of ecommerce and software in all parts of the economy." Dickinson echoes that he initially became interested in insurtech because "there's a host of new data sources that can be used to make the products more efficient." Ingesting and analyzing multiple data streams requires insurance companies to invest in data analytics capabilities and resources. It becomes a virtuous data cycle: the more data that insurance companies can ingest, the better they can understand risk at an individual level and provide more personalized, tailored solutions, even offering tips to customers on how to make their behavior less risky. Improved solutions lead to better customer engagement and more optimal pricing, leading to customers being more willing to share more data to continue to get better products and pricing.

This model is in contrast to the typical insurance model, which pools people's risk and requires those individuals to pay a certain price as a group. Lekas explained that the data that is most useful to an insurance company "is the data that helps segment risk. That data is not always very apparent on why it segments risk exactly and it's most frequently a proxy for behavior." Being able to layer an individual's risk profile, along with the segment they are in, should reduce risk and therefore make pricing more competitive. The more data insurance companies can collect, the more accurate their risk profiling will be. While unique insights into underwriting are essential for insurtech startups, Lazar points out that "the hard thing is you don't really know in some cases how well you've done in that regard for some time because of the delays that often occur between purchasing a policy and making a claim."

The cross-section of Internet of Things (IoT) devices and big data is pivotal to helping the insurance industry innovate. There is now an inundation of real-time data that insurtech companies can use to better understand their customers from devices such as cell phones, watches, and cars. People's lives are increasingly connected by IoT devices in all areas of their lives: at home, in their cars, at work, and on or near their bodies. McKinsey states in its report There's No Place Like [a Connected] Home that as of 2017, there were 29 million connected homes in the US, up from 22 million the year before. The insurance industry is prioritizing IoT data because it empowers them to take a more proactive stance in preventing risk. For example, insurance companies can provide tips and incentivize homeowners to switch their alarms on and stoves off. Some auto insurance companies now offer telematics where consumers can have a device in their car feed information to insurance providers. This data enables auto insurers to create a full picture of consumers' driving behavior and map out various associated risks. Devices in cars could also alert drivers to a potential breakdown or other risks. Research in Accenture's report Technology Vision for Insurance 2017 found that 64% of people wanted more personalized advice and that 57% were willing to share more personal information to get additional benefits. This shows a clear understanding of an exchange of data for more value. In other words, the relationships between insurance companies and their customers have evolved into partnerships.

Incumbents are also taking advantage of this trend. Progressive offers a solution called Snapshot that provides usage-based automotive insurance and it has collected over 25 billion miles of driving data across its usage-based insurance solutions.[21] In 2018, Progressive rolled out a new solution, Smart Haul, a usage-based insurance offering for commercial truck drivers. If drivers share driving data from their electronic-logging devices (ELD) with Progressive, the insurance company promises a minimum of 3% savings on their insurance.

---

21. https://progressive.mediaroom.com/2019-01-17-new-progressive-data-shows-putting-the-phone-down-correlates-to-lower-insurance-claims

MetLife has a solution called My Journey® that tracks drivers' behavior on the road and provides feedback to improve driving and insurance rates.

Insurance companies are also using computer vision to gather more insightful data. For example, Lekas says that roof quality and age are very important factors in understanding homeowners' investment in their homes and houses' ability to withstand storms. Analyzing roofs using computer vision becomes a valuable data input in pricing home insurance. More broadly, Lekas believes there is "tremendous opportunity within imagery interpretation through computer vision because there's so much data about assets that hasn't been available."

A New Customer Experience

As in other areas of fintech, customers are increasingly demanding a positive, frictionless experience from insurance companies, in contrast to the status quo which is often associated with dread and complex paperwork. Insurtech startups have the advantage of starting as customer-centric models. Dickinson believes that for insurtech startups, building trust is not as tough as it might seem: "when you're operating in a market where the incumbents have a Net Promoter Score below cable companies, you've got some leeway. You've got some opportunity." Winning clients over in the first point of contact is key and will create customer stickiness. Lazar recommends three steps to creating a positive customer experience:

"One way is to start with a brand that speaks in a language consumers actually understand. The second thing is to use technology and distribution channels that they're familiar with — whether that's chat, mobile, or desktop web. The third is to over-invest in services in the beginning because people have had such bad experiences historically that their expectations are very low."

"On demand" or "pay-as-you-go" insurance is a prime example of a customer-centric framework in insurance. It marks a dramatic shift in the insurance industry from the "set and forget" approach. This hyper-personalized approach to insurance is based on when people are actually using their assets and when they are therefore at risk. For example, Slice Labs protects property only when homeowners rent out their houses. If they are not renting out their homes frequently, this ends up being cheaper than insuring their homes for the full year or for multiple years. In the article "Will On-Demand Insurance Become Mainstream," KPMG suggests that digital natives expect flexible, dynamic options at their fingertips instead of fixed plans that are difficult to commit to for a long period of time. They state that 93% of millennials would be interested in purchasing on-demand insurance if prices were the same. Consumers pay a premium for the convenience of on-demand insurance as a per unit purchase is more expensive than it would be under an annual policy.[22] While insurance companies sacrifice some customer stickiness with this model, they make a higher margin. One potential issue is adverse selection: customers might only activate their insurance if they are in risky situations. Lekas also believes that on-demand insurance creates friction for users because it forces users to remember that they need to insure themselves in specific instances; however, he acknowledges that "consumers will jump through a lot of hoops to get a cheaper price" when the insurance is compulsory like auto insurance.

Some incumbent insurance companies are shifting their approaches to become more customer-centric but it is more difficult for them because it is not in their companies' DNA the way it is for startups. According to PwC's Global InsurTech Report — 2017, 94% of respondents in the insurance industry identified customer engagement as one of the two most important trends in their field. Research conducted by Bain in its report Customer Behavior and Loyalty in Insurance: Global Edition 2016 shows that insurers want to have more touch points with their customers and own the customer relationship to foster customer loyalty. Bain points out that compared to other financial institutions, like retail banks, insurance companies do not have frequent points of contact with their customers, a problem which has been further exacerbated

---

22. https://home.kpmg/xx/en/home/insights/2017/09/will-on-demand-insurance-become-main-stream.html

by an increase in online aggregators of insurance policies. A customer-centric model helps build consumer trust, which is essential for brands, because as Lekas points out, in insurance, "there's nothing tangible, there's only a promise" that consumers will be covered when something bad happens. From a practical standpoint, he encourages consumers to go beyond branding and understand the financial stability and solvency risk of insurtech startups to make sure they can actually pay their claims.

When Lazar was analyzing insurtech startups at General Catalyst, he carefully studied customer strategies of emerging players, looking to companies with both differentiated and durable advantages and felt that "given the balance sheets and experience of the incumbents, if startups haven't thought through how they can break through the noise, it's going to be tough." He pointed to Lemonade as finding early success in customer acquisition by having unique partnerships with nonprofits, whereby they donate unclaimed money to nonprofits picked by customers. Lemonade's partnerships with nonprofits resonate with millennials due to their social mission. Lazar also finds that it is helpful to "partner with channel partners or agencies where you can borrow their brand halo. Another way to acquire customers could be in the caliber of team you've recruited to showcase that you take underwriting, claims, customer service, and technology seriously." Lazar also suggests "building into core workflows, such as property management systems to help landlords manage their tenants' compliance with things like renters' insurance." Offering product extensions can also work. For example, Fabric is a life insurance company that offers free wills to help with customer acquisition.

Insurtech startups can also take advantage of major operational efficiencies in the age of automation. Brian Hirsch believes that insurance agents are becoming relics of the past. Lekas likes to tell people, "you know the agent that you've never spoken with or met — that person roughly costs you 15% per year every year for your whole life and that adds up to thousands and thousands of dollars." Significantly reducing the number of agents enables insurers to pass on some of the savings to their customers. In addition, Lekas believes that Branch's automated solution will be able to provide superior insights into questions like how much insurance customers should be purchasing. That being said, some consumers prefer to sacrifice some savings and automation to consult with agents, who can provide a level of comfort and understanding when evaluating insurance products. The human relationship can serve to ingrain trust in insurance consumers.

Lekas believes that insurtech startups that employ automation and optimized algorithms that enable them to pass on savings to their customers are destined to grow:

> "I know that an insurance company with a cheaper insurance product will be an insurance company that will grow because that's a very obvious consumer desire. I think that there is inherent good in that because if you believe in the economic benefit of insurance, then making it cheaper should make it available to more people so this will be a way to create value for society as well as to grow a really important and awesome business."

From a regulatory standpoint, insurtech startups can vary in respect to their sales strategy, underwriting capabilities, control over transactions, and amount of risk they bear. There are lead-generation operators, who help create interest in certain insurance products and send those customers to agents or online agencies. Managing general agents (MGAs) can underwrite insurance policies so they have more power over who to insure. Carriers have their own insurance products that they sell and underwrite. Few insurtech startups have obtained underwriting capabilities but those that do, do so to create a barrier to entry. Lazar said of Lemonade, which is an insurance carrier:

> "Lemonade did consider becoming an MGA and the decision was driven by a desire to control their own destiny. When MGAs start, they're small and when they're small that means they're insignificant to their carrier partners or reinsurance partners. We never wanted a scenario where our executive sponsor could get fired at one of those

organizations and the mothership would lose interest in what we're doing, compromising our business. We also wanted to underwrite policies in a unique way that would not conform to the standards of another carrier, so Lemonade had to file their own papers and get those approved. Entrepreneurs should be leaders on the regulatory front, which can create additional barriers to entry."

Security

Similar to other fintech verticals, data security is a major challenge the insurance industry is facing. Companies in other fintech verticals own customer data such as credit and transaction history. Insurance companies can also have health records and other very sensitive personal information. In 2015, Anthem experienced a data breach, compromising 79 million people's health records. As insurers aim to collect more data, such as from IoT devices, there are more entry points for hackers. Lekas recommends that insurance companies "treat personal data as if it's hot to the touch and to automate people out of processes that require them to see or interact with data. It can't be something you figure out on the back-end; it's got to start in the architecture."

The Incumbents

More than in other fintech verticals, incumbent insurance companies are working to partner with insurtech startups.[23] Insurance companies generally do not view insurtech startups as substantial threats; rather, they still view other established insurance companies as their main competitors. Therefore, collaborating with innovative insurtech startups is only going to benefit them. Startups that are left behind without incumbent partners will lose out on access to billions of data points and will have to slowly and carefully build out their own resources.

Many insurance companies are forming venture arms to invest in innovative startups. Interestingly, Accenture revealed in its report The Rise of Insurtech that only 17% of the investments by the 75 top insurers were insurtech

23   https://www.pwc.dk/da/publikationer/2017/pwc-fintech-2-0.pdf

companies. The remainder were in areas that would help insurance companies become more competitive, such as tools in analytics or data protection. For example, New York Life Ventures has invested in startups such as H2O. ai, which aims to democratize machine learning, and Skycure, a cybersecurity company for mobile defense that was acquired by Symantec.

Some insurers are even launching their own startups in-house, such as Allstate, which started Arity, a transport analytics startup. MassMutual helped launch a life insurance startup internally, Haven Life, to target millennials. Incumbents are also holding developer contests; State Farm, for example, held a contest to find a machine learning solution that used dashboard cameras to detect and prevent drivers from becoming distracted.

Incumbents are taking note of innovation and finding ways to actively integrate these solutions into their own offerings. Insurtech startups have the opportunity to find ways to collaborate with incumbent insurance companies or strike out on their own to reach the underserved millennial market as these customers make their first forays into insurance. The opportunity for incumbents and startups to build relationships with each other and fortify one another is massive and those that do will see dividends.

Concluding Thoughts

Tackling the financial industry as a startup is no easy feat. The combination of regulations, security risk, and massive incumbents make this a uniquely challenging industry for startups to make headway. However, improving technology, gaining access to more data, and approaching consumers in a transparent, approachable way while navigating the areas of regulations and security are good starts. Working with financial institutions can provide more scale, customers, and capital than any other relationship will, bestowing a tremendous advantage on startups that are able to forge these key relationships. While these relationships are in the early days, they are likely to provide additional strength and resources to startups in pivotal moments such as economic downturns. There will be startups without these relationships that survive but additional support will help catapult select startups even higher.

Building a startup is difficult. Building a fintech startup is really difficult. But, entrepreneurs need to dream big and run with their vision. I'd like to leave you with these parting words, which Tala CEO and Founder Shivani Siroya said is the best piece of advice she has received: "Be bolder than you think your vision is."

GRACE CHOU
FELICIS VENTURES

In a not so distant past, a family of five would often spend a weekend at the local shopping mall. The parents would shop for linens at Macy's and household appliances at Sears. The children would rush to Game Stop or Toys R' Us for the latest video game or doll. Together, they would shop for pet food at PetSmart, buy clothes from department stores, and read books together at Barnes & Noble. On their way home, the family visited a Blockbuster to rent a movie and a local bodega to buy their ice cream. Less than two decades later, consumer behaviors and values have drastically changed. Technology has led to a swift downfall of several iconic American consumer companies, while creating massive opportunities for consumer-focused entrepreneurs in the $400 billion US consumer market.

How does the average person live, eat, spend, save, travel, sleep? Consumer brands are obsessively focused on answering this question and targeting customers with specific products tailored to make their lives 'better.' Consumer trends and behaviors are difficult to predict and as technology continues to evolve, so do our brand loyalties and preferences. Venture capital funds have capitalized on changing consumer behaviors since the advent of the Internet and supported lucrative brands such as Stitch Fix, Warby Parker, Everlane, Bonobos, Away, Casper, and Dia & Co, as well as massive companies driving the shift in consumer and business behavior, such as Amazon and Shopify. Given the myriad of opportunities and new brands started every day, developing an understanding of consumer as an investment area is complex and daunting. Grace Chou, an investor with Felicis Ventures (a venture capital fund with investments in consumer companies such as Warby Parker, Dollar Shave Club,

Bonobos, Shopify, and Twitch), is an ideal investor to tackle this investment area given her professional experience and unique insight into consumer patterns and behavior.

Grace joined Felicis Ventures after spending a number of years at Walmart eCommerce, an organization that has evolved formidably against the 'Amazon threat.' At Walmart eCommerce, Grace focused on partnerships and investments and developed an expertise in eCommerce and retail. Grace saw the rise of digitally native brands and worked on business model innovations around the world, including the development of Walmart's investment thesis for India. Internationally, Grace led Walmart's $50 million investment in Dada (China's largest on-demand grocery platform) and worked on key initiatives including the Walmart/JD.com partnership. She also worked on acquisitions across a range of technology startups (Adchemy, Luvocracy, PunchTab, Stylr, Yumprint) and transformative eCommerce brands (Jet, Moosejaw, Modcloth, Shoebuy). These experiences have informed a thesis on consumer investing that proves valuable to founders and investors operating within this industry.

In this chapter, Grace shares her perspective on the concept of the jigsaw puzzle I touched on in earlier chapters. She discusses how diverging factors and forces — the cost of starting a retail brand, buying customer loyalty, the Amazon effect, the retail apocalypse — create a perfect storm for consumer entrepreneurs to build game-changing businesses. She also takes a look at the business models that consumer entrepreneurs have stress tested with venture financing, offering entrepreneurs unique insights and anecdotes on launching the next brand that will win over consumers' hearts and minds.

CONSUMER TRENDS AND INVESTING
Grace Chou, Felicis Ventures

Recent History of Consumer Technology

The proliferation of the Internet and mobile phones has been the biggest driver of transformation for consumer products and services over the last two decades. In consumer technology, we saw the rise of eCommerce and direct-to-consumer brands, instant gratification and on-demand services enabled by mobile phones, the impact of social media on commerce and identity, and automated buying and replenishment enabled by subscription services.

Did you buy that online? The rise of eCommerce and direct-to-consumer brands

As retail shifted online, Amazon grew quickly to become the dominant player in eCommerce. eCommerce comprised $258 billion of US retail sales in 2018, with Amazon commanding 49% of the online market (almost 7x the share of next closest competitor eBay). The growth of Amazon meant customers became increasingly trusting and comfortable with making their purchases online. In parallel, we also started seeing the rise of direct-to-consumer ("d2c") brands, as billions of dollars in venture capital started pouring into these companies. Many of these brands have already transformed how shopping is done for entire categories by re-imagining the whole shopping experience — ranging from Warby Parker for eyewear, Third Love for bras, Casper for mattresses, Glossier for beauty, to many more. With the Internet, new brands could reach customers directly and control the entire shopping journey. The barrier of entry to launching a new brand lowered significantly as it became easy to outsource or leverage software tools for the entire stack needed to launch a business — from setting up a website, creating content, developing products, reaching customers, and other retail operations. By cutting out the retail middlemen, brands also had the ability to change their margin structure by going direct-to-consumer and direct-to-manufacturer, owning every step of their production and distribution process while providing an end-to-end brand experience for customers.

By going direct-to-consumer, startup brands were able to fundamentally disrupt large incumbents that have historically dominated their product categories for decades. Especially as millennials came to command significant buying power, they resonated with new brands that valued transparency, quality, personality, and emotional connection. By being agile and working closely with customers, d2c brands are often able to bring products to market in weeks

— while it can take months, or even years, for incumbent players to do the same. Moreover, d2C brands are able to create authentic relationships with their customers and gain direct access to customer data in ways that incumbent brands cannot (example: why Unilever acquired Dollar Shave Club.) Consumers are no longer passive recipients of pre-packaged experiences. A new bi-directional brand-to-consumer relationship emerged as brands could quickly and thoughtfully integrate consumer feedback and data deeply in the product development process.

Meanwhile, we saw many closures of physical stores in the US — this phenomenon was coined by many as "The Retail Apocalypse." However, the truth of the matter was that retail wasn't dying — it was evolving. In fact, total retail spend has continued to grow steadily in the US, from $4.35 trillion in 2012 to $5.35 trillion in 2018. One metric that people often overlook is that while online retail has been growing rapidly, even today it still only accounts for 10% of total retail spend (up from 6% in 2014.) Physical retail wasn't undergoing a one-dimensional apocalypse; it was just evolving to meet the needs of the changing consumer, so certain formats were beginning to decline as they were no longer relevant for the modern consumer. Consumers no longer needed to seek assortment in stores when they could easily find endless options online (especially with two-day shipping by Amazon.) Instead, the role of stores began shifting to be about experience, brand, and emotional connection.

Steph Korey, CEO of Away, calls her physical stores "physical billboards." The next generation of physical stores are no longer simply places to find assortment or restock on goods — they are physical expressions and stories of culture. For example, Winky Lux's beauty pop-ups are referred to as "The Museum of Ice Cream" for beauty — not only are consumers willing to pay an entry fee to enter the stores, they inadvertently assume the role of "nano-influencers," Instagramming their experiences within the stores and sharing the brand with their peers on social media. For brands expanding into physical "experiences," the number of Instagram mentions and tags per store is a critical store metric in context of customer acquisition. These brands are creatively addressing the problem of rising customer acquisition costs (CACs) on social media by building creative concepts that double as indirect ways to advertise on Instagram via user-generated content.

What we saw in store closures was also a bifurcation of retail, which was likely a direct reflection of increasing income bifurcation in the US. What this means is that over the last few years, retail at both ends of the spectrum (premium and price/value-centric) have continued thriving while retail in the middle has declined. Premium grew 80% and price-based grew 37%, but "balanced retail" only grew 2%. It is unfortunate that over 40% of Americans today struggle to cover a $400 emergency expense, which enables value-centric retailers like Walmart to continue growing and thriving across America. Walmart has also been investing heavily in new technology innovation and experiences — from incubating new brands, making transformative eCommerce acquisitions, launching in-store tech, to creating new shopping experiences in virtual reality Internet of Things (IoT), as well as creating verticalized experiences for different categories.

Going forward, we will continue to see retail transform. More spend will continue shifting online. Direct-to-consumer brands will be able to cater to specific customer needs and preferences. Outdated, assortment-focused retail experiences will keep declining, as experience-based retail formats rise. Many d2c brands are already experimenting with and setting up new store fronts — from Winky Lux's "Museum of Ice Cream for Beauty" pop-ups, to Neighborhood Goods, which is building a next generation of shopping malls, to Casper's storefronts with nap pods delivering an "experience" around sleep, to Floravere's first-of-its-kind bridal concept store... the list goes on.

Where's my Uber? The need for instant gratification and the rise of on-demand

The dramatic adoption of mobile led to new consumer expectations of "instant gratification." The phone was the new magical device for near-instant fulfillment of information, products, and services. Hyper-connectivity enabled marketplaces to self-organize quickly and effectively, creating network effects and resulting in the success of on-demand service startups like Uber, Postmates, Instacart, and Wag.

The increased transparency of everyone being online shifted the consumer expectation and definition of ownership, forming a new type of "sharing economy." While one may have never felt comfortable with getting in a stranger's car or sharing your house with other people a decade ago, now it would feel totally strange to live in a world without Uber or Airbnb. Today's consumer has grown comfortable with sharing someone's car (Uber, Lyft), opening up her home (Airbnb, Homeaway), sharing living space (Common, Bungalow), letting others in your home (Amazon Keys, Wag), to sharing people's homes for childcare (Weecare, Wonderschool). Successful startups in this space have focused on protecting trust, prioritizing customer support, and growing and balancing supply/demand while focusing on unit economics and business fundamentals.

How many followers do you have? The rise of the social media influencer

As consumers began spending exponentially more time on their phone, a new concept of our "digital identities" formed. The Internet became an open place for us to not only find information, but also to connect, create, and share via social media. Facebook had 1 million monthly users in 2014, growing to 2.3 billion in 2018 — representing every 1 in 3 people on the planet. Instagram had 30 million users when Facebook acquired it for $1 billion in 2012 — today, it has over 1 billion active users. An average American spends a whopping 2 hours and 22 minutes per day on social apps like Facebook, YouTube, Instagram, and Snap. These platforms have become critical channels for brands to talk directly to their customers.

Social media influencers have become the new curators of today's generation, capable of building powerful and direct relationships and emotional connection with millions of loyal followers. Influencer-led brands like Emily Weiss' Glossier, Kylie Jenner's Kylie Cosmetics, and Rihanna's Fenty Beauty have demonstrated unique capabilities to scale extremely quickly, by leveraging the theme of "people as the new brands" and by delivering an authentic voice and relationship with their loyal, cult-like following. (As a point of reference, Kylie Cosmetics reached $420 million in sales in 18 months directly through her Instagram account.)

Can I subscribe to that? How subscription businesses automate buying and replenishment

There is a "subscription" you can get for most things these days — whether it's for personalized product discovery (Stitch Fix, Ipsy, FabFitFun), replenishment (Dollar Shave Club, Blue Apron, Function of Beauty, Farmer's Dog, Simple Contacts), or content access (Netflix, Spotify, Hulu, Calm, Headspace).

From an investor's standpoint, the advantage of subscription (or subscription-like) business models implies highly recurring and predictable revenue, and that brands only need to spend money to acquire a customer once for multiple downstream purchases (assuming strong retention.)

Successful companies in the space have adopted subscription as a primary business model not because it makes the most business sense from a recurring revenue standpoint, but because it actually turns out to be the preferred way of shopping for consumers they serve — a means to an end, not the end itself. As Kirsten Green of Forerunner Ventures said, "I have never invested in a subscription company. I have only invested in companies where subscription turned out to be the best way to serve the customer."

Key Challenges Consumer Startups Face Today

Rising online CACs and the need to diversify customer acquisition channels

While it has become easier than ever to start a new consumer brand, distribution has become a new challenge for startups in the last few years.

The first wave of consumer startups was able to rise quickly by taking advantage of under-exploited digital marketing channels (e.g. Facebook/YouTube/Google) a decade ago. As a result, we saw the explosive growth of brands like Warby Parker, Glossier, Allbirds, etc. that reached $100+ million in revenues within only a few years.

However, today's consumer startups are experiencing a more matured landscape marked by new industry dynamics. Facebook and Google have duopolized online advertising spend — combined they captured 60% of total spend and contributed 90% of total advertising growth in the US last year. The combination of the explosion of d2c brands and increasingly concentrated channels means that the cost of reaching customers through these digital platforms has increased dramatically. While channels like Google and Facebook were "frontier channels" a decade ago, today they are becoming increasingly competitive, resulting in less effective ad spend. (For reference, Facebook CPM was $0.25 in 2014. In 2018, it grew to $12+). There were around 1 million advertisers on Facebook in 2014 — today, Facebook estimates there are 7 million advertisers on the social platform.

As a result, it is now easier than ever to start a brand, but costlier than ever to acquire customers on the dominant digital channels, and harder than ever to establish differentiation from category competitors while protecting defensibility from Amazon.

To succeed in this current landscape, thriving brands are thinking outside the box, diversifying marketing channels and exploring new frontier channels. For example, many GenZ-focused brands are finding success on less-exploited channels like Twitch and TikTok. Many are seeing success diversifying into the offline world — from podcasts, billboards, TV, to offline "Instagrammable stores." Successful founders need to treat customer acquisition as a data science problem constantly balancing and testing new channels.

Establishing product differentiation in a tidal wave of d2C brands

Besides the rising cost of customer acquisition on dominant digital platforms, the explosion of direct-to-consumer brands in each category has made establishing product differentiation more challenging. A quick scroll through your Instagram will surface dozens of similar direct-to-consumer brands in all different categories — from plants (The Sill, Bloomscape), vitamins (Ritual, Care/of, Zenamins), birth control (Pill Club, Nurx), fresh pet food (Farmer's Dog, NomNomNow, Petplate), shampoo (Function of Beauty, Prose), deodorant (Oars and Alps, Hawthorne, by Humankind, Miro), among numerous startups in other categories. Paying for customers on social media is no longer an effective way to scale a consumer business, as it is increasingly important to have true differentiation via unique customer value proposition, emotional connection, and community.

How to defend against Amazon

As mentioned before, Amazon dominates eCommerce today, accounting for ~50% of online retail spend in the US. It's hard for startups to compete based on price, assortment, or convenience against Amazon. However, it's also important to note that while Amazon is a meaningful threat, the giant also creates many opportunities for startups. This is because as Amazon innovates, it continues to educate and lift consumer expectations in terms of what is possible, as well as what/how they can buy online (e.g. 1-2 day shipping, 1-click buy, voice shopping through Alexa.) In time, this creates opportunities for brands as the consumer is constantly evolving and asking for more. While Amazon has been successful in bringing categories online and pushing the limits of what can be bought online, the opportunity for startups is well captured in this quote from Emily Weiss, CEO of Glossier: "I think Amazon really solved buying, but it killed shopping in the process." Shopping is not just about convenience and certainly not one-size fits all. As Amazon graduates into a mature incumbent (soon to be 26 years old), there is significant room for innovative founders and brands to re-imagine how shopping can be done in this new era.

Investor Perspectives: Areas of Opportunity

Below are a few areas of opportunity that investors in the space have been actively pursuing:

1. Underserved demographics

GenZ: The GenZ population is expected to comprise ~40% of total US consumers by 2020 — the size of this demographic is larger than millennials, and their spending power has come of age, holding $143 billion in direct buying power. While most consumer brands that have been built to date have been focused on millennials, this younger demographic is different in many ways. They grew up not knowing a life without phones, they don't like incumbent brands, they care deeply about social justice and gender equality / human rights and sustainable products. They're also on different channels (Instagram, TikTok, Twitch), shop at different places (Riley Rose, Urban Outfitters), and they resonate with different ways of storytelling/building a brand that incumbents cannot do themselves.

Examples of startups: Blume (personal care + mental health), Co—star (astrology app), Winky Lux (beauty), Downtoshop (mobile shopping)

Investor perspectives: GenZ consumers have an inherent distrust of incumbent, opaque brands and love co-developing products with brands. "Companies like Blume tap into their loyal communities to co-create new products in ways that incumbent CPG brands like P&G and Unilever cannot do themselves" — Victoria Treyger, Partner at Felicis Ventures

Seniors: In the US, the number of Americans 65+ is projected to double from 50 million to close to 100 million by 2060. One in five Americans are expected to be in retirement in the next 10 years. This has also been an overlooked demographic for startups with unique needs and preferences for consumer products and services.

Startup Examples: Mon Ami (matches seniors with college students for tasks and companionship), Honor (at-home care), ElliQ (robots), Togg and SafelyYou (sensors for senior care facilities), Totemic Labs (wearables)

Investor perspectives: "We need to think about the population in a more nuanced way in regard to products and services for seniors and ask questions such as — Who is making the purchase decision? How do they purchase differently? Who is using the product? How do they live and consume products differently?" — Nicole Quinn, Partner at Lightspeed

2. Consumer health

As telehealth regulations become increasingly laxer in the US, several telemedicine startups have emerged, making healthcare products more accessible. Simultaneously, there is an ongoing de-stigmatization of traditionally taboo categories. The healthcare industry is seeing a similar trend to commerce — the consumer is becoming increasingly empowered. There is a lot of opportunity to build trusted brands in this space focused on transparency, trust, accessibility, and experience.

Startup examples: Hims/Hers (prescription telemedicine), Pill Club/Nurx (birth control), Modern Fertility (at home fertility tests), Genneve (menopause care)

Investor perspectives: On modern fertility, "women spend much of their lives thinking about one of two things: how not to get pregnant or how to get pregnant. At the same time, these thoughts are often laced with nervousness, fear, confusion, and embarrassment. For the first time, armed with more insights and knowledge, women should be able to make more informed decisions, adjust the timing of these choices, and feel more confident in their reproductive and health journey." — David Wu, Partner at Maveron

3. Mental health

The topic of mental health is becoming increasingly important in the US. Today, 1 in 5 people have a diagnosable mental illness, and 1 in 20 people struggle with severe mental health in their everyday life. In the meantime, the stigma around mental health is dropping as millennials have driven the focus towards defining wellness as both physical and mental health. Many startups are helping to tackle this challenge — from diagnostics, therapeutics, to many consumer products and services.

Startup examples: Calm/Headspace (meditation), Octave/Two Chairs (next-generation therapy clinics), Woebot (CBT chat bot), Talkspace (online therapy), Alma Campus (WeWork for therapists)

Industry perspectives: "It does feel like a major societal shift. Just a few years ago no one talked about mental health, it was very much in the shadows. As more politicians talk about it, as the media treat it as something normal and healthy to do, more and more people step out of the shadows and into the light. We realize the brain is pretty much the most complex thing in the known universe, it's not surprising it goes wrong every now and then. To be able to talk about that and understand it is a very healthy and positive thing. It just feels like we're at the start. Fifty years ago, the wave began around physical fitness, jogging, aerobics, and now we're at the start of this new wave." —Acton Smith, co-founder of Calm

4. Pets

There are 75 billion dogs and 85 billion cats in the US. More households in America have a dog than a kid, and Americans spend $75 billion on pet care in the US every year. Dogs have become seen as family, and since many millennials are getting married older, they are adopting pets almost as "starter children." The industry is dominated by various incumbents (for example — pet food is dominated by Mars and Nestle, both 100+ year old companies.) Many categories are being re-imagined.

Startup examples: Good Dog (marketplace for breeders/shelters), Farmer's Dog (fresh subscription pet food), Rover/Wag (on-demand pet marketplaces), Fi (GPS dog collar), Small Door (next-gen vet clinic)

Investor perspectives: "Dogs have become a more and more important part of our culture, and, frankly, our day-to-day happiness, over the past few decades. Over $20 billion is spent on pet food annually in the US, and there is a trend towards healthy, premium food over the last decade. But the industry is plagued by issues with food safety and false marketing." — Nikhil Trivedi, Partner at Shasta Ventures

Impacts of Frontier Technologies

Perhaps because many investors seem to be waiting for the next platform/technology wave for the next wave of great consumer businesses to be built, AI assistants and virtual reality (VR)/ augmented reality (AR) seem to have been slower to see mass adoption than what some had hoped. That said, our AI assistants (Google Home, Alexa, Siri) are getting smarter, and while friction still exists, it's not hard to imagine a future where Alexa can enable zero-touch replenishment of everything we need in the home — either by us speaking to her or just by Alexa integrating with IoT devices within the home to automatically detect when things need to be restocked. More than 100 million Alexa devices have been sold to date. Startups like BluTag are building an AI platform that allows brands to build voice-commerce experiences. If voice does take off as a dominant platform for shopping, it will be interesting to think about how brands can better thrive in this ecosystem still controlled by the same giants

— Amazon, Google, Apple — with a much narrower discovery funnel, given search results on voice will be more singular and precise versus surfacing a breadth of products.

Another way that AI has already significantly impacted consumer businesses is in backend processes. For example, Stitch Fix uses a combination of AI and human stylists to deliver personalized fashion recommendations. Brands and retailers are starting to use AI chat bots for customer service and support. AI has also begun to transform the full stack of retail backend infrastructure, from product development, demand and inventory forecasting, marketing automation and analytics, to warehouse robotics for fulfillment.

AR/VR also has the potential to transform the future of shopping and consumer experiences. Several retailers have incorporated AR in the shopping experience (e.g. Ikea launched an AR tool to see how a product would look in your home virtually, Sephora launched a virtual makeup artist, Walmart acquired and incubated Spatialand for next-gen VR shopping experiences), but to date AR/VR has not made as big of an impact as many expected — with 3D content being part of the challenge. Khronos, the developer of OpenXR standard, has recently announced that it is working with a large group of retailers and tech companies to create universal 3D versions of products that can be suitable for AR and VR apps and other online 3D shopping platforms. It's exciting to think about what the potential is if / when VR takes off — as we continue to blur the line between physical and digital, what is the next generation of "omnichannel" and holistic shopping experiences? What if we can use VR to shop entire stores across the world? Startups like Emerge are even working on "VR touch," an experience for people to "touch" virtual objects they see. What if one day you can try on shoes from the comfort of your couch?

It's these kinds of questions that I think about and focus on as I look at the next wave of disruption in the consumer space.

MICHAEL RAAB
SINAI VENTURES

Apple, Facebook, Google, Amazon, Netflix, Hulu, and Spotify have forever changed the media and entertainment industry. Each of these technology companies, all once outsiders to Hollywood or the publishing world, has disrupted movie theatres and movie rental companies, music labels, book publishing and distribution, and continue to change the way consumers engage with content. New business models, applications, and platforms, such as subscription-video-on-demand (SVOD), mobile gaming, and virtual reality (VR) and augmented reality (AR) have grown in market size and value and threaten to steal market share from companies that have been providing entertainment to consumers for several generations. The media and entertainment industry is a fascinating one given it is how consumers all over the world interact with their mobile devices, share and express their creative interests, and spend most of their disposable income. In China, new forms of media and entertainment are emerging that include holographic imaging. In the US, a popular new model of entertainment is the 'choose-your-own-adventure' where TV shows, audiobooks, and podcasts allow the consumer to choose their own ending or storyline as opposed to passively listening to content. As new platforms and concepts emerge within media and entertainment, the opportunity and foresight for a genius founder to predict consumer interests is a meaningful endeavor.

As I emphasized in earlier chapters, the best investors are often those with the insider perspective, and Michael Raab, an investor with Sinai Ventures, has it in spades. Michael began his career at 20th Century Fox in brand and franchise management and eventually worked with the company's digital media division. Prior to joining Sinai Ventures, Michael spent time with the Digital

Consumer Group at Fox Networks, which focused on the future of television distribution for brands including FX, National Geographic, Fox Sports, and the Fox Broadcasting Network. This division built and managed viewing experiences across platforms and services and was charged with creating 21st Century Fox's direct-to-consumer strategy. Bringing this deep experience to Sinai Ventures, Michael has been responsible for investments in top media companies such as Luminary Media and Drivetime, while the fund itself has a history of investing in companies such as Pinterest.

Michael's take on the media landscape encapsulates the concerns and trends that are actively shaping the media industry in real time. Michael compiles the investments that prominent venture capital funds are making, and their specific theses around those investments, against the backdrop of industry changes. As a former insider to a media and entertainment conglomerate, Michael has a unique perspective on media investing that other venture capitalists do not. He understands the business models that work within this segment and shares what metrics founders should be pursuing when launching a media business in the current environment. Even beyond media and entertainment, the insight and lessons he shares will remain relevant for founders operating in any industry that is beginning to adopt frontier technology like virtual reality, augmented reality, and artificial intelligence.

INVESTING IN MEDIA & ENTERTAINMENT TECHNOLOGY COMPANIES
Michael Raab, Sinai Ventures

Global media and entertainment is a $2 trillion industry consisting of filmed entertainment (movies, television, digital video), audio (music, radio, podcasts), publishing (newspapers, magazines, digital publishers), and video games (console, PC, mobile, eSports). The United States represents a third of the global market — over $700 billion in annual revenue, and has traditionally produced the most prolific media assets, which are subsequently distributed around the world. Media, perhaps more than any other industry, has been radically transformed since the advent and mass adoption of the Internet. Prior to the Internet, the vast majority of media and entertainment content was produced and distributed by a select few gatekeepers: movie and TV studios, record labels, book publishers, and newspapers. This control was necessary, as the costs to produce and distribute content was extremely high and out of reach of the everyday citizen. In the past 20 years, the democratization of distribution technology and falling costs of content production have opened the proverbial floodgates and allowed "new" media companies to emerge. However, industry incumbents have thus far survived and adapted, relying on their high-quality (and expensive) talent networks and capital advantages while ramping up investments in promising media startups.

Investing in media startups is a risky gamble, as content is highly subjective, and it's difficult and expensive to produce quality at scale. In fact, entertainment is a hits-driven industry (much like venture capital), where investments in a few "homerun" projects yield outsized returns, covering losses on a majority of other investments. Some venture capital firms explicitly avoid media investments, and founders I've spoken with have expressed with frustration that "Most VCs don't understand media." The truth is, the media industry is a complicated ecosystem, still dominated by a small number of corporate behemoths that are growing even larger with recent mergers and acquisitions. Today, the incumbents continue to have significant advantages over potential disruptors which can be simplified into two categories: 1) talent and 2) capital. The soul of the media and entertainment industry is the talent: writers, journalists, developers, performers, and directors who conceive of new ideas for projects and execute the creation of them. This talent is traditionally supported and guided by high-paid professionals at studios, labels, and publishers whose jobs are to shepherd projects to commercial viability and maintain close relationships with talent. As demand and competition for quality content have increased in recent years due to the on-demand nature of the Internet, prolific creators have commanded record financial incentives, making it even more capital-intensive to produce premium content — a significant barrier to entry for newcomers.

Technologies and innovations that have driven change in media in the 21st century have been streaming video infrastructure, smartphones / mobile video, cloud storage, direct-to-consumer subscriptions / content paywalls, and live streaming. These shifts have primarily affected the distribution and consumption of media, as consumers have a record number of content sources and platforms to choose from.

Recent, Successful Startups in Media & Entertainment

Interestingly, the most successful new media companies to emerge in the past 20 years all found ways to work directly with incumbents, often utilizing their premium content to build audiences and users, rather than creating original content from scratch at inception. This strategy of using proprietary new distribution channels to distribute third-party premium content rewarded Netflix (founded in 1997, IPO in 2002, $154 billion market cap), Spotify (founded in 2006, IPO in 2018, $22 billion market cap), Roku (founded in 2002, IPO in 2017, $10.2 billion market cap), and BAMTech (spun out of MLB Advanced Media in 2015, majority stake acquired by Disney in 2017 at a $3.75 billion valuation), which are some of the most valuable new media and entertainment companies over the past two decades.

Reed Hastings founded Netflix in 1997 with the vision of delivering movies over the Internet, a product the company wouldn't launch for another decade — over five years after its IPO in 2002. From the beginning, Hastings realized two things: 1) it would require content from major studios to make a compelling consumer proposition; and 2) this content would be relatively expensive (for a startup.) So, in the meantime, he built a massive DVD-rental-by-mail service, raising over $100 million in venture funding before IPOing in 2002. In his initial meeting with Ted Sarandos (now Chief Content Officer) in 1999, Hastings reportedly relayed his vision by explaining: "Postage rates are going to keep going up and the Internet is going to get twice as fast at half the price every 18 months. At some point those lines will cross, and it will become more cost-efficient to stream a movie rather than to mail a video. And that's when we get in." Hastings was then able to license streaming rights from major studios, which viewed the revenue as incremental to their bottom line and didn't foresee the massive change in consumption that Netflix was heralding. Always one step ahead, Reed additionally foresaw that studios would eventually pull their content from the platform in order to offer competitive products and began producing original content in 2013. In 2019, Netflix will spend $15 billion on content, reaching well over 700 original series and releasing 80+ original films in an attempt to remove their dependence on third-party content from Disney, WarnerMedia, and other suppliers. As of May 2019, Netflix has a market cap of $154 billion.

Daniel Ek and Martin Lorentzon founded Spotify in Sweden in 2006. Ek, having experienced the ability to access the entire world's music catalog through Napster, realized that "you can't put the genie back in the bottle," and believed that this on-demand access would eventually prevail in some form. At a time when music labels were combative with and threatened by any music download or streaming service, Ek found a way to de-risk their cooperation with Spotify: he guaranteed them the equivalent of one year's worth of revenue to launch in the Swedish market and prove the model. Spotify launched successfully in Sweden in 2008, later gaining the attention of Sean Parker, the co-founder of Napster, who invested in the company through his role at Founders Fund in 2010. Parker joined Spotify's board and personally negotiated with Warner and Universal Music Group on behalf of Spotify, which launched in the US in 2011. After completing a direct listing on the New York Stock Exchange in April 2018, the company has a market cap of $22 billion as of May 2019.

BAMTech, the video streaming infrastructure platform originally pioneered by MLB's Advanced Media Group to stream MLB baseball games went on to take on third-party clients beginning in 2005, including CBS' March Madness, The WWE Network, HBO Now, Playstation Vue, PGA Tour Live, NHL Live, MLS Live, and Hulu Live TV. After officially spinning out of MLB Advanced Media in 2015, Disney acquired a controlling stake in the company in 2017 at a valuation of $3.75 billion. Today, Disney is utilizing BAMTech's streaming infrastructure technology to launch Disney+, their forthcoming direct-to-consumer product set to launch in November 2019.

Other notable media technology companies pioneering distribution technology relied on someone other than incumbent media conglomerates to produce content: consumers themselves. YouTube, founded in 2005, enabled anyone to upload videos to its platform, and was quickly acquired by Google in 2006 for $1.65 billion. Twitch, spun off from Justin.tv in 2011, enabled video gamers to live-stream their gameplay, and was acquired by Amazon in 2014 for $970 million.

21st Century Challenges and Learnings

Companies relying on original content and third-party distribution channels have had a tougher time reaching and sustaining scale. Founded in 2007, Zynga, the social and mobile video game studio made famous by "Farmville's" viral success on Facebook saw explosive growth — raising over $866 million in venture funding in just over four years. After IPOing in December 2011 at a valuation of $7 billion, the company has shrunk to a market cap of $5.7 billion as of May 2019. Ventures focused primarily on advertising-supported business models have not fared well compared to subscription businesses. Native digital publishers have yet to exit with valuations over $1 billion, and the most successful exits occurred as acquisitions between 2010-2015. Business Insider (founded in 2007) was acquired by Axel Springer in 2015 for $442 million. The Huffington Post (founded in 2005) was acquired by AOL in 2011 for $315 million. The Bleacher Report (founded in 2007) was acquired by Turner Broadcasting in 2012 for $175 million. Digital publishers that weren't acquired during the heyday of Facebook's publisher-friendly algorithm have struggled in recent years. Mic Network (founded in 2012) was sold in a fire sale to Bustle for a reported $5 million in November 2018. Mic had previously raised over $60 million in venture capital, and was at one point valued over $100 million. Mashable (founded in 2005) was acquired by Ziff Davis in 2017 for under $50 million, after raising $46 million in venture funding and being valued at $250 million in an investment round led by Time Warner in 2016. Vox Media (founded in

2003 and last valued at $1 billion during a 2015 fundraising round) and Buzz-feed (founded in 2006 and last valued at $1.9 billion during a 2016 fundraising round) have both faced layoffs and significant revenue target misses since their last fundraises.

The struggles of these companies highlight the challenges facing new-comers in media and entertainment over the past decade and still today — FAANG. Facebook, Amazon, Apple, Netflix, and Google. Digital publishers that depended on ad-driven revenue models found that Google and Facebook sucked the proverbial air out of the room, amassing over 50% of the digital ad market. Amazon's impressive entrance into ad sales is also projected to skyrocket over the next few years. Further, the startups that depended on these platforms for distribution — Buzzfeed (Facebook), Zynga (Facebook), AwesomenessTV (YouTube / Google), and Maker Studios (YouTube / Google) — found that depending on third-party distribution channels could put their business at risk with the simple change of an algorithm; and they had no control over that. The two primary concerns of media companies — content and distribution — face tough competition by FAANG, which own the largest distribution networks in the world, and are now self-interested media companies, investing billions of dollars in original content annually.

Strategic Partners and Prolific Venture Investors in Media & Entertainment

Media startups face an interesting dynamic: since the vast majority of pre-mium content is still produced and distributed by a small number of legacy media conglomerates, there are few exit opportunities beyond scaling large enough to go public. Content isn't a defensible moat, as media companies have superior talent networks and capital to invest in popular content trends. Incum-bent media conglomerates also have active corporate development teams, and routinely invest in startups to either: 1) secure a stake in a high-growth media technology company; or 2) learn from savvier technology challengers to inno-vate on their own strategy.

Notable media investments and acquisitions by media incumbents include: In the past five years, AT&T has made mega-acquisitions of Time Warner (home of Warner Bros., HBO, TNT, and TBS, among other properties) and DirecTV. This combined entity also has investments in the video space (Quibi, Cheddar, Philo, Eko), gaming (Discord), and XR (Magic Leap, 8i, NextVR). The company's investments in the digital publishing space (Mic Media, Mashable, Refinery29) have struggled in recent years.

Disney has a fantastic track record of acquisitions in the 21st Century, most recently acquiring 21st Century Fox. Other acquisitions have included IP holders (Marvel Entertainment, Lucas Film) and production / distribution technology (Pixar, BAMTech). Disney also owns a controlling stake in Hulu, and has invested in Roku, Quibi, Caffeine, FuboTV, along with a handful of XR companies (Dreamscape Immersive, Jaunt, Within) and daily newsletter theSkimm. One of Disney (and Fox's) early digital media investments, Vice Media, has been written down in valuation significantly by the company in recent years.

In the past 15 years, Comcast NBCUniversal has acquired video distribution companies (Sky), content companies (Dreamworks Animation SKG, Oxygen Media) and advertising technology (Freewheel). Comcast has also invested in video companies (Quibi, Cheddar), gaming (Upcomer, FanDuel), digital publishers (Axios Media, NowThis Media, Vox Media, Buzzfeed, Re/Code, PopSugar), and XR companies such as Baobab Studios, NextVR, and AltSpaceVR.

While AT&T / Time Warner, Disney / 21st Century Fox, and Comcast NBCUniversal represent the most active strategic investors in media and entertainment companies, other media companies have also made select acquisitions and investments. This includes Discovery Networks (acquired Scripps Networks, Oprah Winfrey Network, HowStuffWorks; invested in Philo, FuboTV, Group Nine Media), Sony (acquired Funimation; invested in Quibi, Eko, and Soundcloud), Viacom (acquired Pluto TV, AwesomenessTV, and VidCon; invested in Quibi, Roku, DEFY Media), CBS (acquired Last.fm, CNET Networks; invested in Syncback), Lionsgate (acquired Starz; invested in Quibi, Immortals, Tubi TV, TellTale Games), MGM (acquired EPIX; invested in Quibi,

Dreamscape Immersive, Eko, Tubi TV), and AMC Networks (invested in Philo, FuboTV, Dreamscape Immersive, MiTu).

While some traditional venture capital firms avoid media-related investments altogether, there have been a handful of prolific VC investors in the sector.

Lerer Hippeau has been a leading investor in digital publishers over the past decade, with investments including Buzzfeed, Refinery29, Mic Media, Axios, Spanfeller Media Group, NowThis Media, Pando, Green Matters, Herb, Fatherly, and Thrillist Media Group among others. The firm is also investors in podcast studio Wondery and "monster" video company CryptTV.

Greycroft has seen exits for investments in Huffington Post, Pandora, AwesomenessTV, Elite Daily, and Maker Studios, and currently has investments in sectors such as gaming (Discord, Caffeine, FanAI, Gamer Sensei, Scopely), video (Overtime), XR (TheWaveVR, UploadVR, Omnivirt), and publishers (Axios Media, theSkimm).

New Enterprise Associates (NEA) has previously exited Snap, SAY Media, Upworthy, SPIN Media, Stitcher, and Tivo, and currently has investments in subscription podcasts (Luminary), video (Masterclass, Philo), publishers (The Players' Tribune, goop), and gaming (PlayVS).

Lightspeed Venture Partners previously exited investments in Sna, Flixster, IGN Entertainment, Mic Media, and eMusic, and is currently invested in video (Cheddar), gaming (HQ Trivia, Illumix), audio (Audius, Dose FM), and publishers (goop, Girlboss Media)

Kleiner Perkins Caufield Byres (KPCB) previously exited media-related investments in Spotify, Snap, Audible, Shazam, and Flipagram, and is currently invested in audio (Audius, Soundcloud), video tools (Kapwing), XR (Ubiquity6), and gaming (Blitz eSports).

Greylock Partners, which previously exited investments in Pandora and Music.ly (which merged with TikTok after being acquired by Bytedance), has current investments in gaming (Discord, Caffeine, Roblox), mobile video (Mammoth Media), and open publishing platform Medium.

RRE has invested in a variety of digital publishers (Business Insider, Huffington Post, Buzzfeed, TheOutline, Spanfeller Media Group, theSkimm), video (Vine), XR (TheWave VR, 8i), and blockchain technology (MediaChain).

Current Trends and Companies

The founders and startups currently gaining momentum in media are focused on delivering premium content via proprietary distribution channels, building subscription platforms, and creating production and engagement tools for new forms of media and entertainment. Digital publishers have faced difficulties in recent years, as content consumption has shifted to video and third-party platforms have prioritized their own content instead of promoting publishers. Today, the most common high-growth media startups are niche video platforms, content aggregators acting as virtual multichannel video programming distributors (vMPVD), original subscription video-on-demand (SVOD) platforms, gaming engines and platforms, podcast companies, and subscription publishers. It's unclear whether these challengers will succeed in the long term, as they face direct competition from tech and media giants that can afford to operate similar services as loss leaders and have massive distribution reach. Recent exits in the media and entertainment sector have included widely distributed, advertising-supported businesses such as Pluto TV, Cheddar, Gimlet Media, and Anchor. While these exits were generally viewed as "successful," they only amounted to $50-$350 million in exit valuations — decent, but by no means venture "home runs" for most investors.

Pluto TV (founded in 2013, $52 million raised) was acquired by Viacom for $340 million in January 2019. Pluto provides a widely distributed, free, advertising-supported video streaming platform with content from Warner Bros, Lionsgate, MGM, Bloomberg Media, and Cheddar, among others. The platform has over 12 million monthly viewers and partnerships with smart TV manufacturers. Pluto TV was founded in 2013 by Tom Ryan (former SVP of digital strategy & development at EMI Music) and Ilya Pozin (former founder and CEO at Coplex). Viacom, whose businesses have suffered in the age of SVOD, hopes to leverage Pluto to build world-class, ad-supported TV products.

Cheddar (founded in 2016, $54 million raised) was acquired by cable TV provider Altice USA for $200 million in April 2019. Cheddar is a subscription video platform that broadcasts live networks Cheddar (a business news network) and Cheddar Big News (a non-partisan general news network.) Cheddar was founded by Jonathan Steinberg, the former COO of Buzzfeed, and is available on a variety of over-the-top (OTT) platforms or through a $2.99/month direct-to-consumer subscription. Cheddar reportedly generated $27 million in 2018 revenue.

Spotify went on an acquisition spree in Q1 2019, acquiring three podcast-related companies: Gimlet Media (founded in 2014, $28.5 million raised) for around $230 million, Anchor.FM (founded in 2015, $14.4 million raised) for about $107 million, and Parcast (founded in 2016) for $56 million. Spotify's podcast company acquisitions were strategic — if the company can get listeners to more podcasts (and less music), it will pay lower royalties to music labels and publishers.

Notable venture-backed companies capitalizing on trends in technology and consumer behavior include Quibi, Luminary Media, fuboTV, Philo, Eko, Unity Technologies, Niantic, Discord, and Caffeine. These companies remain private, and although some have found traction, their success is still uncertain.

Quibi (short for "Quick Bites") is a new venture launched by Jeffrey Katzenberg (founder of Dreamworks SKG and former Chairman of Walt Disney Studios), and led by Meg Whitman (former CEO of HP and eBay) aimed at creating premium short-form mobile video content. Katzenberg knows first hand the difficulty and expense of creating premium original content, and thus raised an astounding $1 billion for Quibi from nearly every major studio before launching any product. Quibi is producing serialized, movie-length stories told in "bites" of 10-20 minutes. The platform is targeting consumers ages 25-35, and will have a two-tiered subscription, with the lower-priced tier supported by advertising. The company is reportedly looking to raise an additional $1 billion prior to its platform launch in April 2020.

Luminary Media raised nearly $100 million from investors before launching to the public in April 2019. Matt Sacks, a former Principal Investor at New

Enterprise Associates, founded Luminary in 2018 with the objective of bringing a better user experience to podcasts through an ad-free subscription platform with exclusive premium content. Luminary is taking a page out of Netflix's playbook, acquiring exclusive distribution rights to the most popular podcasts in order to create a compelling consumer proposition. By introducing a subscription model to the podcast industry, Luminary has the opportunity to multiply the annual revenues of podcasts, which are consumed by 48 million Americans on a weekly basis — yet only brought in $314 million in revenue in 2017.

fuboTV ($151 million raised) is a sports-focused vMVPD offering live streams from the NFL, MLB, NBA, and NCAA, as well as general entertainment from FX, AMC, CBS, and NBC, among others. Subscriptions to fuboTV start at $55/month, and the service has a reported 250,000 subscribers as of October 2018. fuboTV was founded in 2014, and Co-Founder and CEO David Gandler was previously a VP of Ad Sales at DramaFever, a subsidiary of Time Warner.

Philo ($83 million raised) is a vMVPD with subscription packages ranging from $16/month (40 channels) to $20/month (52 channels). Philo's CEO, Andrew McCollum, was a co-founder at Facebook. As of January 2018, the service had 50,000 subscribers.

The gaming industry is also in the midst of profound change and innovation, as technology companies like Google, Amazon, and Microsoft invest in cloud gaming infrastructure, allowing consumers to play games without owning a console or downloading any content. At the same time, publishers are experimenting with business models, such as offering subscriptions to a catalog of titles to users instead of charging a la carte. The video game technology companies that have gained the most traction and attention from investors are developer tools, game engines, communication and engagement technologies, and distribution platforms.

A recent development in media technology is that of interactive storytelling, or "choose-your-own-adventure" style television and films, most notably demonstrated by Netflix's release of Black Mirror: Bandersnatch in December 2018. Walmart has invested $250 million in a joint venture with Eko, an interactive media company founded in 2011, which previously raised over $36 million from investors including Sequoia Capital Israel, Intel, and MGM Studios. CtrlMovie, another interactive media startup, has partnered with 20th Century Fox to produce and distribute choose-your-own-adventure films in movie theaters, allowing moviegoers to vote on storylines.

Discord ($279 million raised, $2 billion valuation) was originally founded by Jason Citron in 2012 as Hammer & Chisel, a game development studio, but has since pivoted to create a voice and text chat platform for gamers. Discord is free to use, but for a $4.99 monthly subscription, users can access premium features like HD streams, custom emojis, and animated avatars. Streamers have utilized Discord to build and interact with their followings. Citron has commented on the importance of distribution: "Even if the product is right and the distribution channel exists, if you don't know how to find the distribution channel and get the word out in the right way, you can have the right product and it doesn't matter." As of May 2018, Discord reported having 130 million registered users.

Caffeine ($146 million raised to date) is a social broadcasting platform for gaming, entertainment, and creative arts. Caffeine was founded in 2016 by Ben Keighran (former Product Design Lead for Apple TV) and Sam Roberts (former Senior User Experience Designer at Apple.)

Despite the recent hype around eSports — organized competitive multiplayer games and leagues — it isn't yet clear which assets (if any) are of venture scale. Ownership of eSports leagues and teams are likely to be similar to professional sports teams — more valuable as trophy assets for high networth individuals than an entity that can continuously scale and create outsized returns. Further, eSports teams and leagues face something that physical sports haven't faced: they become irrelevant more quickly as new games are released. Fortnite was an unpredictable success that supplanted the popularity of other video games. As discussed above, investing in content (video game developers / publishers), is high risk — case in point: Telltale Games' recent fall from grace after initially being heralded as an innovative developer for its video game based on The Walking Dead.

While the growth-stage companies discussed above represent where investors have made their bets over the past few years, there is no guarantee of their ultimate success. New challengers, startups, and technologies are continually looking to build the next big thing, while investors are continually revising their theses on the sector and hoping to fund the next big thing.

Perspectives and Theses of Media Venture Investors

As venture investing is not a consensus sport (and in fact, contrarians are often the victors), I'd like to present multiple theses on investing in media and entertainment companies from venture capitalists.

First, my own perspective as an investor at Sinai Ventures:

As demonstrated by the past 20 years, the most valuable venture-scale media companies have three things in common — what I refer to as "the three Ts": technology, timing, and team. These companies realize that shifts in technology and consumer behavior are the major opportunities to creating multi-billion dollar companies, and that it's imperative to time your go-to-market correctly. It's very difficult to beat the incumbent media conglomerates at quality content, but if you can leverage their content (or convince consumers to produce content for you) on your proprietary distribution channel, you have an opportunity to acquire consumers on your platform and scale quickly. Reed Hastings knew Netflix streaming wasn't feasible in 1997 — so he built a company that was ready to take advantage of technological shifts in 2007. Daniel Ek took the risk of guaranteeing music labels their revenue to gain their trust and prove the subscription music streaming model. Since many people and companies usually have the same idea and vision, ultimately success or failure is determined by the execution of a strategy. The strength and experiences of the team behind an early-stage company is the best indicator of the likelihood of strong execution and ultimately, success.

My thesis in the media space is simple, and twofold: 1) Make something people are willing to pay for; and 2) Own distribution. Netflix, Spotify, Roku, YouTube, and Twitch are historic examples, with Unity Technologies, Discord, Caffeine, Drivetime Media, and Luminary as likely future success stories.

Other investors and venture firms have publicly commented on their own theses in the media and entertainment sector. Here is a sample of viewpoints:

Nicole Quinn, Partner at Lightspeed Venture Partners has publicly commented:

"Success in media isn't about churning out content to attract as many eyeballs as you possibly can. It never was. It's about finding the right audience. It's about building a community of common interest and then connecting its members to products and services. It's quality, not quantity."

"There isn't just one way to generate revenue for a media business. Advertising revenue alone may not be the way forward but there are multiple other ways in which media founders are able to grow and monetize their customer bases."

On the future of media: "We don't yet know what the next technology platform will be but we do know that people in any community will continue to buy things (physical, digital and experiential.) Companies will transcend across platforms if they have a true brand and a strong enough community."

Jon Goldman, Venture Partner at Greycroft has publicly commented:

On gaming: "If you're a media company and you're not taking gaming seriously, you're being shortsighted. Historically, there's just been a coterie of media executives who've looked at video games as options for merchandising. In their heart of hearts they really just want to make movies or TV. That's a mindset that, in terms of hours of engagement, the opportunities around social, around cooperative and competitive play — it's the most important form of media. You can't ignore it."

"I'm excited by the potential of that technology to allow multi-genre gaming. You really could have a game where people can drive and shoot and explore, where you combine all different types of gameplay. That would enable an even more social experience, where people could be involved in the game together, but play the genres they like, play the role that fits their interest."

Rick Yang, Partner at New Enterprise Associates (NEA) has publicly commented:

On NEA's investment in PlayVS: "As the venture industry searches for the next wave of consumer social innovation happening outside of the established players, we believe that gaming is at its core. Gaming has always been a huge market, with 2.2 billion gamers and $109 billion in revenue worldwide in 2017. But something's different now as it's become mainstream. A larger part of the population is now not only playing a wide range of games, they're also watching via Twitch and building strong communities via Discord. While the broader ecosystem is still nascent, it's clear to see the pieces coming together across consumers, publishers, brands, publishers, and the infrastructure required to take off. There are also more and more studies showing the benefits of gaming for kids and the multiple types of positive impacts: cognitive, motivational, emotional, and social."

NEA's blog states:

"The media world has undergone a dramatic shift over the course of the last decade, and the $40 billion sports media market is (finally) undergoing its transition from traditional to digital distribution. This tectonic shift creates huge opportunities for new entrants to compete for audience and market share in one of the most valuable and largely untapped markets for start-ups."

David Sze, Partner at Greylock Partners has publicly commented:

On their investment in Roblox: "Over the past several years, the gaming industry has undergone a transformation driven by technological advancements, such as mobile and cloud, and new gaming tools and platforms. Historically, consoles and PCs dominated the gaming market, but the rise of mobile and online games and live streaming services have ushered in a new generation of players and game creators. The traditional game company model relies on internal or contracted developers building titles to be published primarily as standalone games. The goal is to make hit games that can be turned into brands and franchises with many sequels or extensions (think Call of Duty, Star Wars Battlefront, or even Overwatch and Fortnite.) These models are heavy on top-down game design, expensive development costs and are hit franchise driven. Roblox is a completely different mode — more YouTube than Netflix. Roblox lets anyone create and play interactive, 3D multiplayer casual games. Individuals or indie developers can easily create and build new games for a massive community of Roblox users who are constantly looking for new content. And players can immerse themselves in the Roblox platform world of these games while also making social connections and playing with friends. Most importantly, Roblox functions as a social network — users can friend other users to interact and play games together. It's one of the core reasons many people decide to stay and spend time in Roblox. Players can play with friends and make new friends while discovering new games. And, as players become more engaged, more developers build for the platform, which in turn creates more game variety and more users. At Greylock, I've spent much of my career investing in companies and products that have strong network effects that connect people together. Roblox has built just that — a platform that garners a community across the world, which continues to organically grow month over month."

Bertelsmann Digital Media Investments' website states:

"BDMI partners with emerging digital media companies to share expertise, to make industry connections and to drive growth. We focus on three sectors:

Online Video: From over-the-top television to viral videos to social media stars, video continues to be a disruptive force in the media industry

Next Gen Media: Companies leveraging unique content, technology, social media and new business models to build loyal audiences

Publishing Technology: Companies that help publishers create, distribute and monetize content."

RRE Ventures' blog states:

"We live in a post-portal world in which content travels freely through different messaging channels (email, text, Snapchat, Slack, a multitude of messaging services) and across major social media platforms (Facebook, Twitter, Google, YouTube). Successful distribution today depends on promotion, broad appeal, and your audience's willingness to engage, react and share. Understanding these platforms and the forces that drive engagement and proliferation are critical if you want your content to achieve meaningful distribution. For media businesses that depend on advertising, this seems counterintuitive since better ad experiences have the potential to unlock major new revenue streams. Innovating around the advertiser's experience has actually created a vast amount of value and we wish we saw more companies focused on this."

"We believe that in every media format, the important thing is to give the brand advertiser a means to engage the audience emotionally, just as the content does. At BuzzFeed, Jonah Peretti recognized this and drove the creation of the sponsored content model. This gave brands a fresh medium to tell a story through shareable content, while holding them accountable for engaging the audience. Today, there are more ways than ever for publishers to be true partners to a brand, helping hone their voice and find their targeted audiences. BuzzFeed's test-and-learn approach lets brands explore new formats like quizzes, shorter-than-short form content, and no-sound-required video. These explorations have opened up entirely new revenue streams for BuzzFeed in the form of cross-platform branded content packages that are integrated with the company's owned and operated site and apps. It's one of the reasons the company has continued to grow at a terrific rate. Today, we welcome the ad innovations from SnapChat, with Lenses that overlay a brand lifestyle on our own and publisher driven Discover channels that include short, high-quality video ads. Now it feels like we are getting something new that works for brands, though a lot of what's happening in those channels feels a lot like TV. We look forward to seeing new innovations in ad experiences that captivate audiences and advertisers alike."

Frontier Technology in Media and Entertainment

Today's most commonly hyped frontier technologies — XR, blockchain, and artificial intelligence — are extremely relevant to the media and entertainment industry and will likely capture billions of dollars of value in the next few years.

XR (AR / VR / MR)

Media companies have been some of the most fervent investors in XR — defined as the category of virtual reality (VR), augmented reality (AR), and mixed reality (MR) — as many view these platforms as the next frontier and platform for entertainment. At the moment, the sector is in "the trough of disillusionment" of The Gartner Hype Cycle. After Facebook acquired Oculus in 2014, investors poured capital into VR startups with unrealistic expectations around market timing and consumer adoption in the short term, and have generally been disappointed by traction to date. Media companies, realizing that movie attendance was declining and cord-cutting was increasing, began investing in VR, believing it could be the next mass media distribution channel.

Media companies were some of the first to realize (intentionally or not) that VR may be better suited, at least initially, as Location Based Entertainment (LBE) installments for a vast majority of consumers who aren't in a rush to purchase their own hardware. Dreamscape Immersive ($41 million raised from 21st Century Fox, Warner Bros. AMC, MGM, Nickelodeon, IMAX, and Steven Spielberg), The Void (undisclosed funding from Disney), SPACES ($9.5 million raised from investors including Comcast Ventures), and SandboxVR (over $70 million raised from Andreessen Horowitz and others) are creating physical locations for interactive, multiplayer VR experiences. These companies are installing locations at theme parks, movie theaters, and shopping malls — and in some cases are providing reduced or even free rent to encourage the installments, which they hope will bring increased foot traffic to their dying retail hubs. These installments are riding the consumer trend of seeking "experiences," such as escape rooms and Instagram installments. The big challenge for LBE VR is to transcend the novelty, cultivate reasons for repeat visits, and solve the peak traffic issue — not being able to handle demand on a Saturday afternoon while having little to no demand on Tuesday morning.

Since VR has yet to find its "killer app," it's still unclear whether virtual reality will be more than a new gaming platform (in a media context.) The most popular VR content to date have been interactive games such as Beat Saber, as opposed to 360 degree video or VR films. Film and television studios are betting that VR can provide a new distribution and monetization channel for filmed content, but it is not yet certain whether this content is a compelling consumer proposition. The most promising venture investments in VR are most likely in content tools, distribution technology, and networks (excluding hardware) — not in content companies. Founded in 2012 by Herman Narula, Rob Whitehead, and Peter Lipka, Improbable ($603 million raised, $2 billion valuation) is building the toolset to create "virtual worlds" for gaming and entertainment, similar to Unity Technologies.

AR / MR media and entertainment applications in the immediate future are most likely gaming (again), advertising, and data. Founded in 2011 by John Hanke and Phil Keslin, Niantic ($470 million raised, $4 billion valuation) has had the most financially successful AR application to date with "Pokemon Go," which has brought in over $2.5 billion in revenue and over 800 million downloads since launching 2016. The company's next launch is a Harry Potter themed AR game due to be released in the second half of 2019. Advertising applications of AR / MR are likely to be pioneered by Google. On the data side, inside-out tracking for spatial positioning means companies like Facebook (through Oculus), Magic Leap, Google, and Apple will now have cameras inside your home, with the ability to recognize objects, products, and brands. Needless to say, this data is highly valuable (and sensitive.)

Blockchain

Blockchain technology has a few potential applications within the media and entertainment industry, including digital rights management / royalty payment and microtransaction options for paid content. Today, digital rights and royalty payments for music, TV shows, and films are primarily tracked, recorded, and paid out via individual databases (sometimes excel sheets) held by multiple independent organizations. This regularly results in disputes and unpaid royalties to the tune of millions of dollars annually. Smart blockchain contracts could ensure that everyone involved in the creation of a piece of content gets their share of revenue generated by it. Stem Disintermedia (founded in 2015) is building solutions for the music industry that would create decentralized databases on the blockchain, allowing third parties to transparently and immediately license content, while simultaneously providing reimbursement for all rights holders. Audius (founded in 2018, $5.5 million raised to date) is creating a decentralized platform for the distribution, attribution, and monetization of audio content.

Blockchain technology is also being considered for creating new monetization models for content creators, such as microtransactions. Utilizing cryptocurrency / digital currencies, consumers could pay pennies or fractions of a penny to consume content such as articles, music, and video. The pendulum has shifted in digital publishing from free, ad-supported models, to paywalls and expensive upfront subscriptions. How many subscriptions are consumers willing to pay for? Spotify already pays music labels $0.006—$0.0084 per stream, which is supported by subscribers' monthly fees or advertising revenue. What if consumers paid this fee directly, without paying a subscription fee or being exposed to advertising? The proposition is certainly compelling for many consumers, who currently overpay for content relative to their consumption. Currently, paywalls on publishers' websites demand high upfront payments, regardless of a user's consumption. Mycro Media is looking to unbundle the exuberance of subscription publishers by empowering consumers to purchase access to only the articles that interest them for a nominal fee. Micropayments have the ability to align consumption with cost and ensure that content creators are fairly compensated.

Artificial Intelligence (AI)

Early use of artificial intelligence (more accurately, machine learning) was leveraged by companies like Netflix to power recommendations, content targeting, and personalization for consumers. Now, companies such as Brud (founded in 2014, over $25 million raised to date) are looking to use machine learning to scale content creation for the first time. Production of high-quality entertainment is expensive primarily because it is not scalable and takes an incredible amount of human effort to create. Brud is betting that it can create entertainment properties and stories using machine learning and algorithmic content creation.

Machine learning (ML) and natural language processing (NLP) are also being utilized by companies like Papercup.ai to translate audio from video content into different languages in real time, while maintaining the intonation, emphasis, and emotion of the original speaker. This significantly expands the reach and audience of filmed content, whether YouTube videos or major motion pictures.

The media and entertainment industry has changed more in the past 10 years than it had in the prior 50, thanks to the immense shifts in distribution and production technology and costs. The most successful new media technology companies over the past 20 years have demonstrated that the highest value is in creating compelling consumer propositions, proprietary distribution platforms, and infrastructure, communication and engagement tools. Today, we're on the brink of even quicker innovation and disruption as new technologies like XR, AI, and blockchain demonstrate the potential for even better consumer experiences.

LAURA CHAU
CANAAN PARTNERS

Facebook (with its acquisitions of WhatsApp and Instagram), Twitter, LinkedIn, and Snap dominate social interactions online and have expanded their reach to become global juggernauts within social networking. The thought of an entrepreneur launching a new social network amidst this competition often seems like an untenable idea. Building a genuine sense of community, fostering conversation, adding utility for diverse populations, and maintaining privacy and security are all challenges these companies continue to face. Laura Chau, a Principal with Canaan Partners, takes a contrarian view. Laura believes that there are opportunities for new social networks to emerge where these existing networks begin to hit their 'breaking points' and that as consumer behaviors evolve, so too do their interests in how they interact with one another or share pieces of themselves online. In this chapter, Laura shares her perspective on the challenges and opportunities of social networks.

Canaan Partners is an early-stage fund with a storied 32-year history that has made it a mainstay player in the venture ecosystem across the US. On the consumer side, Canaan has invested in companies such as TheRealReal, Instacart, Turo, Ro, Ladder, and Match.com. Laura is a two-time graduate of Stanford University, with a B.S. and an MBA, and is supporting the next generation of consumer investing as a Principal with Canaan's 11th fund. Before joining Canaan, Laura was one of the first of 20 employees at Kabam, the mobile gaming startup that was acquired in 2017 for $800 million. At Canaan Partners, Laura has led investments in Coterie and Jumpcut in addition to working closely with the firm's investments in companies such as Cuyana, Kustomer, Cargomatic, and World View.

As Laura thinks about online communities and interaction, she offers a discerning perspective on the foundational reasons why companies such as Facebook, Twitter, and Snap were specifically built, and how those companies have evolved in recent years. Unlike other investors who are outsiders to the industries that they cover, Laura offers personal perspectives in this chapter. She is an avid user of social platforms — be it the larger incumbents or new and novel approaches to social interaction — and balances her curiosity and enthusiasm as a user with the intellectual hurdles she must cross to prove that a social network is truly gaining the attention of users beyond herself.

SOCIAL MEDIA: A GAME OF STATUS
Laura Chau, Canaan Partners

Introduction

In 2019, the impact and reach of social media is undeniable. Facebook serves 2 billion unique users every month, Snapchat users post over 3 billion snaps every single day, and even the guy who artfully makes my Sunday morning lattes is an Instagram influencer. In tech and venture, social companies are the holy grail of Silicon Valley. They are the investments that VCs become famous for — like Chris Sacca and his early bet on Twitter, or Jim Goetz who turned $60 million into $3 billion with his bet on WhatsApp. The importance of social within this community is so pervasive that the founders of social companies are often the de facto template for budding entrepreneurs who could "build the next Facebook" or "become the next Evan Spiegel."

Yet there comes a point when these social networks hit their peak. In fact, most of the social media giants of today started 10-15 years ago — nearly an entire generation back. Today, as their growth begins to slow, they must acquire new companies to stay relevant, and for many, their original value proposition morphs — now in favor of revenue, margin, or user growth.

What is perhaps most notable about many of these social media companies is that they are in fact, no longer social. Most social media companies initially rose to prominence through a small, controlled community: Facebook with Harvard students, WhatsApp through private group messages, Snapchat's domination of 1:1 photo messages with your friends. This feeling of being pulled in by a friend or confidante allowed these platforms to grow virally: one friend inviting 10 of their pals; those 10 inviting another 10 and so on. However, now that we've hit maturity on these platforms, nearly all have taken a turn from intimate social network to social media with broadcasting as the core use case. In early 2019, Mark Zuckerberg proclaimed that Facebook had hit this peak — functioning as a "townsquare" — when now the goal is to get back to a "living room." With this shift towards broadcasting and a massive growth in network size, most of these companies are, I argue, no longer social media platforms. They are status media platforms.

The Building Blocks of Social

Let's first start by examining what actually makes something social. In the common lexicon, social is most commonly used to refer to social networks and social media. While the two share quite a bit of overlap, they are still distinct classifications. A social network is ultimately a communication platform, with 1:1 interactions at its core. Unsurprisingly, it also has strong network effects, such that the more people who are using it, the more valuable the content and the service itself becomes. Social media is typically a platform that broadcasts information from one to many. Facebook, for example began purely as a social network, requiring a double opt-in to be "friends" and a direct communication channel via your personal wall (and while this wall was public, your friends would have to purposefully seek out your wall to view it.) Facebook has also now become a social media platform, given the nature of the Newsfeed that broadcasts information about your friends, friends of friends, or trending news. Twitter on the other hand, was a social media site from the start — an open broadcast of your thoughts available for all to see. That's perhaps why Twitter quickly became overrun with celebrities — it was a novel method to communicate with a fan base. Ashton Kutcher could tweet out something mildly provocative about what he ate for breakfast, creating a feeling of social closeness with his fans without having to communicate individually with each of them via DMs or replies.

Platforms will often blur the lines between social media and social network, even changing where they fall on the spectrum over time. Snapchat is a great example as something that began purely as a social network, but now straddles both. Again, with messaging at its core, users would send 1:1 snaps back and forth between friends. Even the interface discouraged sending snaps to mass audiences as you had to individually select everyone's name. Eventually, Snapchat moved to allow you to snap large groups of friends and eventually post stories to anyone you were connected with (and even those you didn't know) — perhaps the company's most impactful feature contribution to modern media. Then, once Discover was added, providing short-form video and news content, Snapchat was fully a social media app in addition to still being a social network. Users had the option to choose which aspects of the service to use.

Regardless of whether something is classified as social media or a social network, there are five characteristics that underlie anything that is inherently social. I refer to these as the "Social Pillars."

1. *Community and Conversation:* A platform must enable connection. It could be one-to-one or it could be one-to-many, but the ability to build some type of community and have a form of discourse is critical. Facebook and Twitter are clear examples of apps that capitalized on this pillar early. Others like Whisper or Meerkat had an early surge of success because of this community element, but failed to deliver on the remaining pillars.

2. *Utility:* There must be some useful aspect to the tool to keep users engaged. This might be messaging to stay in touch with friends, a source of news, or a method to save photos of interior decorating ideas

you've found on the Internet. Without true utility, social companies will be novel for a moment but will quickly fall to the wayside as soon as that novelty is exhausted (RIP Yo).

3. *Entertainment:* It might be obvious, since social is almost synonymous with "fun," but social apps need to have some element of entertainment. This type of entertainment is often separate from the utility of an app (though they can be the same — ask any bride who has gotten sucked into an endless pinning frenzy of wedding inspiration on Pinterest.) It's important for any social app to have some core element of entertainment, while also continually evolving what makes it novel and fun.

4. *Privacy and Control:* This is perhaps more of an honorary mention. While privacy is not a characteristic that is required to be inherently social, I argue that it is becoming table stakes in today's era for an app to become successful. This is in part due to the proliferation of social data and the backlash from Cambridge Analytica and Facebook. It's also a generational shift as Gen Z increasingly cares about privacy and has grown up in an age of Snapchat where shared moments are meant to be just that — ephemeral moments in time.

5. *Status:* As humans, we all seek status at our core (remember Klout?). And to reach the success and scale that entrepreneurs' dreams and VCs' careers are built upon, a social platform must deliver a mechanism for status to be amassed. This is a pillar that a social app does not necessarily need to have from the beginning. However, I argue that any successful social app will inevitably end up with a status element over time.

The Shifting Footprints of Social

Now the quality or strength across each of these pillars can vary wildly for each social platform. At the end of the day, each platform has its own unique footprint based on its performance within these pillars. These footprints will inevitably morph over time as the feature set changes, user behavior shifts, and the networks themselves evolve. Below are rough illustrations of a few social platforms as I see them as of 2019.

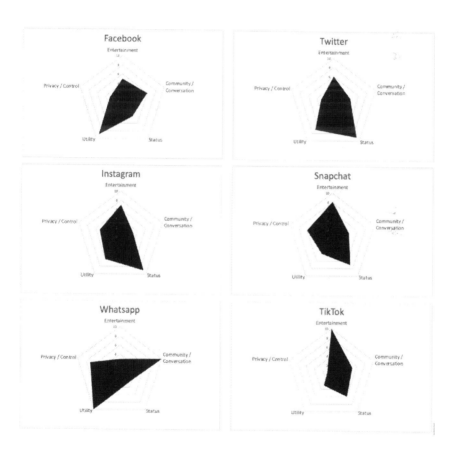

Let's look at Twitter as an example. When Twitter first launched in 2006, it was high on the entertainment and community/conversation pillars. The service was intended to be a fun way to update your friends on your status or what you were doing, no matter how frivolous. Even the name of the company reinforced this idea of frivolity — the dictionary defines the word "Twitter" as "a short burst of inconsequential information." Twitter was both a form of entertainment (sending fun updates via SMS to the web) and a form of community (bringing groups of friends together to stay more connected on the others' moods and activities.) The concepts of status, privacy or utility were not even on the radar. In fact, Twitter Co-Founder Ev Williams famously quipped about the app, "Who ever said things have to be useful?"

Well, fast forward to 2019, and Twitter's footprint across these five pillars has shifted significantly. It turns out that Twitter and its users found a way to make the service extremely useful. For many, Twitter is a first destination for news. It has been used effectively to sway public opinion and win elections. Businesses use it to communicate with customers (and customers use it to complain publicly and get refunds.) Twitter's elements of status and conversation have also changed. Over time, a certain form of tweet has emerged as one that is worthy of attention or virality. You know it when you see it — pithy, funny, perhaps a bit cutting and sarcastic. It might read a bit like a fortune cookie. It likely has a meme attached as well. It is these types of tweets that get retweeted and amass new followers for a user. And those retweets and follower counts are what provide status on the platform. Given how public your tweets and follower count are, many feel pressure to chase these status metrics. But in doing so, conversation is squashed. If users must communicate in fortune cookie format to gain status, they are no longer authentically sharing and messaging with their group of friends as they once did. And on top of that, the tweets that get the most airtime are those fortune cookie quips from individuals who have already amassed significant followers. It becomes a vicious cycle where status is king and conversation is an unfortunate casualty.

This is all to demonstrate that the pillars underlying social platforms are universal. They exist in all social apps at some level, yet the strength of each will inevitably shift over time. And as they shift, it opens up opportunities and entry points for new social platforms to emerge (more on this later.)

The Social <> Status Tipping Point

There is a common theory with most social media companies that there is a point for each service that a user must reach to unlock value in the service. For Facebook, it might be once you have three or more friends. Or in the early days of Instagram (pre-Explore tab), it might be once you've followed five active accounts so that your feed is regularly refreshed with new content. It's at these points some of the pillars are made accessible — you can't have conversation without friends. You can't be entertained without content from others.

The ease of clearing this early hurdle is a predictor of the virality and growth of an emerging service. However, there is a similar hurdle faced by mature social media platforms that acts in the opposite way. Once you reach a saturation point of your audience, you are actually dis-incentivized from posting more.

Consider Facebook. As a teenager, once your parents and grandparents are your friends and can see what you post, how likely are you to share your actual thoughts (or photos from the party you snuck out to)? This is the same phenomenon that drove teens on Instagram to develop "Finstas" — or "Fake instagram" accounts. On these accounts, teens would sporadically post parent-approved content to uphold an image for their unknowing parents. They would then host the content that felt authentic to them with their friends on a completely separate account, hidden from their parents' reach.

Even I have felt the breaking point of Instagram lately. In celebrating a recent birthday, there were many friends I wasn't able to invite. I found myself nervous that those in attendance would post photo evidence of the gathering, outing me to those who weren't invited. It wouldn't be a FOMO-inducing experience of the kind that Instagram thrives on, but rather one that would cause potentially uncomfortable social tensions. The ever presence of Instagram was making in real life (or "IRL") experiences feel stressful, just because of the potential reach of the audience. Instagram recently released a feature where you can designate your "close friends" to help mitigate this issue. This is an indication that Instagram already recognizes the need to provide more control and smaller groups to encourage people to post more often.

I believe Instagram and Facebook have hit that tipping point — the point where the accumulation of status tilts the scales such that these social media companies transform into status media companies. You can tell this has happened when your social group on a platform becomes too big or varied that you no longer want to post authentic content; or when your usage of the platform becomes solely about content that will get you status. The pure social elements have disappeared and status reigns king.

Using the Social Pillars to Guide Investment Opportunities

When it comes to finding the investment opportunities within social, it becomes a function of where the gaps lie between the existing landscape of social platforms and the shifting needs of each generation. More tactically speaking, when looking at the unique footprints of the existing social platforms of today: Which pillars are they delivering on? And for which demographics? And which pillars have the most white space?

A budding social platform can arguably emerge with any one of these five pillars as its primary value proposition. However, given the network effects often so inherent in social platforms, reaching escape velocity out of the gate can often be the difference between long-term success and failure. Given that, the budding platforms that take advantage of the white space in the current social landscape will likely have the best chance of making an initial impact. Revisiting the footprints of today's social platforms overlaid across the five pillars, we see that many of the platforms are delivering on status and utility. This makes sense given that many of these platforms are mature and have already hit that "status tipping point," as well as found ways to become a utility in everyday life, enabling stickiness and engagement. Thus, looking at the white spaces, we see that Community/Conversation, Entertainment, and Privacy/Control offer the most opportunity for a new social platform to gain traction. I'll share a few case studies on the opportunities I see within these pillars.

1. Community/Conversation: Slack as a Social App

As platforms reach that tipping point and transition into status media, they also begin to lose those characteristics that allowed for authentic community and conversation. Thus, as social apps mature and move away from their early versions of community-based platforms to status media platforms, a white space opens up for new social platforms to provide community and conversation, thus restarting the natural cycle of social apps.

Perhaps one unlikely app, given its enterprise roots, that provides a great template for a social platform leveraging conversation, is Slack. Teams and entire workplaces have flocked to the product as a replacement for email and chat apps. It makes communicating at work and gathering/sharing information faster and richer — so much so that 10 million office workers log into the app daily, actively using it for ~90 minutes during weekdays, and staying logged into the app for ~10 hours/day during the week.

But let's examine Slack purely as a social app. Slack, as a messaging platform, has conversation at its core. It also has a strong sense of community. All members are invited, and often are already connected through an existing IRL community (e.g. an entire start-up office, a recreational soccer league, a collection of individuals interested in retail and fashion.) By this nature, community exists based on affinity, interests, proximity, or a common goal. Within Slack, conversations are then organized in two ways: 1) in channels — a further subdivision into topic areas from the general community so that those who are interested or relevant to that topic can communicate with one another without spamming the broader group, thus increasing engagement and participation. And 2) direct messages — private messages that are 1:1 or in small sub-groups of the overall community, functioning similarly to any messaging app.

Slack is not purely an app that indexes high on community/conversation. Utility is a clear strength given its numerous integrations with services like Twitter, Salesforce, and Dropbox, making communication and the sharing of information at work both faster and richer. Entertainment is certainly at play as well — if you've ever worked at a startup using Slack, you've been subject to (or have heavily participated in) the onslaught of gifs, memes, and polls that seem to take place at lightning speed. I've long wondered, for all the benefits and efficiency that Slack provides as a utility, how much of that is lost to the time suck that is random Buzzfeed articles posted for everyone in the office to see, debate about whether Dave should wear a onesie to the office or sing Eye of the Tiger if your team hits its quarterly sales goal, or meme wars about the fact that the Cheez-Its were discontinued in the kitchen.

For all of its strength on these three pillars, I would argue that Slack falls short on the privacy and status pillars. Given the fact that employers could be peering over your shoulder, users may be wary to share on the platform — but that is also just a nature of messaging within any enterprise. That said, Slack has done a great job of taking community and conversation as an entry point to build an effective, engaging social app, whether the market values it as that or not.

This focus on community can be seen in the broader social ecosystem. Real life communities like The Wing have become a new form of social group. Facebook has been experimenting with Facebook Groups and finding new ways to help smaller interest groups together. We have entered an era some refer to as "the unbundling of Facebook" where individual apps or online groups are created specifically for affinity groups or interest areas — apps for runners, groups for immigrants in specific cities, or platforms for make-up lovers looking to share product and application tips. I expect that we will continue to see new apps, and new features within existing platforms, that foster tighter communities around shared interests or goals in the way that Slack has modeled.

2. Utility: WhatsApp and the Suppression of Status

While services like WhatsApp and Messenger share the conversational elements above that make Slack a great social platform, these messaging apps really shine when it comes to utility. Sure, they foster community amidst your friend group, provide entertainment with Bitmojis and inside jokes galore, and offer a certain level of privacy and control with the limited size of a community (and the end-to-end encryption in the case of WhatsApp.) Yet their primary purpose is to communicate information quickly and effectively. This is utility at its finest.

In fact, the utility of these messaging apps is perhaps so strong that it actually limits the ability of status to be a dominant pillar. There are few ways within WhatsApp to acquire more social capital than the others in your group. You may be the wittiest or share the most helpful information, but there is no mechanism to earn a badge or likes for such behavior. And while not ephemeral in the same concept as a snap or a story, your messages often go by so quickly such that the funny gif you sent this morning is long forgotten by lunchtime. Thus, there is no manner in which to store an indicator of status within the app. Status is suppressed by the nature of the utility.

As a result, WhatsApp (or any pure messaging tool for that matter) is perhaps the most authentic of social apps. It is real time and the one most closely tied to your real person and life. In fact, the idea of a "persona," which is the foundation of many social platforms, doesn't really exist within WhatsApp. The person you present on WhatsApp is the same person you are in real life. You message largely the same way that you speak. Compare that to someone's Instagram feed or TikTok account, which is littered with expertly crafted styles and images. Oftentimes these styles even vary significantly across platform for the same person — a result of the fact that the crowds they are gathering status from differ on each platform and reward different styles or behaviors.

So what does this tell us about the merit of utility when it comes to social apps? First and foremost it is that apps with strong utility from the outset are less likely to hit the status media tipping point early in their lifecycle. However, this does not mean that apps that index high on utility are immune from this tipping point. Just look at the steps WhatsApp and Facebook Messenger have taken to add a stories feature to their platforms — each is now at over 500 million daily active users (DAUs.) Stories have added a new layer of social that prizes entertainment and status through the crafting of personas. The question now is when these platforms will tip to status media. We will likely hit a point where the messaging groups become too large, or a mechanism to track status (views, likes, hearts) becomes so strong, or the type of content that is "valued" becomes too prescribed, that the scales ultimately tip. And at that point, WhatsApp will tip into the land of status media, opening up opportunity for the next wave of social messaging players.

3. Entertainment: The Rise of TikTok

TikTok, as of mid-2019, has had one of the most meteoric rises of a social app in years. TikTok is an app focused on Gen Z (41% of their users are between 16-24) that allows users to post fun, 15-second videos, usually set to music. Many of these videos are in the form of lip-syncing, as well as creative trending challenges, memes, and duets. In the first half of 2019, it was the third most downloaded app worldwide, after WhatsApp and Messenger, and boasts over 1.2 billion monthly active users (MAUs) and 500 billion daily active users (DAUs.) For context, Instagram has 1 billion MAUs, YouTube has 1.9 billion MAUs, and Facebook has 2 billion MAUs. The app formally launched only one year ago under the TikTok brand (though Bytedance, the parent company, had launched the Chinese version, Douyin, in 2016, and bought the US company, Musical.ly, in 2017 for $1 billion — combining the two entities to create TikTok.) And I should mention, this app is sticky. The average user is opening the app eight times per day, for a total of 52 minutes each day.

So how did TikTok pull off such massive growth in a crowded social landscape? They put entertainment and novelty front and center. Posting a 15-second clip of you lip-syncing to "Old Town Road" by Lil Nas X probably sounds like a waste of time to most. But the pure frivolity of such an act is what makes it so special — especially amidst a sea of social apps that increasingly feel onerous with influencers and brands jockeying to present the perfect millennial life.

Another thing that TikTok got right was that it created a new platform to amass status for a generation that was seeking it. The average Gen Z kid was introduced to platforms like Instagram and Twitter once those platforms were fully mature and had already tipped into status media. Amassing their own following and status would be difficult for most — these platforms were saturated and rising above the fray was reserved for only a select few new entrants.

TikTok, on the other hand, presented a brand new platform tailor made to give this generation a reasonable opportunity to achieve status. The TikTok algorithm for the user feed also intelligently supports this. Every user's feed is curated "for them" — serving up content from any users who may be interesting to that individual. This means that it is easier for any one person to "go viral" as it is not based on the number of followers that person has, but rather on the quality of that content and how it might resonate with other users. Layer on the trending challenges and duets that are common on the platform and you end up with a creative platform that provides users first and foremost with entertainment, but also with a fair chance to achieve status.

4. Privacy & Control: Brud, Identity, and Storytelling

Privacy and control have become an everyday part of the conversation about social platforms. Facebook has been plagued by this topic for most of 2018 and beyond. TikTok is under constant scrutiny given the heavy surveillance of its Chinese app, Douyin, and has been fined for illegally storing information for its youngest users below the age of 13. Gen Z has grown up as a generation much more concerned about their online identities than those who came before them. They are accustomed to the form factor of disappearing messages and photos from Snapchat. They have finsta accounts, as I mentioned before, to control the image they portray to their parents. They are constantly culling their pictures on Instagram, as it would be tacky to have more than 25 photos posted at a given time (compared to the average millennial who has every embarrassing tagged photo from college still visible on their profile.) In short, Gen Z has become obsessed with owning their online identity.

Enter Brud. Brud is the company behind artificial influencers like Lil Miquela and Bermuda. They have devised deep identities and dramatic story arcs for these lifelike characters, garnering millions of followers on Instagram. These characters have released pop singles with millions of streams on Spotify, they have partnered with brands like Prada and Calvin Klein, and even gotten tattoos from the hottest celebrity tattoo artists. Brud has acknowledged what much of Gen Z has already picked up on — social media today is largely real humans being fake. It is humans broadcasting their life to achieve status. Now, Brud is taking fake humans to broadcast fake lives as well. But because there is no premise of these lives actually being real, there are fewer limits to what artificial influencers can do. It is storytelling at its finest. And people are happy to buy into it.

I believe that Brud is just the beginning. While today Brud acts as a studio, carefully crafting the stories of these specific influencers, one can imagine a day when any user on the Internet can create their own avatar or artificial character and craft their own unique story. This will give users a new level of control — an ability to choose, and create, the life they portray to the rest of the world. We are already doing it today on Instagram, picking and choosing the moments we share, spending hours getting the perfect selfie with the perfect filter to show off that perfect weekend at the beach. Avatars and artificial influencers will take this storytelling to the next level. It removes the limitations of the physical world to allow users to express themselves in a new way.

Conclusion

You may have noticed that in evaluating opportunities for investment across the five pillars, I spoke to all except Status. This is because Status is an inevitability with all social platforms. In some cases it may be a starting point, but in all cases it is an end point. Every successful social app will find itself a part of the Social <> Status cycle.

The Social <> Status Cycle:
- A social company is born with some unique footprint across the five social pillars.
- As that company matures, it will seek to satisfy the natural desire of users to amass status, adjusting its feature set and thus its footprint across the social pillars.
- Once one's social group on that platform becomes so large that it disincentives authentic content, that platform has tipped into status media.

- Once a social company tips to become a status media company, a void is left in the social landscape for more authentic interactions across the remaining four pillars.
- New social companies will enter the ecosystem to fill that gap and eventually provide a new platform for amassing status to rising generations.

This is the natural evolution of social apps. It means there will always be opportunities for new social innovations — the holy grail in Silicon Valley. This is a cycle we have seen play out, and one that we will inevitably see again. It will continue because it is based on the natural human desire for community, utility, entertainment, (increasingly) privacy, and most certainly — status.

SHEFALI BHARDWAJ
ZS ASSOCIATES

Healthcare is an industry that is difficult to navigate as an investor or operator given ever-changing regulation and technological advancements. Despite its complexity, it is also one of the most compelling industries for entrepreneurs or venture capitalists who want to see technology improve humanity in meaningful ways. For a chapter focused on the healthcare industry, I wanted to identify someone who had spent several years developing a focused perspective on the industry by interacting with the major players in the ecosystem. Shefali Bhardwaj, a healthcare advisor with ZS Associates, fit the bill.

With ZS Associates, Shefali works closely with pharmaceutical companies, hospitals, and fortune 500 companies as they navigate the healthcare landscape from a commercial perspective. Prior to ZS, Shefali worked with PricewaterhouseCoopers (PwC) as a consultant to many of the large payors and beneficiaries within the healthcare ecosystem. While at PwC, Shefali authored a whitepaper on the Affordable Care Act and how it would impact American citizens and continued this focus on healthcare while earning her MBA from Columbia Business School.

For the purpose of this chapter, Shefali focuses primarily on consumer health. As health data becomes increasingly more accessible to consumers through electronic health records, diagnostics, at-home kits, and wearables, the consumer healthcare industry has exploded with new applications through companies such as Ro, Hims, and Modern Fertility. Shefali offers her perspective through a background informed by the incumbents within this industry.

THE DIGITAL HEALTH REVOLUTION
Shefali Bhardwaj, ZS Associates

A Recent History of Digital Health

We live in one of the most transformational times in human history brought about by a digital revolution which is impacting each and every industry. Healthcare is no exception. Traditional paradigms are shifting and being redefined. Patients are now consumers, managing their healthcare experience from their own homes and personal devices. While patient centricity, and an emphasis on value, are at the heart of this transformation, much of it is propelled by digital disruption in the industry. With more than three billion people worldwide connected to the Internet, harnessing the power of digital connectivity is key to solving some of healthcare's greatest challenges. This chapter will explore how we got to this point in the digital health revolution, what digital health really means, and what key leaders, investors, and entrepreneurs feel about the industry today and where it is headed.

The healthcare industry has long been ripe for change. For decades, the US health industry has operated in a system of silos — hospitals, insurance companies, government institutions, pharmacies, drug makers, medical device-manufacturers, and employers. Today, healthcare operates more like an ecosystem of players all orienting themselves to compete for a consumer that is now more informed. No longer are patients playing a passive role in the process but are in control of their own data and the healthcare experience. The industry has been forced to re-evaluate strategies and align business models with consumer-driven industries like hospitality and retail.

So why is digital health so relevant now versus 10 years ago? What has been the impetus for change?

Mobile Phones and Wearables Empower Patients

The rise of mobile phones has enabled a rising trend of the patient as the consumer, able to make instant decisions about their own health with the click of a button. The digital/mobile revolution has given rise to online pharmacies, health tracking applications, and secure doctor-to-patient communication platforms. These shifts have allowed for the delivery of treatment without a patient ever having to step into a doctor's office and one major technological breakthrough has empowered the patient like never before: wearables.

The introduction of Fitbits, Apple Watches, Garmin watches, Whoop, and a host of other wearables have allowed consumers to track health fundamentals accurately. The wearables market grows each year exponentially and only halfway through 2019, over 150 million wearable units were sold internationally generating over $30 billion in revenue. While these numbers are astounding and clearly indicate high consumer adoption at the intersection of health and technology, the impact wearables can have on human health has only begun to scratch the surface. For most healthy people, mass market wearables such as the FitBit or the Apple Watch have had minimal impact on their lives, aside from tracking steps, measuring sleep patterns, and more frequently checking heart rate. These consumer products create convenience but are not essential to patients with serious health concerns. There are however a growing group of entrepreneurs focused on developing the next generation of wearables for patients with specific needs.

For patients who suffer from chronic diseases — diabetes, heart conditions, asthma — the rise of the mobile phone and wearable devices has been transformative. It has not only improved the patient experience, but it has also enabled doctors to treat patients in a much more precise way. There are several examples of wearables feeding specific, indicative and high-impact health data to a mobile phone. These include the 'smart bra' that leads to early-detection of breast cancer, contact lenses that detect early signs of glaucoma for at-risk patients, and smart glasses that help people with cerebral palsy browse the Internet and perform better at their jobs. Larger players are investing heavily in the wearables market as well. IBM partnered with Pfizer to create wearables that help track the progression of Parkinson's disease. Larger risk-bearing entities, such as health insurance companies, continue to explore ways to empower patients to monitor their own health indicators. Most recently, Aetna has partnered with Apple to allow members to purchase an Apple Watch, but then "pay it off" through healthy behavior. The hope is that improved patient outcomes will continue to reduce overall costs to the healthcare system.

While wearables and mobile phones have provided more access to healthcare and health data, a challenge that continues to persist is privacy. In 2019, over 503 breaches compromised the health records of over 15 million people, and healthcare cybersecurity has continued to see investment from VCs. With new regulations like GDPR in place and on the horizon, we may see a reinstatement of consumer confidence in sharing their data with healthcare technology companies. Healthcare cybersecurity is a field that has grown in favor with venture capitalists looking to protect consumers as they continue to track and gain access to important and sensitive data.

Direct to Consumer Options

Mobile technology and wearables have also given rise to the consumerization of healthcare whereby patients are now operating as consumers of the healthcare experience. Much like other industries, healthcare consumers are seeking services through their phones, in the comfort of their own homes, or through very tailored and convenient experiences that serve their exact needs. This has put immense pressure on incumbent healthcare companies that have always viewed healthcare services as a utility. These organizations — hospitals, pharmacies, health insurance companies — have been disrupted by a new wave of digital health companies that bring the consumer focus from other industries (e.g. retail, technology, finance) to healthcare, where the consumer or patient experience is largely broken.

In women's health, companies such as Maven Clinic and Modern Fertility are transforming the way in which women approach fertility decisions. These companies have taken usually stressful, anxiety-driven experiences for women in their childbearing years — who either want to prevent a pregnancy or start planning for a pregnancy — and made them much more easier to navigate. Raising close to $50 million to date, Maven Clinic offers an online clinic that focuses on women's healthcare and the family, with a larger goal of keeping more moms in the workforce. Since its founding in 2015, Maven has delivered care to almost 200,000 patients and currently has more than 1,300 health specialists in its network. Katherine Ryder, the founder and CEO of Maven said to Forbes:

"I started talking to a lot of women, and it was really clear that… the problems really revolved around access to care and just getting better information in a sea of misinformation online. [Maven] in very nuanced ways, tries to help better the lives of working mothers and new mothers."

Similarly, Modern Fertility is transforming the fertility-testing space by offering a $159 at-home hormone test kit, accompanied by a consultation with a nurse, to help women make informed decisions about when to have babies. The global fertility-testing industry is a nearly $400 million market that is projected to grow to almost $600 million by 2020. Currently, most doctor-prescribed blood tests are handled by industry leaders Quest Diagnostics and LabCorp. The pitch to young women is: "if you have the tools to start monitoring your fertility the same way you should continuously monitor your credit scores — you can make more informed decisions, whether it's freezing your eggs or trying to conceive sooner rather than later."

These companies, along with a host of others such as Ro, Hims and Helix are contributing to the shift of the patient as the consumer, enabling individuals to proactively make decisions about their health with information that historically has been largely unavailable or difficult to obtain. According to a McKinsey study, consumers continue to want more from the healthcare industry, with coverage ranked as most important, followed by customer service, cost, and access. The types of relationships consumers have with tech innovators such as Amazon, Google, and Apple are the types of interactions they want from healthcare organizations. With healthcare companies being so deeply embedded in consumers' lives, they are uniquely positioned to create this experience. But there is a long way to go, and likely no perfect path or single company to get us there.

AR/VR and AI applications in healthcare

Alongside the rise in mobile technology, technology trends such as AR/VR and AI, are just beginning to make strides in healthcare. In the last decade, there have been thousands of investments in companies that utilize AI in healthcare. The majority of activity has occurred in the last three years, signaling that healthcare investors see promise in this space. According to an Accenture report, healthcare AI applications can potentially generate more than $150 billion in yearly savings for the US healthcare economy by 2026.

A large proportion of these companies are deep learning startups focused on medical imaging analysis with the hope of lowering costs, improving accuracy, and saving time for doctors through enhanced detection and diagnosis. Experts predict operationalizing AI platforms across healthcare workflows would result in a 10-15% productivity gain over the next couple of years.

Let's take the example of breast cancer — one of the most prevalent forms of cancer. X-ray based mammography is an effective screening tool for detecting cancer, but what many women may not realize is that breast screening programs produce a high level of false positive results — meaning, women are informed that they may have cancer when in fact they don't. Unfortunately, this is particularly the case in the US, where x-rays are generally reviewed by a single, expert radiologist (whereas in Europe, two independent radiologists read each study.) The inability to confidently rule out the possibility of cancer in complex cases frequently results in women being asked to return for further imaging or studies or even a biopsy (an invasive screening procedure.) This leads to unnecessary anxiety and has broader implications around efficiency and cost to the healthcare system. That's where companies like Kheiron Medical Technologies are transforming breast cancer screening. Initial data from over 5,000 patients showed that AI-based analysis was as good as conventional physician interpretation.

In addition to medical imaging, repetitive and time-consuming tasks, such as scheduling appointments, are a sweet spot for AI companies. Cleveland's MetroHealth System had a 10-35% no-show rate at its four hospitals before bringing AI into its operational decision-making in late 2017. During a 2018 US News Healthcare of Tomorrow panel on AI, MetroHealth's chief strategy and innovation officer Karim Botros shared that MetroHealth used AI to quantify that select patients had a high likelihood of not showing and double booked those patients in order to not waste providers' time.

Another example is the company Kit Check, which sells machine learning to help hospitals identify drug diverters by identifying high-risk hospital employees who may be stealing drugs. The system scores them on a range of metrics, such as physical location, documentation and timing behaviors. These technologies trickle into all parts of the healthcare system, creating the potential to reduce overall drug spend.

Efforts to Reduce Regulatory Burdens

Unlike other industries, the healthcare industry faces high regulatory burden. To keep pace with rapid disruption, the FDA has taken measures to pave the path for new digital health products through the Digital Health Software Pre-Certification program, which streamlines the approval process. Since the introduction of this regulation, there has been an increase in digital health companies receiving FDA Breakthrough Device designation. Earlier this year, Paige.AI, a digital pathology start-up, received the first such designation for AI in cancer diagnosis.

A recent report by PwC found that only 42% of pharmaceutical executives said they were actively developing digital therapeutics in 2018; of those 42% said they would begin doing so in the next two years, and 58% said they are planning to in the next three to six years. Despite these trends that have enabled the rapid innovation and growth in the digital health space, not all companies have had success stories we hear about in the news such as Flatiron Health, Livongo, and 23andMe. In fact, many are questioning whether digital health is in a "bubble," with valuations skyrocketing. Michael Greeley, a co-founder of Flare Capital, offers a different perspective:

"The US healthcare market is over $3 trillion, which is nearly 15x the US. advertising industry. Given the enormity of the market opportunities, it feels more than large enough to absorb the amount of capital being invested today. It has taken a decade to reach the $8 billion investment pace we will see this year. I just don't conclude we are in a bubble. When we saw bubbles created in other sectors, it was often around uncertain business models and when too much capital flooded in too quickly. We have crystal clear business models here addressing enormous market opportunities."

The Future of Digital Health: What's next?

There is no one-size-fits-all platform in digital health today, and it's unlikely that there will be one for the future. The industry is complex and constantly changing. So, what does the future look like?

Remote Monitoring and Disease Management

Medicine is reaching a problem of epic proportions. By 2030, assuming there are no changes to how primary care is delivered, there will be a projected deficit of up to ~50,000 primary care physicians to meet the needs of the US population. Today, chronic disease (such as heart failure, hypertension, and diabetes) is primarily managed by PCPs, which takes up the majority of healthcare expenditures, and accounts for nearly one-fifth of our GDP. With this challenge on our hands, it will be critical for innovative digital health technologies to address efficient and rapid disease management. Remote monitoring of patients through effective disease management tools (e.g. Bluetooth-enabled blood pressure cuffs or a portable sleeve that can detect when DVT-blood clots are formed.)

Gene Editing / CRISPR

It has been less than a decade since scientists first learned how to splice the human genome in a precise and reliable way, using a tool called CRISPR. This has opened a realm of possibilities related to addressing disease-causing mutations and actually curing genetic diseases ranging from sickle cell anemia to certain types of cancer and even blindness.

As with most breakthrough innovation in healthcare, the use of CRISPR has led to heated debates from opponents who cite ethical or security concerns. On the ethics front, some believe the use of CRISPR is tampering with what nature intends and will create a society in which certain types of genetic traits are considered superior to others. On the security front, an extreme and dystopian example of healthcare data and CRISPR in the wrong hands can be seen through the concept of *genome hacking*. John Sotos, the Chief Medical Officer at Intel, has been hired to focus on Cancer Moonshot, a program investing in *precision medicine* to identify the genetic signature of a tumor and create a virus that will kill cells with that specific signature. The intended result would be a complete cure to all forms of Cancer. At a conference, Sotos shared an alternate reality in which this type of genome targeting can lead to genome hacks, in which 'hackers could supercharge pharmaceutical sales by spreading the genes for treatable illness, induce alcohol or meat intolerance or even deafness or blindness, create a hyper-susceptibility to STDs, or sun sensitivity.' While such radical concepts may well be fear mongering, data breaches and privacy laws around health data sharing have really come into question.

While we are still far from the scientific community feeling comfortable to use CRISPR in the US, medical professionals have already experimented with it abroad. In 2018 in China, a scientist announced that he had already used CRISPR to permanently alter the genomes of twin girls to be immune to HIV infection. Editas Medicine and Allergan recently announced a more accepted form of gene editing, one that would change genetic defects in cells that don't get passed onto the next generation. The companies are currently enrolling patients born with a congenital vision disease into what will be the first US test to determine if CRISPR can fix a mutation in the cells of a living human body. Other ongoing trials, including one from Vertex Pharmaceuticals and CRISPR Therapeutics that is treating blood disease, rely on treating patients' cells outside the body and introducing them back to the body so that they would outnumber the diseased cells. While the scientific and ethical application of CRISPR is still being explored and defined in its early stages, this will undoubtedly be a defining component of the future of digital health.

Direct-to-consumer Diagnostics

After the widely publicized Theranos scandal, the diagnostics industry remains to be disrupted. There are several emerging companies that are venturing to take on industry giants — Quest and LabCorp. On the genetic testing side, companies such as 23andMe.com, Helix, and Color are becoming common. On the routine testing side, niche at-home diagnostic companies like Modern Fertility (for women's fertility) and EverlyWell (for food sensitivities) are emerging. With increased competition in diagnostics and testing, LabCorp and Quest are taking note and also entering into collaborations with other retail and pharmacy outlets to accommodate consumers. Sonora Quest, a subsidiary of Laboratory Sciences of Arizona, just launched a new service "My Lab ReQuest," which is a DTC service including a limited menu focused on wellness health profiles. It also includes screening for allergies, diabetes, and cardiovascular health. Several trends are continuing to shape the direct-to-consumer laboratory testing market including the growing demand for early disease detection and diagnosis, personalized medicine, and the importance of remote disease monitoring.

Mental Health Management

Approximately 57 million adults had mental health or substance-use conditions in 2017, and about 70% of them received no treatment, according to federal estimates. When people do get treatment, it's often not effective and rarely a long-term, sustainable solution. While the growth in this space has been slow, many large healthcare organizations are leading efforts to address mental health as a holistic part of their overall health. "The evidence continues to mount that mental health and physical health are intimately entwined," said Dr. Don Mordecai, a national leader for mental health and wellness for Kaiser Permanente, where providers are experimenting with apps that connect patients and behavioral health providers.

Intermountain Healthcare, one of the nation's largest providers, has "taken a cultural approach to normalizing mental health as part of a routine part of care. The mental health activity is not just the responsibility of the mental health staff," said Brenda Reiss-Brennan, the health system's director of mental health integration.

Other tools, such as Talkspace, are finding success in the digital application of mental health and counseling services. Talkspace is one of several companies, including Ginger and BetterHelp, offering low-cost, high-tech alternatives to traditional, in-person therapy visits. The emergence of therapy apps comes at a time when insurers are facing lawsuits and complaints from advocates and regulators over the persistent difficulty many people face getting care for mental health and substance abuse. As our country continues to grapple with the growing mental health challenges, health insurance companies, pharmaceutical companies, and providers will continue to innovate to ensure help is accessible to those who need it most.

Advice and Perspectives from Investors

How do investors decide what to invest in? How do they distinguish between one solution over another? And how can they tell which company will be successful? Like any other industry, finding the "next big idea" will always be nuanced and involve being in the right place at the right time. In my conversations with healthcare venture capitalists who have invested in many of the companies mentioned in this chapter, there are a few things investors look for repeatedly that have led them to invest in the right companies at the right time.

- Strong clinical validation and buy-in
- Experience and a deep understanding of the regulatory environment
- Partnerships and integration with existing incumbents is helpful

With the healthcare market being valued at nearly $3.5 trillion, there is no shortage of opportunity. As large, non-healthcare companies like Amazon, Google, JPMorgan, and even BestBuy look to enter the space, we can expect even more financing and M&A activity then we've seen in the past decade. With examples like Amazon outbidding Walmart to acquire PillPack (estimated $800 million) and JPMorgan acquiring InstaMed (estimated $500 million), capital is flowing heavily into startups attempting to disrupt healthcare. For entrepreneurs building in the healthcare industry, there is now a foundation for a promising path to continued innovation and disruption in this space.

Sources & Resources

Rock Health: *Beyond Wellness for the Healthy*, Digital health and Consumer Adoption, 2018

Automated Chronic Disease Management to Scale Care, MobiHealth, 2019

Engaging Behavioral Health Patients through Digital Tools, Modern Healthcare, 2019

How AI Could Shape the Health Tech Landscape, Healthcare Dive, 2019

FINDING GENIUS

368

RESOURCES

Books on entrepreneurship and venture capital
Secrets of Sand Hill Road, by Scott Kupor
Venture Deals, by Brad Feld & Jeffrey Busgang
Measure What Matters, by John Doerr
The Lean Startup, by Eric Riess

Podcasts worth listening to
a16z Podcast on topics of technology and venture capital
How I Built This with Guy Raz
Masters of Scale with Reid Hoffman
The Twenty Minute VC with Harry Stebbings

Resources for venture capital and building a startup
AngelList
John Gannon's Blog
F6S: Startup accelerators, competitions, and incubators
Pitchbook & CrunchBase
Product Hunt
VC Finder: An online list of VC funds and investors and their areas of focus

Newsletters
Axios
Strictly VC
Term Sheet
Morning Brew

Printed in Great Britain
by Amazon